PENGUIN BOOKS

A VIETNAM WAR READER

Michael H. Hunt is the Everett H. Emerson Professor of History Emeritus, the University of North Carolina at Chapel Hill. His major books include *The American Ascendancy*, *The World Transformed: 1945 to the Present* and *Lyndon Johnson's War: America's Cold War Crusade in Vietnam, 1945–1968*.

American and Vietnamese Perspectives

A VIETNAM WAR READER

EDITED BY
MICHAEL H. HUNT

PENGUIN BOOKS

PENGUIN BOOKS

Published by the Penguin Group
Penguin Books Ltd, 80 Strand, London WC2R ORL, England
Penguin Group (USA) Inc., 375 Hudson Street, New York, New York 10014, USA
Penguin Group (Canada), 90 Eglinton Avenue East, Suite 700, Toronto, Ontario, Canada M4P 2Y3
(a division of Pearson Penguin Canada Inc.)
Penguin Ireland, 25 St Stephen's Green, Dublin 2, Ireland (a division of Penguin Books Ltd)
Penguin Group (Australia), 250 Camberwell Road, Camberwell, Victoria 3124, Australia
(a division of Pearson Australia Group Pty Ltd)
Penguin Books India Pvt Ltd, 11 Community Centre, Panchsheel Park, New Delhi – 110 017, India
Penguin Group (NZ), 67 Apollo Drive, Rosedale, North Shore 0632, New Zealand
(a division of Pearson New Zealand Ltd)
Penguin Books (South Africa) (Pty) Ltd, 24 Sturdee Avenue, Rosebank, Johannesburg 2196, South Africa

Penguin Books Ltd, Registered Offices: 80 Strand, London WC2R ORL, England

www.penguin.com

First published by The University of North Carolina Press 2010
Published in Penguin Books 2010
1

Printed in England by Clays Ltd, St Ives plc

978-0-141-04702-7

www.greenpenguin.co.uk

To the students

in my Vietnam War course at

Colgate University, UNC–Chapel Hill,

and Williams College (1978–2008),

whose enthusiasm for these documents

fed my own.

Contents

----

5. The View from the Ground, 1965–1971 *123*

Preface

The prolonged and bloody conflict widely known as the Vietnam War touched the lives of many people in many different social and political situations. There is thus not one or two perspectives on it but a great variety. Incorporating that variety is an interpretively urgent goal yet one of the most difficult tasks faced by anyone confronting that conflict.

In shaping this volume, I have made some practical editorial decisions:

- Limiting the documents that appear here to a carefully selected representative sample from a large and still growing body of evidence. In the interest of providing diverse points of view, I have done considerable excerpting, sometimes cutting sharply.

- Focusing tightly on Americans and Vietnamese at war and thus excluded materials that deal with the allies that Hanoi and Washington recruited, including Soviet, South Korean, Australian, Philippine, and Thai. Also missing are the Cambodians and Laotians, who felt the side effects of the struggle in Vietnam with special intensity. So too have I left out the accounts of young people worldwide — in places as far flung as Paris, Tokyo, and Mexico City — who responded to the war with a passion that defines the time.

- Giving Vietnamese and Americans equal time. In what follows, American policy makers and soldiers share the spotlight with the Vietnamese, who were their main antagonist and whose land took the main pounding. Thus the seven chapters here go well beyond the dates normally associated with the U.S. war (1965–1973) and include not just the Communist leaders defying Washington but also early nationalists, ordinary activists and soldiers, peasants, and those on the Saigon side. In the interest of balance, I have included a fair sample of official Vietnamese documents (internal and public) even though some are available only in rough translations and are couched in what may seem formulaic Marxist terminology. My interest in balance has also led to a decision in treating the societal dimensions of war to give Vietnamese a heavy emphasis in chapter 1, offset by devoting all of chapter 6 to developments within the United States.

- Devising a format that is meant to be engaging and user-friendly. The overall arrangement of the documents is chronological so that Vietnamese and American views on particular issues and during particular phases of the war are again and again juxtaposed, thus inviting attention to the interplay between the actors and comparisons among them. I have provided only the background information essential to moving through materials sprawling across some seven decades and dealing with topics as exotic as Vietnamese nationalism and communism and the contested countryside. My introduction sketches the misconceptions surrounding the war and the various stages in its evolution. Accompanying that introduction are a guide to abbreviations, a detailed chronology, and a map of Vietnam. Each of the seven documentary chapters opens with a brief overview of the main themes and questions raised by the documents to follow and includes background information for each section and each document within each section. A brief concluding section at the end of the final chapter gives readers a chance to reflect on what they have learned and offers some general questions to facilitate that task. Throughout I have tried to keep my own views on a leash so that readers will feel free to grapple on their own with the important questions still surrounding the Vietnam War.

- Editing of the source texts in a way that follows a consistent set of guidelines and that keeps editorial clarifications and corrections to a minimum. Spellings and italics follow the source texts. In changing capitalization and inserting ellipses, I have followed the "rigorous method" of *The Chicago Manual of Style*.

The main goal of this collection will have been realized if readers find they can critically engage the evidence gathered here and, from that evidence, formulate their own, historically grounded sense of what the Vietnam War was about.

It is a pleasure to acknowledge those who have helped make this volume possible. Once more I owe thanks to the University of North Carolina Press: foremost my editor, Chuck Grench; his assistant, Katy O'Brien; Paul Betz, who brought order to the manuscript and the production process; Vicky Wells, my patient guide on copyright issues; Anna Laura Bennett, who provided thoughtful and meticulous copyediting; and Kim

Bryant for a design done with flair and care. I received helpful advice in the early stages of this project from Pierre Asselin and Allan M. Winkler. Christopher Goscha as well as Winkler provided incisive comments on the first full draft. At a pivotal point Rosalie Genova read the manuscript with a keen editorial eye and sharp pedagogical sense, while Peter Agren made sensibly ruthless suggestions on tightening the documents. Will West did yeoman service checking the accuracy of the documents excerpted here. Finally, my thanks to Jon Huibregtse for permission to draw in the introduction on my "Studying the Vietnam War: Between an Implacable Force and an Immovable Object," *New England Journal of History* 54 (Spring 1998): 45–61.

Introduction
The Vietnam War: From Myth to History

For most Americans today, the history of the Vietnam War is like a play that unfolds in ways quite different from the audience's preconceptions. Ticket holders take their seats expecting a drama about American soldiers. But once the curtain goes up, there are some surprises — the Vietnamese characters dominate the stage at the outset, the American characters arrive late (soldiers among the last), the play proves far longer than anticipated, and the plotline takes some unfamiliar twists. This collection of documents — snippets from a real drama — should also shatter some expectations that readers carry in their heads. The materials gathered here suggest that the Vietnam War was not mainly about U.S. soldiers and that it spanned a good deal more than the decade of direct U.S. combat.

MISUNDERSTANDING AN UNPOPULAR WAR

Many Americans feel instinctively that they know the Vietnam conflict in large measure because of popular myths and misconceptions incorporated and propagated, if not actually created, through the movies and other widely consumed U.S. media. Hollywood, with its trademark capacity for neat packaging and simple messages, tackled the war in the late 1970s, and in a steady output over the following decades, it became the single most important source for public memory. One movie critic commented wryly, "Since 1977, Hollywood has been succeeding where Washington consistently failed: namely, in selling Vietnam to the American public."[1] The Hollywood version of the war — perpetuated in DVDs and television reruns — worked its magic above all by draining the war of much of the controversy that would have gotten in the way of entertainment. In often powerful, frequently reiterated images, Vietnam became a fantasy world where Americans tested their manliness, underwent youthful rites of passage, embarked on perilous rescues, suffered personal corruption, or replayed frontier dramas with the Vietnamese as the

1. Thomas Doherty, "Full Metal Genre: Stanley Kubrick's Vietnam Combat Movies," in *Perspectives on Stanley Kubrick*, ed. Mario Falsetto (New York: Hall, 1996), 307.

"wild Indians." Seldom do the serious political issues raised by the war come into view, and the Vietnamese rarely figure as anything more than bit players in an American drama.

What comes across most forcefully in Tinseltown products is the notion that Vietnam as a disembodied force somehow made a victim of Americans. Witness the treatment of soldiers in combat films such as *Go Tell the Spartans* (1978), *Apocalypse Now* (1979), *Platoon* (1986), and *Hamburger Hill* (1987). The theme of victimization is also central to the movies that show veterans returning home twisted in mind and ruined in body. The once normal young Americans made into psychopaths, paraplegics, and enraged muscle men inhabit such films as *Taxi Driver* (1976), *Coming Home* (1978), and the Rambo series (1982 and 1985). Some, such as *The Deer Hunter* (1978) and *Born on the Fourth of July* (1989), manage to develop both themes—the wounds inflicted on soldiers in the field and in the lives of warriors back home. *Forrest Gump* (1994), perhaps the most widely viewed of these films, offers a lighthearted version of this conventional story line of the soldier as victim during and after the fighting. These stories of victimization have reduced the war to easily grasped terms to reach and hold a broad audience. Their appeal may be rooted in the way soldiers as victims serve as stand-ins for their country whose innocence the war destroyed. Personal victimization becomes an easily understood expression of national victimization.

Public opinion polls conducted in the early 1990s suggest a popular acceptance of Hollywood's simple but symbolically loaded version of the war.[2] Consistent with the view that Vietnam somehow managed to do bad things to the United States, about 70 percent of those surveyed held that the Vietnam commitment was a mistake (up from around 60 percent in the early 1970s, during the last phase of U.S. troop involvement, and virtually unchanged when the question was asked again in 2000). Nearly as many (68 percent) carried the indictment further and said that Vietnam was not a "just war." Also consistent with Hollywood's portrayal, the public strongly identified with the American soldier. Overwhelmingly (87 percent) the public thought favorably of those who served and sacrificed

2. The polling data in this and the following paragraphs come from George Gallup Jr., *The Gallup Poll: Public Opinion, 1990* (Wilmington, Del.: Scholarly Resources, 1991), 47–50; George Gallup Jr., *The Gallup Poll: Public Opinion, 1993* (Wilmington, Del.: Scholarly Resources, 1994), 228; George Gallup Jr., *The Gallup Poll: Public Opinion, 1995* (Wilmington, Del.: Scholarly Resources, 1996), 228; and *Gallup Poll Monthly*, November 2000, 44.

in a conflict that respondents thought was more costly in American lives than any other in the twentieth century. (In point of fact, each of the two world wars resulted in more Americans killed in action than did Vietnam.) In line with the fixation on victimization, a substantial majority (69 percent) regarded veterans as ill used by their government and unappreciated by their countrymen. Indeed, 64 percent believed U.S. officials so indifferent that they had abandoned servicemen to permanent captivity in Southeast Asia.

Where Hollywood provided less clear guidance, Americans were more divided in the early 1990s polls. They split evenly on whether any good came out of the war, such as slowing the advance of communism in Southeast Asia or contributing to the decline of communism worldwide. Respondents also split when asked whether American warriors died in vain. Fifty-one percent said "yes," while 41 percent answered "no." Finally, the public divided on how to appraise the protest movement at home. In 1990, 39 percent of respondents had a favorable view, and the exact same percentage had an unfavorable view. Asked three years later about dissent from another angle — whether draft avoidance by all legal means was justified — the public again divided (with the "no's" outnumbering "yes's" 53 to 41 percent).

HOW HISTORY MATTERS

What is remarkable about the films and the polls is their omissions. Popular conceptions of the war have little room for the Vietnamese, even though the war was fought on their soil, resulted in deaths and injuries in the millions, and imposed lasting societal costs. Vietnamese appear at best on the periphery, limited to cameo appearances. The enduring American images of the Vietnamese at war — the shadowy foe darting through the underbrush or lying crumpled on the ground, the prostitute camped outside an American base, the child in frightful flight from napalm — first appeared in contemporary media. Soldiers' memoirs and Hollywood films have perpetuated this extraordinarily limited, invariably superficial, and often caricatured treatment. So dim has the public sense of the Vietnamese political context grown that a fifth of those polled in 1990 thought that the United States had fought alongside, not against, North Vietnam.

Because the popular view of the Vietnam War focuses on Americans in combat and thus is concerned only with the period of direct U.S. engagement, it is fundamentally ahistorical. The U.S. war was but one phase in a string of conflicts in Vietnam that began with the struggle against the French and continued as an insurgency against the U.S.-backed government in Saigon, which in turn morphed into the American war that spilled over into Cambodia and ultimately gave way to the ceasefire war of 1973–1975. Within each of these phases, the nature of the conflict varied from place to place (for example, large cities versus remote villages; highlands versus river deltas). And because this long-lasting, far-flung struggle incorporated elements of social revolution, national liberation, and civil war, it swept up a wide variety of people, turning their lives upside down.

As the documents that follow suggest, the Vietnam War was not a single, neatly played out drama featuring the Americans, and it was never primarily about U.S. soldiers. It was more like a long, loosely unfolding story by a playwright who had lost control of his plot and players. Characters wander onto the stage, often barely mindful of the other members of the cast. They deliver their lines, often speaking past each other. And then they exit, sometimes never to reappear. They don't even agree on the name of their shared drama. What Americans call the Vietnam War their Vietnamese foe thought of as the American war or "the war of resistance against American aggression."

Even the chronology of the play is off-kilter. For Vietnamese the war had its roots in the nineteenth century; it encompassed at least three generations, going back to resistance to the French conquest. By the time the play reached the final act in the 1970s, virtually all segments of Vietnamese society had made an appearance—from nationalist intellectuals to political activists, to peasants pulled into the struggle, to ordinary soldiers, to those who hitched their fortunes to the French and then American causes. The Americans walked onto the stage relatively late—in the 1940s—and even then acted only as minor players, largely unaware of previous plot developments. Despite their late appearance, an impressive range of Americans did manage to get into the act. They included, notably, a string of seven U.S. presidents, well over 3 million Americans who saw service in Vietnam, and many ordinary Americans who felt the war's effect in deepened social ferment and political embitterment at home during the late 1960s and early 1970s.

OVERVIEW OF COVERAGE

The Vietnam War drama as it is arranged here opens with a long prologue (chapter 1) running up to 1954. It is dominated by elite Vietnamese in the grip of nationalist fever and by country folk with practical concerns about livelihood and social justice. A liberation movement harnessing these two groups begins to take shape in the 1920s and 1930s. The entrance during the 1940s and early 1950s of U.S. policy makers preoccupied by a world war and then the Cold War conveys the first hints of trouble to come. In the first act (chapter 2), the fate of South Vietnam emerges as a source of deepening discord among the assembled cast of Vietnamese and American characters. Initiatives pursued by Washington and countermeasures by Hanoi raise the tensions so that, by the end of 1963 and the beginning of the second act (chapter 3), the two parties are already close to blows. Though facing the prospect of war with the United States, leaders in Hanoi prove relentless in their program to bring the South under control and thus plunge Lyndon Johnson into some strikingly Hamlet-like moments before he decides on a major armed response. The third and fourth acts (chapters 4 and 5) carry us through the thrust and parry of war. Strategists search for a way to prevail, while ordinary Vietnamese and Americans try to come to terms with privation and death. Chapter 6 introduces a kind of Greek chorus — Americans commenting at a distance on a war that is producing ever greater domestic dissension. With both sides at last exhausted, the play moves to a resolution. Shakespeare was right in observing that "good plays prove the better by the help of good epilogues." For the Vietnam War, an epilogue (chapter 7) treats the end to the fighting among Vietnamese in 1975 and examines the various ways those touched by the war sought to make sense of it once the guns had gone silent. As the curtain comes down, those who have followed this sprawling drama with its large cast have a chance to decide for themselves what it means rather than accepting uncritically what Hollywood and political pundits have suggested.

QUESTIONS TO CONFRONT

To some extent, the sources collected here ask us to think about how fearsome war can be for those caught up in it and how unpredictable its effects may turn out for those who presume to command its course. But beyond those points applicable to any war, a set of difficult but fundamental questions arise from this particular conflict that are worth keeping in mind in reading the documents to come:

- What brought Americans and Vietnamese to blows? How did hopes and fears on each side contribute to this outcome?

- What calculations led U.S. leaders to intervene in Vietnam and defend their position there despite nagging private doubts and rising public dissent? Were there genuine alternatives to the interventionist path they followed?
- What led Vietnamese leaders to confront the Americans, and how did they ultimately overcome their vastly greater power? Can the outcome be explained essentially in terms of what the Vietnamese did, or do we need to focus on what the Americans failed to do?
- How well did the two sides understand each other, and how did their conceptions (or misconceptions) influence their decisions?
- How was the war experienced by ordinary Vietnamese and Americans?

History, like any good play, should leave you thinking—and wanting to learn more. Good places for further inquiry are the collections from which many of the documents in this reader are drawn (cited in the source notes). Going to the original will provide a sense of context not fully conveyed by the sharply edited items included here. A substantial body of scholarship is also available to assist in further exploring the many issues raised by the Vietnam War.[3]

3. For general information on the war, see David L. Anderson, *The Columbia Guide to the Vietnam War* (New York: Columbia University Press, 2002), which includes an annotated bibliography of key publications, films and documentaries, and electronic resources. A fuller list of readings — scholarly works as well as memoirs and documents — can be found in the up-to-date online guide maintained by Edwin E. Moïse, *Vietnam War Bibliography*, http://www.clemson.edu/caah/history/FacultyPages/EdMoise/bibliography.html. Gary R. Hess, *Vietnam: Explaining America's Lost War* (Malden, Mass.: Blackwell, 2009), helpfully links the enormous literature to the chief points of controversy that have swirled about the war. A good source for maps is the collection of the History Department at the U.S. Military Academy online at http://www.dean.usma.edu/history/web03/atlases/vietnam/VietnamWarIndex.html.

Guide to Abbreviations

ARVN	Army of the Republic of Vietnam (the Saigon government's regular ground forces fighting with U.S. units and advisers against Communist-led Vietnamese forces)
CIA	Central Intelligence Agency
COSVN	Central Office for South Vietnam (the Vietnamese Communist Party's political-military headquarters responsible for directing the struggle in the South)
DRV	Democratic Republic of Vietnam (created in 1945 with its capital in Hanoi; renamed Socialist Republic of Vietnam in 1976)
GVN	Government of Vietnam (in Saigon)
JCS	Joint Chiefs of Staff (heads of the four U.S. armed forces plus a chair appointed by the president)
MACV	Military Assistance Command, Vietnam (the command center for U.S. forces; created in February 1962)
NLF	National Liberation Front (the Communist-directed united front; created in December 1960)
PAVN	People's Army of Vietnam (DRV's army)
SDS	Students for a Democratic Society
SEATO	Southeast Asia Treaty Organization
SVN	South Vietnam (Republic of Vietnam with its capital in Saigon)
VC	Viet Cong (literally Red Vietnamese, a term loosely applied by Americans and their South Vietnamese allies to NLF cadre and troops and/or PAVN forces)

Chronology

1955–1956 Diem consolidates control in South and rejects nationwide elections stipulated by Geneva settlement.

1959 Diem's repressive policy leads Communist leaders to endorse military as well as political struggle in South and to open supply line (Ho Chi Minh Trail) to sustain it.

1960 National Liberation Front created as anti-Diem united front in South Vietnam; U.S. military advisers rise to 900.

1961 NLF success in countryside forces President Kennedy to increase military support.

1962 Kennedy agrees to neutralization of Laos (July). China signals support for DRV in looming contest with United States.

1963 Buddhist-led protest movement culminates in Diem's overthrow and assassination by South Vietnamese generals (November). Military government distracted by infighting.

1964 U.S. destroyers are reportedly attacked twice by North Vietnamese torpedo boats in Gulf of Tonkin, and Congress passes Gulf of Tonkin resolution allowing President Johnson to retaliate against aggression in Southeast Asia (August). First DRV combat units move down Ho Chi Minh Trail in late fall; U.S. military advisers number slightly over 23,000.

ESCALATION

1965 Soviets pledge support to DRV. Johnson begins sustained bombing ("Rolling Thunder") against DRV (February) and sends first U.S. combat units to fight in South (March). First major antiwar protest in Washington (April). Johnson announces major increase in U.S. ground forces (July). U.S. and DRV units clash for first time in Ia Drang valley (November). Nguyen Van Thieu and Nguyen Cao Ky stabilize Saigon military government.

1966–1967 U.S. forces (approaching half million mark) follow strategy of attrition, but PAVN and NLF forces keep fighting with aid from Soviet Union and China. March on Pentagon (October 1967) with public now evenly split on war.

1968 Tet Offensive (late January–February): NLF forces attack cities all over South, including Saigon, but are beaten back with heavy losses. American media and public opinion register shock. Johnson calls for peace talks and renounces another term in White House (March). My Lai massacre (March). Protesters and police clash in Chicago during Democratic National Convention (August).

WAR'S END

1969 President Nixon promises to end war, presses Vietnamization, withdraws U.S. troops, and begins campaign of secretly bombing Cambodia. Henry Kissinger and Le Duc Tho begin secret talks in Paris (August). Major demonstrations against Nixon's lack of progress toward peace (October–November).

1970 Cambodian neutralist Prince Norodom Sihanouk overthrown by General Lon Nol (March). U.S. forces invade Cambodia (April–June), setting off nationwide campus protests. Senate repeals Gulf of Tonkin resolution and bars U.S. military presence in Cambodia (June).

1971 Saigon forces defeated in campaign into Laos (February–March). U.S. veteran discontent evident in Winter Soldier Investigation (February) and Dewey Canyon III protest in Washington (April).

1972 DRV forces launch major (Easter) offensive (March) provoking Nixon to heavy bombing of DRV (Linebacker I). Preliminary peace terms concluded in Paris (October). Nixon's insistence on revisions leads to Christmas bombings of DRV (Linebacker II).

1973 Paris peace accords (January): withdrawal of all U.S. troops; return of American prisoners of war; and settlement of South Vietnam's future by peaceful, political means. Congress cuts off bombing of Cambodia (June).

1974 Fighting between DRV and Saigon forces intensifies. President Ford renews U.S. commitment to South Vietnam (August).

1975 DRV launches major offensive (March). Congress rejects emergency military aid, and Saigon falls (April). Flight of Vietnamese abroad begins (numbering more than 1 million over following fifteen years). Pol Pot's Kampuchean Communist Party (Khmer Rouge) overthrows Lon Nol regime in Phnom Penh (April) and establishes People's Republic of Kampuchea.

POSTWAR

1976 Vietnam formally reunified as Socialist Republic of Vietnam.

1979 Vietnam overthrows Khmer Rouge and occupies Cambodia; China retaliates with attack across Vietnam's northern border.

1980s Vietnam struggles to rebuild economy, with Nguyen Van Linh
       launching market-oriented reform program (1986).
1989   Vietnamese troops leave Cambodia.
1995   United States and Vietnam establish diplomatic relations.

A
VIETNAM
WAR
READER

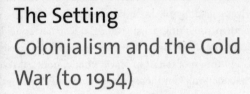

The Setting
Colonialism and the Cold War (to 1954)

The Vietnam War story begins with patriotic ancestors who opened the drama decades before their country had even begun to penetrate American consciousness. Three generations of well-educated, politically engaged Vietnamese faced French colonial control as a force that was penetrating and upending their world. They made liberation from that control their prime concern in life.

The French presence loomed ever larger and more ominous between the 1840s and the 1890s. Naval expeditions and diplomats extended a grip over Vietnam as well as Cambodia and Laos (collectively dubbed Indochina by the French). The rich Mekong Delta of southern Vietnam (known as Cochin China) was the first to fall. It came under direct rule during the 1860s. The rest of Vietnam — Annam and Tonkin — was soon reduced to the status of a protectorate in which a humiliated monarchy remained nominally in charge. But in fact a French governor-general held sway over all of Indochina. The influx of some 40,000 to 50,000 French settlers and of French capital added cultural and economic dimensions to Vietnamese political subordination.

At the outset — across the latter half of the nineteenth century — scholar-officials loyal to the ruling dynasty mounted a desperate but ineffectual resistance to French conquest. Their failure to turn the tide put in question the established order, which was dominated by a monarchy modeled after China's and by Confucian social values. Vietnamese intellectuals began to explore the sources of their country's vulnerability and to consider ways to revitalize and liberate their country.

These concerns led the second generation of patriots to nationalist ideas early in the twentieth century. Under the sway of those ideas, they discovered the importance of building popular unity, creating a strong government to lead the people and resist international pressures, and drawing instruction and support from other countries, such as Japan, whose nationalist programs were proving successful. These pioneer nationalists were products of an educational system geared to create officials to staff the state bureaucracy, and so they instinctively assigned themselves a leading role in finding a substitute for the old, failed monarchy and in remaking society along lines they considered modern. In undertaking these tasks, they carried forward a sense of the special obligation of men of talent to play a public, political role. At the same time, their nationalism incorporated a special faith in the capacity of Vietnamese to resist foreign domination. In this they built on widely retailed legends of heroic resistance against Chinese domination and invasion.

The third generation, active in the 1920s and 1930s, faced perplexity and frustration. The old monarchical resistance had sputtered out. French prejudice and self-interest were discrediting moderate nationalists who had embraced the idea of enlightened colonial tutelage. Revolutionary plots repeatedly failed in the face of repressive security forces. Given the formidable obstacles to developing a nationalist consciousness and creating nationalist organizations, the educated class began searching farther and farther afield for models and insights. As they conceived the task of liberation in ever more expansive terms, they took an ever more critical view of the flaws of Vietnamese society—from gender inequality to class exploitation, to servile subordination to the colonial presence, to official corruption, to popular illiteracy.

Ho Chi Minh is the most famous member of this third generation. By the early 1940s, Ho had scored two major achievements that established his reputation and inspired nationalist hopes. The first, effected in the context of Japanese military expansion into Southeast Asia, was to translate broad ideas about revolution and independence into workable policies. In 1941, just as Japanese forces were taking charge in Indochina, Ho returned home at the head of the Viet Minh. This Communist-led organization would win broad popular appeal and spearhead the independence cause. The Viet Minh at first made its target the Japanese occupation army and the French who had acquiesced to Japanese control. With the unexpectedly early end of fighting in the Pacific in mid-1945, Ho and his colleagues seized power and declared Vietnam independent. The "August Revolution" of that year resulted in the creation of the Democratic Republic of Vietnam (DRV). Ho became president of the new state. With his close associates Pham Van Dong, Vo Nguyen Giap, and Truong Chinh, he would direct the next phase of the independence struggle against a France determined to reassert its colonial prerogatives. The resulting conflict would last nearly eight years (late 1946 to mid-1954). Ho abandoned the cities in favor of a strategy of broad political mobilization led by the Viet Minh. On the battlefield his forces resorted to a mix of guerrilla and conventional warfare to harass and ultimately exhaust the enemy. Diplomatically Vietnam's Communists had by 1950 emphatically put themselves on the side of the Soviet-led world communist movement, and they looked hopefully to the new Communist China for practical support.

Ho's second major achievement was establishing the Communist Party's legitimacy as the leading resistance force with an effective appeal to a wide range of ordinary Vietnamese. The key to this accomplishment was melding rural with nationalist concerns. Vietnamese Communists had embarked in the 1930s on finding ways to mobilize peasants, far and away the largest part of the population. Along the way they discovered the importance to villagers of land and livelihood.

The same wartime context in which Ho consolidated party control and advanced the independence cause also turned the attention of American policy makers to French Indochina. In 1940 and 1941, President Franklin Roosevelt started worrying about Indochina along with the other tottering European colonial domains in Southeast Asia. The Japanese attack on Pearl Harbor drew the U.S. military deeply into the Pacific struggle and raised the question of the postwar status of colonial territories now in Japanese hands. In response Roosevelt offered qualified support for decolonization, but his successors — Harry Truman and Dwight Eisenhower — shifted to full acquiescence to the restoration of French control and then to full-throated support even as the French effort faltered and then collapsed.

This chapter's documents on the deep roots of the Vietnam War raise some fundamental questions:

- What fears, hopes, enmities, and ideals gripped Vietnamese confronted with French domination of their country? How did those concerns vary over time and between politically engaged elites and peasants?
- To what extent did Ho Chi Minh's evolving views emerge from earlier nationalist attitudes, and to what extent were they shaped by communism?
- What concerns led Presidents Truman and Eisenhower to a commitment in Vietnam?

- Why in the final analysis did Vietnamese and American leaders fail to find common ground on the seemingly shared principle of self-determination?

EMERGENCE OF A NATIONALIST VISION

French domination provoked a class of Vietnamese trained in the Confucian classics and oriented toward political service to engage in an ever deeper and more desperate search for a way to end Vietnam's humiliating condition. Open resistance to the French had failed by the turn of the century and planted grim doubts about the capacity of Vietnamese to liberate themselves or even to survive as a society in a world of rapacious powers. Dealing with this grim realization fell to a new set of nationalist intellectuals and activists who emerged at the start of the twentieth century. Some among them favored revolutionary struggle, while others preferred a nonviolent reformist program as the more realistic course.

1.1 Nguyen Dinh Chieu, funeral oration honoring peasants who fought the French, 1861

This well-known southern writer (1822–1888) represents the proto-nationalist resistance directed against the French and a collaboration-minded royal court. In the poem that follows, Chieu champions popular armed struggle. But, however defiant, he and like-minded advocates of resistance failed to create a peasant army strong and durable enough to drive out the French.

The only things you knew were ricefields and water buffaloes.
    You lived according to the village's customs.
Digging, plowing, harrowing, replanting were your usual
    occupations. . . .
You were not professional soldiers . . . experienced in military life
    and training. You were but inhabitants of villages and hamlets
    turned partisans to serve the cause of righteousness. . . .
In your hands, a pointed stick; you did not ask for knives or helmets.
The match for your gunpowder was made of straw; but this did not
    prevent you from successfully burning the missionary house.
For a sword, you used your kitchen knife; yet you were able to behead
    the enemies' lieutenant.
Your officers were not compelled to beat the drums in order to urge you

forward. You advanced on your own, clambering onto the barricades. You looked upon the enemy as if he did not exist.

You were not frightened by the French who shot large and small bullets at you. You forced your way into their camp, risking your life as if you had no material body.

Some of you stabbed, some struck so eagerly that the French soldiers and their mercenaries lost heart.

You screamed in the forefront, you shouted at the rear regardless of the enemies' gunboats, their ships, or their rifles. . . .

You preferred to die fighting the enemy, and return to our ancestors in glory rather than survive in submission to the Occidentals and share your miserable life with barbarians. . . .

O, the smoke of your battle has already dissipated, but your right conduct shall be recorded for a thousand years.

1.2 Phan Boi Chau, call for Vietnamese to awaken, 1907

Chau (1867–1940) was a leading proponent of revolutionary nationalism. He was trained in the Confucian classics and passed the qualifying exam to become an official. Instead he became a voice for anticolonial resistance. He held up Japan (where he lived for a time in exile) as a model for Vietnamese modernization and a potential source of support for Vietnamese independence. The extract included here comes from The New Vietnam, *one of Chau's many works. The French authorities banned the book and in 1925 arrested, tried, and convicted the defiant Chau of subversion. He spent the rest of his life under confinement.*

Our soil is fertile, our mountains and rivers beautiful. Compared with other powers in the five continents, our country is inferior only to a few. Why, then, do we suffer French protection? Alas, that is simply because of our deep-rooted slave mentality; it is because of our inveterate habit of depending on others for over two thousand years. We gladly accepted the colonization of the Han, the Tang, the Song, the Yuan, the Ming [all powerful Chinese dynasties]. As slaves, we served them; we lacked human dignity. Today our enemy the French are very ingenious. They despise us, claiming that we are weak; they lie to us, because they consider us stupid. . . . They trample over our people; they hold our fathers and brothers in contempt; they treat us like buffaloes and horses; they suck the sweat and blood from our people; and yet they dare broadcast loudly to the rest of the world that France is here to protect the Indochinese country. Oh! Compatriots, the country is ours; the people are ours. What interest does France have here for her to come and protect our country?

Ever since France came to protect us, Frenchmen hold every lever of power; they hold the power of life and death over everyone. The life of thousands of Vietnamese people is not worth that of a French dog; the moral prestige of hundreds of our officials does not prevail over that of a French woman. Look at those men with blue eyes and yellow beard. They are not our fathers, nor are they our brothers. How can they squat here, defecating on our heads? Are the men from Vietnam not ashamed of that situation? . . .

After modernization we shall determine the domestic as well as foreign affairs of our country. The work of civilization will go on, day after day, and our country's status in the world will be heightened. We shall have three million infantrymen, as fierce as tigers, looking into the four corners of the universe. Five hundred thousand of our navy men, as terrifying as crocodiles, will swim freely in the boundless ocean. We shall send ambassadors into every country of Europe, America, Japan, the United States, Germany, England. These countries will make ours their first ally. Siam [Thailand], India, and other countries of the South Seas will look up to our land as an enlightened example. Even the big countries of Asia, such as China, will be brother countries to ours. The enemy, France, will be afraid of us; she will listen to us, ask us for protection. Our flag will fly over the city of Paris, and our colors will brighten the entire globe. At that time the only fear we shall have is that we won't have enough time to protect other countries. All the shame and humiliation we have suffered previously, which resulted from being protected by others, will have become potent medicine to help us build up this feat of modernization. Commemorative monuments will be erected; a thousand torches will illuminate the entire world. The wind of freedom will blow fiercely, refreshing in one single sweep the entire five continents. Such will be the victory of our race. How pleasant that will be!

1.3 Phan Chu Trinh, open letter to French governor-general Paul Beau, 1907

Trinh (1872–1926) was Phan Boi Chau's equal in fame among the early-twentieth-century nationalists. He too was trained in the classics, passed

*the qualifying exam for royal service, but veered off into nationalist dissent.
But unlike Chau, Trinh was skeptical about seeking outside support, whether
from Japan or anywhere else. And rather than promote resistance, he looked
to enlightened French tutelage to bring his troubled country into the modern
world. His involvement in a peasant uprising in 1908 led to his arrest and left
him politically sidelined until his death.*

Since Vietnam was placed under their protection, the French have built
roads and bridges; they have improved communication through the construction of railroads and steamships; they have established post offices
and telegraph lines: all these works are indeed very useful to Vietnam. . . .

. . . [Y]et how is it that [the Vietnamese people] all have reached the
lowest level of their subsistence, that they are about to witness the destruction of their race? What are the causes of this predicament? . . .

. . . The first one, as I see it, resides in the fact that the Protecting Power
[France] gave too great a liberty to the Vietnamese mandarins [officials in
the bureaucracy]. . . .

Knowing, for some time, that the Protecting Power favors and never
punishes them, the Vietnamese mandarins . . . who are greedy become
more so, counting on their corruption to climb up the hierarchical lad-
der. Those who are lazy become even lazier, counting only on their apathy
to remain in their position. . . . They paid no attention whatsoever to the
people's complaints. . . .

The second cause resides in the fact that the Protectorate has always
regarded with contempt the people of Vietnam, resulting in a segrega-
tion syndrome. . . . Seeing that our mandarins are corrupt, our people un-
intelligent, our customs in decay, the French despise our people, who, in
their judgment, have no national dignity. Therefore, in their newspapers,
books, conversations, or discussions, they usually express the contemp-
tuous opinion that the Vietnamese are barbarians and comparatively not
much different from pigs. . . .

If France is really interested in changing her policy, she should employ
only those mandarins who have talent; give them authority and power;
treat them with propriety; show them sincerity; deliberate with them over
the best means to promote the good and eradicate the evil; open up new
ways for the people to earn their living; provide the scholar-students with
the freedom of discussion; widen the freedom of the press so as to know
the people's sentiments; put an end to the abuses of the mandarinate by
resorting to just punishments and fair rewards. Furthermore, if, little by

little, the legal system is improved, the mandarinal examinations abolished, the educational system renovated, libraries built, teachers trained, commercial and industrial knowledge encouraged, the taxes and corvée [required labor] systems ameliorated, then the people will quietly devote their efforts to do their work well. The scholar-students will discharge their duties with joy. At that time people will only fear that France will abandon Vietnam. Who would and could see her as an enemy?

. . . The only way for us to keep our territory and to allow our race to survive on this globe is to have a capable teacher to educate us and regard us as his pupils; to find a good mother who would treat us like her own children, raise us and take good care of us, with confidence and with affection.

HO CHI MINH'S RISE TO PROMINENCE, 1919–1945

The following items trace the rise of the leading figure in the Vietnamese liberation struggle from obscurity to national prominence. Ho Chi Minh was born in 1890 in a northern province noted for its anti-French resistance into a distinctly patriotic family. He knew personally the leading nationalists. Educated at first in Vietnam, Ho went abroad in 1911 to learn the secrets of Western power. During his development as a political leader between the late 1910s and the 1940s, he time and again invoked in his writings the proud resistance of earlier generations.

_____

1.4 Recollections of discovering Communist anticolonialism in July 1920

Ho settled in Paris in the late 1910s and hit his political stride, recapitulating as he went the views of an older generation. Under the name Nguyen Ai Quoc (Nguyen the Patriot), he joined other Vietnamese exiles in June 1919 in petitioning the victors in World War I for administrative reforms along the lines advocated by Trinh (document 1.3). Ho and his colleagues were ignored even by that champion of self-determination, U.S. president Woodrow Wilson. The French Socialist Party, to which Ho turned, also proved indifferent to the aspirations of the colonized.

In mid-1920 Ho's views took a revolutionary turn in the spirit of Chau (document 1.2). Here, in a recollection prepared in 1960 for the Soviet review Problems of the East *on the occasion of Vladimir Lenin's ninetieth birthday,*

Ho recalls his stunning encounter with an essay by Lenin that threw the support of the recently established Communist International behind oppressed peoples struggling against colonialism. Ho found attractive the notion that the "working masses" (including peasants) in Vietnam and other colonies were to combine with the proletariat in the developed countries and spearhead world revolution. According to the conventional Marxist formulation of the time, revolution in the colonies would sweep to power bourgeois nationalists, who would in turn yield to a socialist tide in their countries.

After World War One, I made my living in Paris, at one time as an employee at a photographer's, at another as painter of "Chinese antiques" (turned out by a French shop). I often distributed leaflets denouncing the crimes committed by the French colonialists in Viet Nam.

At that time, I supported the October Revolution [the 1917 seizure of power by the Bolsheviks in Russia] only spontaneously. I did not yet grasp all its historic importance. I loved and respected Lenin because he was a great patriot who had liberated his fellow-countrymen; until then, I had read none of his books. . . .

Heated discussions were then taking place in the cells of the Socialist Party, about whether one should remain in the [Socialist] Second International, found a "Second-and-a-half" International or join Lenin's Third [Moscow-based Communist] International[.] I attended the meetings regularly, two or three times a week, and attentively listened to the speakers. . . .

What I wanted most to know — and what was not debated in the meetings — was: which International sided with the peoples of the colonial countries?

I raised this question — the most important for me — at a meeting. Some comrades answered: it was the Third, not the Second International. One gave me to read Lenin's "Theses on the national and colonial questions". . . .

In those Theses, there were political terms that were difficult to understand. But by reading them again and again finally I was able to grasp the essential part. What emotion, enthusiasm, enlightenment and confidence they communicated to me! I wept for joy. Sitting by myself in my room, I would shout as if I were addressing large crowds: "Dear martyr compatriots! This is what we need, this is our path to liberation!" . . .

. . . [F]rom then on, I . . . plunged into the debates and participated with fervour in the discussions. Though my French was still too weak to express all my thoughts, I hit hard at the allegations attacking Lenin and the Third International. My only argument was: "If you do not condemn colonialism, if you do not side with the colonial peoples, what kind of revolution are you then waging?"

1.5 Statement on behalf of the new Indochinese Communist Party, 18 February 1930

During the 1920s and 1930s, Ho worked as a full-time revolutionary supported by the Soviet-backed Communist International. In 1930 he pulled a fragmented Vietnamese communist movement into a single party (known for its first two decades as the Indochinese Communist Party). The following excerpt was written in Canton, a center of Vietnamese political activity, and appeared under one of Ho's pseudonyms (Din).

Though Ho was never interested in Marxist theory or in theoretical controversies, he did make conventional Marxist ideas an essential part of his worldview. He saw international affairs in terms of conflict between capitalist-dominated countries embarked on an imperialist course abroad and the emerging socialist camp led by the Soviet Union. He accepted the inherent superiority of the socialist system. And he took as a given the inevitable collapse of capitalism, the victim of its mounting crisis of overproduction and social unrest at home, warfare generated by rivalry among competing capitalist states for foreign markets, and revolutionary resistance in the colonial world. What above all else engaged him was Lenin's notion of a tight, disciplined party organization as a way of speeding the inevitable advance of progress, not to mention marshaling limited resources against a more powerful foe. Ho devoted his energy and ingenuity to building the party as an essential, effective instrument of liberation and winning broad support for it, including among the peasants Chieu had written in praise of (document 1.1). Ho's devotion to organizing Vietnamese to fight reflected this Marxist's still deeply nationalist impulses.

Workers, peasants, soldiers, youth and school students!
Oppressed and exploited fellow-countrymen!
Sisters and brothers! Comrades!

Imperialist contradictions were the cause of the 1914–1918 World War. After this horrible slaughter, the world was divided into two camps: one is the revolutionary camp which includes the oppressed colonial peoples and the exploited working class throughout the world. Its vanguard is the Soviet Union. The other is the counter-revolutionary camp of international capitalism and imperialism. . . .

That war resulted in untold loss of life and property. . . . French imperialism was the hardest hit. Therefore, in order to restore the forces of capitalism in France, the French imperialists have resorted to every perfidious scheme to intensify capitalist exploitation in Indochina. They have built new factories to exploit the workers by paying them starvation wages. They have plundered the peasants' land to establish plantations and drive them to destitution. They have levied new heavy taxes. They have forced our people to buy government bonds. In short, they have driven our people to utter misery. They have increased their military forces, firstly to strangle the Vietnamese revolution; secondly to prepare for a new imperialist war in the Pacific aimed at conquering new colonies; thirdly to suppress the Chinese revolution; and fourthly to attack the Soviet Union because she helps the oppressed nations and the exploited working class to wage revolution. World War Two will break out. When it does the French imperialists will certainly drive our people to an even more horrible slaughter. If we let them prepare for this war, oppose the Chinese revolution and attack the Soviet Union, if we allow them to stifle the Vietnamese revolution, this is tantamount to letting them wipe our race off the surface of the earth and drown our nation in the Pacific.

However, the French imperialists' barbarous oppression and ruthless exploitation have awakened our compatriots, who have all realized that revolution is the only road to survival and that without it they will die a slow death. This is why the revolutionary movement has grown stronger with each passing day: the workers refuse to work, the peasants demand land, the students go on strike, the traders stop doing business. Everywhere the masses have risen to oppose the French imperialists.

The revolution has made the French imperialists tremble with fear. On the one hand, they use the feudalists and comprador bourgeoisie [a class dependent on foreign capital] to oppress and exploit our people. On the other, they terrorize, arrest, jail, deport and kill a great number of Vietnamese revolutionaries. If the French imperialists think that they can suppress the Vietnamese revolution by means of terror, they are grossly mistaken. For one thing, the Vietnamese revolution is not isolated but enjoys the assistance of the world proletariat in general and that of the French working class in particular. Secondly, it is precisely at the very time when the French imperialists are frenziedly carrying out terrorist acts that the Vietnamese Communists, formerly working separately, have united into a single party, the Indochinese Communist Party, to lead the revolutionary struggle of our entire people.

1.6 Proclamation of the Viet Minh–led independence struggle, 6 June 1941

Building Vietnam's Communist Party provided Ho a springboard for launching the Viet Minh in 1941. It would serve as a vehicle for attracting all types of his compatriots to the independence cause.

Now, the opportunity has come for our liberation. [German-occupied] France itself is unable to help the French colonialists rule over our country. As for the Japanese, on the one hand, bogged down in China, on the other, hampered by the British and American forces, they certainly cannot use all their strength against us. If our entire people are solidly united we can certainly get the better of the best-trained armies of the French and the Japanese. . . .

Dear fellow-countrymen! A few hundred years ago . . . when our country faced the great danger of invasion by Yuan [Mongol-led Chinese] armies the elders ardently called on their sons and daughters throughout the country to stand up as one man to kill the enemy. Finally they saved their people, and their glorious memory will live for ever. Let our elders and patriotic personalities follow the illustrious example set by our forefathers. . . .

Dear fellow-countrymen!

National salvation is the common cause of our entire people. Every Vietnamese must take part in it. He who has money will contribute his money, he who has strength will contribute his strength, he who has talent will contribute his talent. For my part I pledge to follow in your steps and devote all my modest abilities to the service of the country and am ready for the supreme sacrifice.

1.7 Declaration of independence, 2 September 1945

The headway the Viet Minh made during World War II allowed Ho to seize power in Hanoi in August 1945. Early the next month, he stood before a cheering crowd in central Hanoi and declared the colonial era at an end. His name

was now a household word among patriotic Vietnamese. The striking invo-
cation of the lines from the U.S. independence declaration was part of a cal-
culated attempt to get Washington to deliver on its wartime embrace of the
principle of self-determination. Ho also nominally disbanded the Commu-
nist Party (which would not be formally revived until 1951, as the Vietnamese
Workers' Party), created a broad coalition government to run the DRV, and
appealed directly to the Truman administration for support. With the United
States in a globally dominant position, with no prospect of Soviet backing,
and with the French bent on restoring control throughout Indochina, this con-
ciliatory approach made good sense.

"All men are created equal. They are endowed by their Creator with certain unalienable Rights; among these are Life, Liberty and the pursuit of Happiness." . . .

Those are undeniable truths.

Nevertheless, for more than eighty years, the French imperialists, abusing the standard of Liberty, Equality and Fraternity, have violated our Fatherland and oppressed our fellow-citizens. They have acted contrary to the ideals of humanity and justice.

Politically, they have deprived our people of every democratic liberty.

They have enforced inhuman laws; they have set up three different political regimes in the North, the Centre and the South of Viet Nam in order to wreck our country's oneness and prevent our people from being united.

They have built more prisons than schools. They have mercilessly massacred our patriots. They have drowned our uprisings in seas of blood.

They have fettered public opinion and practised obscurantism [hindering the spread of knowledge].

They have weakened our race with opium and alcohol.

In the field of economics, they have sucked us dry, driven our people to destitution and devastated our land. . . .

We, the Provisional Government of the new Viet Nam, representing the entire Vietnamese people, hereby declare that from now on we break off all relations of a colonial character with France; cancel all treaties signed by France on Viet Nam, and abolish all privileges held by France in our country.

The entire Vietnamese people are of one mind in their determination to oppose all wicked schemes by the French colonialists.

We are convinced that the Allies . . . cannot fail to recognize the right of the Vietnamese people to independence.

A people who have courageously opposed French enslavement for more than eighty years, a people who have resolutely sided with the Allies against the Fascists during these last years, such a people must be free, such a people must be independent.

THE POPULAR APPEAL OF REVOLUTION

Revolutionary sentiment spread through Vietnamese society in the early twentieth century, not only gripping the imagination of educated city dwellers but also reaching into the countryside. In these excerpts we get insight into the diverse ways ordinary Vietnamese became converts to the cause of liberation.

1.8 Nguyen Thi Dinh on her political awakening in the 1930s

Born in 1920, Dinh grew up in a poor family in Ben Tre province, a fertile part of the Mekong Delta known for its revolutionary tradition going back to uprisings in the 1860s. The Communist Party maintained a presence there from the 1930s despite repeated rounds of French repression. Dinh followed her activist brother into party work while still in her teens and married another activist, who died in prison. Dinh herself was subsequently jailed by the French during the early 1940s. She participated in the Viet Minh seizure of power in her province in 1945 and assumed in the 1960s a prominent role in the southern resistance as the deputy commander of the National Liberation Front (NLF) armed forces (formally known as the People's Liberation Armed Forces). In late 1965, just after the start of the Vietnam-U.S. war, Tan Huong Nam recorded Dinh's story, which was published in Hanoi in 1968. This account of a political coming-of-age is especially revealing of the opportunities the revolutionary cause opened to women.

The family reading noted in the first paragraph is the classic novel Luc Van Tien *by Nguyen Dinh Chieu, the prominent nineteenth-century southern scholar and foe of the French whose poem in praise of peasant resistance (document 1.1) was probably written in Ben Tre. This novel in verse, which tells of the triumph of a young couple over wicked people, affirms both Confucian ideas of virtue and the Buddhist faith in the ultimate victory of good over evil.*

Whenever we had nothing to do at night, we would gather around the oil lamp . . . and listened to my brother read [Chieu's novel]. . . . Sometimes . . . I wept and the neighbors also wept. Once in a while, my father nodded his head in approval and commented:

—This story teaches people all the virtues they must have in life: humanity, kindness, filial piety, courage, determination and loyalty. . . .

. . . I hated those in the old days who abused their power, position and wealth to harm honest people. . . . On one occasion, the landlord in the village came to my house and demanded paddy [unmilled rice] in a threatening manner. My parents had to hastily prepare food and wine to regale him. We were out of chickens then, so they had to catch the hen about to lay eggs which I had been raising, and slaughter it for him to eat. When he finally left, his face crimson with all the drinking, I broke down and cried in anger, and demanded that my mother compensate me for the hen. In that period (1930) I noticed that my brother Ba Chan came and went at odd hours. Sometimes men came to the house, sat and whispered for a while and then disappeared. One day, I heard whispers in the room, I looked in and saw my brother hand to my father a piece of red cloth embroidered with something yellow inside [a hammer and sickle flag of the Communists]. . . .

. . . [M]y older brother Ba Chan was suddenly arrested by the puppet village officials who took him and jailed him. . . . It was Muon, the same Canton Chief—the tyrannical landlord who had come to my house to collect rent, drink and swallow my hen which was about to lay eggs—who now angrily hit the prisoners with a walking stick while drinking and shouting. . . .

. . . My brother was not the only one who was tortured, many other old and young people were also tortured. Many men were beaten until they passed out, blood trickling from their mouths, heads and feet, and dyeing the cement floor a greyish and purplish color. . . . I just stood there, frozen, and wept in anger. . . .

. . . My brother was not released until half a year later. We wept with joy. He loved me even more than before because I was the only one in the family who had taken care of him during his imprisonment. I asked him:

—You didn't do anything to them, then why did they beat you up so brutally?

He smiled and said:

—Of course I did something, why not?

—You mean you were a subversive?

—Don't be silly! I make revolution to overthrow the landlords who are oppressing and exploiting us, like Canton Chief Muon, and also to overthrow the French who have stolen our country from us.

He explained to me at great length, but I did not understand anything more than that the Communists loved the poor and opposed the officials in the village. My love for my brother and the men who had been jailed blossomed and deepened with such new and significant events. . . .

. . . [In 1936] the movement was on the rise. People from many areas frequently came to hold meetings in my house. My brother Ba Chan persuaded me to help and cook for them. I agreed at once. They all treated me with affection like my brother Ba. They were all good people and my parents were very fond of them. . . .

. . . [B]esides cooking when they came to hold meetings I was given the job of delivering letters, propagandizing people in the hamlets and village to join mutual aid associations and rice transplanting and hoeing teams, encouraging people to buy the "Dan Chung" (People) newspaper, and mobilizing women. . . . Whatever task I was given I performed with a lot of zeal. . . .

. . . After succeeding in a few tasks, I became very eager to operate and wanted to leave because if I stayed home a lot of chores, such as cooking, working in the ricefields and tending the vegetable garden, would get in the way of my work. I began to move around more [on party business]. Some nights I stayed out and came home very late. My parents were afraid I would become "bad" and said, "State affairs are not for girls to take care of. And even if women can do it, they must be very capable. What can our daughter Dinh do? If she's caught, she'll confess everything and harm others." At that time, I had reached the puberty period and caught the attention of many youths in the village. Several sent matchmakers to my house to ask for my hand. My parents wanted to accept and give me away in marriage to put an end to their worries, but I absolutely refused to go along. I often confided to my brother Ba:

—I only want to work for the revolution, I don't want to get married yet.

1.9 Truong Nhu Tang on his conversion to the nationalist cause in the mid-1940s

This offspring of a well-to-do Saigon family was an unlikely nationalist recruit. His grandfather, a Confucian scholar, had worked for the French administration. His father was determined to see his son well educated, gainfully employed, and thus able to add to the family's already substantial wealth. To that end Tang attended the best French schools open to Vietnamese and then moved to France for pharmacy studies. His nationalist awakening there offers more testimony to the power of the ideas Ho promoted and the striking personal appeal that Ho himself exercised. Many other youths embraced the revolution as Tang did, without ever joining the Communist Party or fully accepting its principles and policies. Disowned by his family, Tang eventually returned to Vietnam to teach school while actively supporting the Viet Minh in the anti-French struggle. He later served as an NLF organizer in Saigon and as a top-ranking member of the NLF leadership. He and other southern activists became increasingly restive under Hanoi's control of the NLF in the latter stages of the anti-American war. Tang fled abroad in 1975, dismayed by the realization that the North was going to dominate the South. His ultimate disillusionment with the revolution makes all the more poignant and convincing his recollections here of how he became a convert to the liberation cause.

Each Sunday we would gather at my grandfather's house to visit and also to listen as he taught us the precepts of Confucian ethics. He would remind us of our duty to live virtuous lives, lives of personal rectitude and filial piety. And he would talk about the five cardinal ethical principles: *nhon, nghia, le, tri, tin* ("benevolence, duty, propriety, conscience, and faithfulness"). There was nothing abstract or dry about his exposition. Instead he would weave his story around the adventures and exploits of ancient Chinese heroes and sages, whose lives illustrated one or another of these virtues. For boys especially, he would tell us, there are two unshakable necessities: protection of the family's honor and loyalty to the nation. . . .

At the Chasseloup Laubat [an exclusive Saigon school for children of the French colonial administrators and select Vietnamese] we spoke and wrote exclusively French, and we learned, along with mathematics, science, and literature, all about the history and culture of *nos ancêtres les Gaulois*. . . . About our own country we remained profoundly ignorant, except for what we read in the final chapters of our history books, the ones on France's colonial empire, *France outre-mer*. . . . It wasn't until after I had begun secondary school that I began to realize that I was—in some ways at least—different.

The scene of my initiation into the mysteries of colonialism was the lycée schoolyard during recess. As the games we played became rougher and more competitive, my Vietnamese friends and I learned that we, in contrast to our French schoolmates, were part of a racial entity sometimes called *nhaques* (peasants), sometimes *mites* (a derogatory abbreviation of *Annamite*, the French term for Vietnamese). . . . Soon shock gave way to anger, and recesses were occasionally punctuated with brawls, which mirrored the hatreds felt by many of our elders. . . .

[In 1946 Tang moved to Paris to pursue pharmaceutical studies. There he and other students met with Ho, who was then in France seeking recognition of the DRV's independence.] I was immediately struck by Ho Chi Minh's appearance. Unlike the others, who were dressed in Western-style clothes, Ho wore a frayed, high-collared Chinese jacket. On his feet he had rubber sandals. . . . [H]e gave off an air of fragility, almost sickliness. But these impressions only contributed to the imperturbable dignity that enveloped him as though it were something tangible. . . . Ho exuded a combination of inner strength and personal generosity that struck me with something like a physical blow. He looked directly at me, and at the others, with a magnetic expression of intensity and warmth.

Almost reflexively I found myself thinking of my grandfather. There was that same effortless communication of wisdom and caring with which my grandfather had personified for us the values of Confucian life. I was momentarily startled when Ho reached his arm out in a sweeping gesture, as if he were gathering us in. "Come, my children," he said and sat down on the steps. We settled around him, as if it were the most natural thing in the world. . . . He told us to call him Bac Ho—Uncle Ho—instead of Mr. President. Then he began asking each of us in turn about our families, our names, our studies, where we were from, how old we were. He wanted to know too about our feelings toward Vietnam's independence, a subject on which most of us had only the vaguest thoughts. . . .

When Ho realized that among our group there were students from the North, South, and Center of the country, he said gently, but with great intensity, "*Voila!* the youth of our great family of Vietnam. Our Vietnam is one, our nation is one. You must remember, though the rivers may run dry and the mountains erode, the nation will always be one." . . . Ho went on to say that, when he was born, Vietnam was a nation of slaves. . . .

Eighty years of slavery had diminished the nation; now it was time to re-establish the heritage given to us by our ancestors and recover from our backwardness. If our people were to gain an honorable place among the peoples of the world, it would depend largely on us, on our efforts to study and learn and to contribute to the national family.

It was a message that combined ardent and idealistic nationalism with a moving personal simplicity. Ho had created for us an atmosphere of family and country and had pointed to our own role in the great patriotic endeavor. Before an hour had passed, he had gained the heart of each one of us sitting around him on those steps. . . .

. . . Against what I knew to be my father's deepest wishes—not to mention his explicit orders—I was now on my way to becoming a rebel. . . . In my mind's eye, I began to envision a radical westernization of Vietnam along the lines of Japan's miraculous industrialization of the late nineteenth and early twentieth centuries. There seemed to me no reason that Vietnam, newborn to independence but full of hard-working, intelligent citizens, could not adopt the best from the world's political and economic cultures: the American approach to economics, the German scientific spirit, the French fervor for democracy.

1.10 Peasants in the Red River Delta on their reaction to the Viet Minh in the late 1940s

The testimonies collected by French scholar Gérard Chaliand in October–November 1967 offer insight on the revolutionary appeal in the northern countryside. We hear from peasants in Hung Yen province in the Red River Delta, a region longer and more densely settled than Nguyen Thi Dinh's Mekong region and distinctly poorer. They recall the anti-French sentiment, the poverty, and the injustice that made the countryside a Viet Minh stronghold.

a. Tuan Doanh (a member of the Hung Yen provincial committee of the Communist Party)

Historically, our province has been a battlefield ever since . . . the second and third centuries. The marshes and reeds provided an excellent terrain for guerrilla warfare in the lowlands, and the dense vegetation stopped the enemy from advancing. There were also major battles against the Mongols in the thirteenth century. It is fair to say that the peasants of Hung Yen have had to withstand continual attempts at invasion throughout their history, in addition to long periods of drought and flooding. They've had the French to contend with, too! . . .

The first [Communist] Party cell in the province was set up in 1930. . . . By 1940, repression or no repression, we were able to get on with our propaganda work and agitation. Each militant was required to establish contact with several villages . . . and do his best to establish nests of sympathizers. This went on from 1940 until 1944. There were very few professional revolutionaries in the area — no more than four or five in the entire province; the rest did ordinary jobs as well as working for the Party. And then, round about 1943 or 44, we started making military preparations. On a very small scale, mind: we had no arms and ammunition as yet. . . .

On 9 March 1945 came the Japanese *coup* toppling the colonial administration. . . . The French were in such disarray that they could do nothing to stop us. Side by side with the armed conflict, the masses were incited to lay hands on the stocks of rice held by the Japanese. . . . The communal rice-stocks in the possession of the village elders . . . were shared out, together with the supplies appropriated by the Japanese. In addition, all taxes were withheld. As a result of these steps, starvation was averted in the province. . . . This seizure of rice for public use finally removed the peasants' uncertainties about the revolution. . . .

In August 1945, we took over every district in the land. . . . Suddenly we found ourselves enjoying independence and freedom. The mood of the country was unbelievable: people were burning with enthusiasm. I shall never forget those times.

And then, in December, the French invaded us again. . . .

After 1949 the people living in the delta became [the target of French forces]. . . . [O]ur army and cadres could not be dislodged; the peasants continued to hide them. A complete network of underground shelters and communication trenches was established, stretching for tens of miles, with exits in or on the outskirts of villages. As the war dragged on, it became possible to conceal and accommodate whole regiments and, eventually, whole divisions.

b. Phan Van Ha (a thirty-six-year-old commune party secretary)

My own family were landless peasants: all they had was a house and a small yard. They were hired labourers, working for landowners. . . .

I was eleven when my father died, after an illness, at the age of fifty-four. My mother died of starvation during the great famine of 1945. I was fourteen at the time. We were a family of six. . . . My little sister and I took jobs, looking after landowners' children. . . . At that time, I ate one meal a day: rice with fig-leaves, and usually a soup made from rice and bran. There were no vegetables: all we had was rice and salt. One of my sisters died of starvation in 1945; another was killed during a bombardment in 1948. And one of my brothers was killed in the army in 1953. That leaves the three of us. . . .

. . . The landowners used to hold huge feasts and make the villagers contribute. Some of them had three wives. They ate meat or chicken every day. When you were working for them, you got a few sweet potatoes in the morning and some rice at midday. That was for heavy labour. . . . If they wanted to grab a peasant's land, they would plant some liquor in his home (the colonial administration had exclusive rights to liquor) and tip off the authorities. The peasant was duly prosecuted and had to sell his plot. That is how my uncle was dispossessed. And another thing: peasants would run into debt whenever the taxes fell due. The interest rate was 50 per cent for a period of six months. They would just manage to pay off the interest. The debt itself was never disposed of. . . . The poorer a family was, the greater the attempts to make it sell its land, fall into debt and move to another part of the country. . . . In 1943 the village notables [individuals with influence based on their wealth or education] decided to put pressure on my family. At their bidding a man came to my uncle's house, feigned insanity and set fire to the place. . . . [M]y two uncles were arrested for laying hands on the notables. There was pandemonium at the district court. In the end, my uncles had to sell all they owned to pay for the trial and were sentenced to three months' imprisonment. We had already lost three saos [about a third of an acre] as a result of the liquor incident, and now the last four saos had to be sold. We had nothing left. In 1945, the young uncle to whom all this had happened was the first person in Quoc Tri to join the self-defence forces; afterwards, the whole family served in the Resistance.

DEEPENING U.S. ENGAGEMENT IN INDOCHINA, 1943–1954

Within one decade, under three presidents — Franklin Roosevelt, Harry Truman, and Dwight Eisenhower — U.S. policy toward French Indochina moved from qualified verbal support for independence to heavy material support for an embattled colonial army. Accordingly Ho Chi Minh and other Vietnamese Communists came to view the United States not as a likely patron but as an increasingly formidable obstacle to their revolution.

1.11 U.S. policy shifts from self-determination to Cold War containment, 1943–1950

Roosevelt, like his successors in the White House, viewed Indochina through the prism of global concerns. The World War II crusade against expansionist powers—Germany, Italy, and Japan—had dominated Roosevelt's attention, with priority given to putting together a coalition to secure victory. To rally support, Roosevelt made self-determination one of the main war aims. While decolonization was high on his agenda, the president still thought of independence for young, emerging nations such as Vietnam as something for the distant future. The onset of the Cold War early in the Truman presidency changed the global context and made self-determination less important than good postwar relations with France and containment of Soviet influence. Some of the most vulnerable points in the Cold War struggle were colonies moving toward independence and seemingly at risk of disorder or a Communist takeover. The return of French forces to Indochina in late 1945 and the onset of fighting between them and a Communist-led Vietnamese resistance put the Truman administration on a path toward intervention even as it called attention to the legitimate claims of Vietnamese nationalists. In early 1950 the Truman administration made a highly consequential commitment to back the French. Truman gave his formal approval. The outbreak of the Korean War in June made urgent the new program of support for the French. The U.S. treasury was soon covering the bulk of France's war costs, and the U.S. military dispatched its first advisers to the war zone.

a. President Franklin D. Roosevelt and Premier Joseph Stalin, discussion at the Tehran conference, 28 November 1943

THE PRESIDENT said that . . . he felt that many years of honest labor would be necessary before France would be re-established. He said the first necessity for the French, not only for the Government but the people as well, was to become honest citizens.

[Stalin] agreed and went on to say that he did not propose to have the Allies shed blood to restore Indochina, for example, to the old French colonial rule. . . .

THE PRESIDENT said he was 100% in agreement with Marshal Stalin and remarked that after 100 years of French rule in Indochina, the inhabitants were worse off than they had been before.... He added that he had discussed with [Chinese leader and U.S. ally] Chiang Kai-shek the possibility of a system of trusteeship for Indochina which would have the task of preparing the people for independence within a definite period of time, perhaps 20 to 30 years.

b. State Department policy paper on postwar Asia, 22 June 1945

At the end of the war, political conditions in Indochina, and especially in the north, will probably be particularly unstable. The Indochinese independence groups, which may have been working against the Japanese, will quite possibly oppose the restoration of French control. Independence sentiment in the area is believed to be increasingly strong....

French policy toward Indochina will be dominated by the desire to reestablish control in order to reassert her prestige in the world as a great power. This purpose will be augmented by the potent influence of the Banque de l'Indochine and other economic interests. Many French appear to recognize that it may be necessary for them to make further concessions to Indochinese self-government and autonomy primarily to assure native support but also to avoid unfriendly United States opinion....

The United States recognizes French sovereignty over Indochina. It is, however, the general policy of the United States to favor a policy which would allow colonial peoples an opportunity to prepare themselves for increased participation in their own government with eventual self-government as the goal.

c. National Security Council report 64, "The Position of the United States with Respect to Indochina," 27 February 1950

[T]he threat of communist aggression against Indochina is only one phase of anticipated communist plans to seize all of Southeast Asia....

A large segment of the Indochinese nationalist movement was seized in 1945 by Ho Chi Minh, a Vietnamese who under various aliases has served as a communist agent for thirty years.... In 1946, he attempted, but failed to secure French agreement to his recognition as the head of a government of Vietnam. Since then he has directed a guerrilla army in raids against French installations and lines of communication. French forces which have been attempting to restore law and order found themselves pitted against a determined adversary who manufactures effective arms locally, who received supplies of arms from outside sources, who maintained no capital or permanent headquarters and who was, and is able, to disrupt and harass almost any area within Vietnam (Tonkin, Annam and Cochinchina) at will.

The United States has, since the Japanese surrender, pointed out to the French Government that the legitimate nationalist aspirations of the people of Indochina must be satisfied, and that a return to the prewar colonial rule is not possible. The Department of State has pointed out to the French Government that it was and is necessary to establish and support governments in Indochina particularly in Vietnam, under leaders who are capable of attracting to their causes the non-communist nationalist followers who had drifted to the Ho Chi Minh communist movement in the absence of any non-communist nationalist movement around which to plan their aspirations. . . .

[Conclusions:] It is important to United States security interests that all practicable measures be taken to prevent further communist expansion in Southeast Asia. Indochina is a key area of Southeast Asia and is under immediate threat. . . .

Accordingly, the Departments of State and Defense should prepare as a matter of priority a program of all practicable measures designed to protect United States security interests in Indochina.

1.12 Ho Chi Minh, denunciation of deepening U.S intervention, January 1952

Ho took note of rising U.S. support for the French, which he interpreted in terms of his assumptions about intense economic competition among capitalist states. He concluded that Americans were bent on elbowing the French out. For support against this powerful new foe, Ho looked to his Communist neighbor to the north. China's recently victorious Communists quickly lined up behind the Viet Minh, providing from 1950 onward strategic guidance, troop training, and substantial matériel.

At the very beginning of the war, the Americans supplied France with money and armaments. To take an example, 85 per cent of weapons, war materials and even canned food captured by our troops were labelled "made in U.S.A.". This aid had been stepped up all the more rapidly since June 1950 when the U.S.A. began interfering in Korea. American aid to the French invaders consisted in airplanes, boats, trucks, military outfits, napalm bombs, etc.

Meanwhile, the Americans compelled the French colonialists to step up the organisation of four divisions of puppet [Vietnamese] troops with each party footing half the bill. . . .

The French colonialists are now landed in a dilemma: either they receive U.S. aid and be then replaced by their American "allies", or they receive nothing, and be then defeated by the Vietnamese people. To organise the puppet army by means of pressganging the youth in areas under their control would be tantamount to swallowing a bomb when one is hungry: a day will come when at last the bomb bursts inside. However not to organise the army on this basis would mean instantaneous death for the enemy because even the French strategists have to admit that the French Expeditionary Corps grows thinner and thinner and is on the verge of collapse.

Furthermore, U.S. aid is paid for at a very high price. In the enemy held areas, French capitalism is swept aside by American capitalism. American concerns like the Petroleum Oil Corporation, the Caltex Oil Corporation, the Bethle[he]m Steel Corporation, the Florid[a] Phosphate Corporation and others, monopolise rubber, ores, and other natural resources of our country. U.S. goods swamp the market. The French reactionary press . . . is compelled to acknowledge sadly that French capitalism is now giving way to U.S. capitalism.

The U.S. interventionists have nurtured the French aggressors and the Vietnamese puppets, but the Vietnamese people do not let anybody delude and enslave them.

People's China is our close neighbour. Her brilliant example gives us a great impetus. . . . Can the U.S. interventionists, who were drummed out of China and are now suffering heavy defeats in Korea, conquer Viet Nam? Of course, not!

1.13 The Eisenhower administration response to the collapsing French position in Indochina, March–April 1954

When Dwight Eisenhower took over from Truman in early 1953, he held to the established Indochina policy even as the French faltered and struggled to break a Viet Minh siege of their garrison at Dien Bien Phu. The new president and his secretary of state described the U.S. commitment in broad terms

*that were to become staples in U.S. officials' discussions of Vietnam: Ho was
a threat to the genuine independence of Vietnam, Indochina was a domino
whose fall would have far-reaching repercussions, and U.S. policy could not
afford to repeat the appeasement that had brought on World War II.*

a. Secretary of State John Foster Dulles, address to the Overseas Press Club in New York, 29 March 1954

The Communists are attempting to prevent the orderly development of independence [of Vietnam, Laos, and Cambodia]. . . .

The scheme is to whip up the spirit of nationalism so that it becomes violent. That is done by professional agitators. Then the violence is enlarged by Communist military and technical leadership and the provision of military supplies. In these ways, international Communism gets a strangle-hold on the people and it uses that power to "amalgamate" the peoples into the Soviet orbit. . . .

"Amalgamation" is now being attempted in Indochina under the ostensible leadership of Ho Chi Minh. He was indoctrinated in Moscow. . . . [He worked with a Soviet agent] to bring China into the Soviet orbit. Then Ho transferred his activities to Indochina.

Those fighting under the banner of Ho Chi Minh have largely been trained and equipped in Communist China. They are supplied with artillery and ammunition through the Soviet-Chinese Communist bloc. . . . Military supplies for the Communist armies have been pouring into Viet-Nam at a steadily increasing rate.

Military and technical guidance is supplied by an estimated 2,000 Communist Chinese. They function with the forces of Ho Chi Minh in key positions — in staff sections of the High Command, at the division level and in specialized units such as signal, engineer, artillery and transportation.

In the present stage, the Communists in Indochina use nationalistic anti-French slogans to win local support. But if they achieved military or political success, it is certain that they would subject the People to a cruel Communist dictatorship taking its orders from Peiping and Moscow.

The tragedy would not stop there. If the Communist forces won uncontested control over Indochina or any substantial part thereof, they would surely resume the same pattern of aggression against other free peoples in the area.

b. President Dwight Eisenhower to British prime minister Winston Churchill, 4 April 1954

I am sure that like me you are following with the deepest interest and anxiety the daily reports of the gallant fight being put up by the French at Dien Bien Phu. . . .

But regardless of the outcome of this particular battle, I fear that the French cannot alone see the thing through, this despite the very substantial assistance in money and matériel that we are giving them. . . . [A]nd if they do not see it through, and Indochina passes into the hands of the Communists, the ultimate effect on our and your global strategic position with the consequent shift in the power ratio throughout Asia and the Pacific could be disastrous. . . . It is difficult to see how Thailand, Burma and Indonesia could be kept out of Communist hands. This we cannot afford. The threat to Malaya, Australia and New Zealand would be direct. The offshore island chain would be broken. The economic pressure on Japan which would be deprived of non-Communist markets and sources of food and raw materials would be such, over a period of time, that it is difficult to see how Japan could be prevented from reaching an accommodation with the Communist world which would combine the manpower and natural resources of Asia with the industrial potential of Japan. . . .

. . . [W]e failed to halt Hirohito, Mussolini and Hitler by not acting in unity and in time. That marked the beginning of many years of stark tragedy and desperate peril. May it not be that our nations have learned something from that lesson?

Drawing the Lines of Conflict, 1954–1963

In mid-1954 the future of South Vietnam began to emerge as a major bone of contention between U.S. cold warriors and Vietnam's Communist leaders. The defining event was the French defeat at Dien Bien Phu in the spring. A Viet Minh army, built up by former history teacher Vo Nguyen Giap with help from the newly installed Communist regime in China, won a decisive victory. French domestic support for the distant colonial struggle had evaporated and with it the last hopes of France's holding on to Indochina. President Dwight Eisenhower had considered last-minute military measures to rescue the beleaguered French garrison but encountered congressional reluctance and finally bowed to international pressure for a diplomatic solution.

The result was a major international agreement reached at Geneva. In July representatives from both sides of the Cold War divide (the Soviet Union, China, the United States, Britain, and France), along with the states emerging from the dissolution of the Indochina colony (Ho Chi Minh's DRV and the French-created government in Saigon, as well as Cambodia and Laos), came to terms ending the French era. Vietnam, as well as Laos and Cambodia, gained independence. But rather than handing the Vietnamese Communist Party an unambiguous victory, the conference limited immediate DRV control to the territory north of the seventeenth parallel, with roughly half of Vietnam's 27 million people. The conference also called for a cooling-off period before any attempt at unification. The contending forces were first to be separated into North and South, and then in 1956, national elections were to bring together the two parts of the temporarily divided country.

For the Eisenhower administration, the Geneva agreement was a serious setback to the fundamental Cold War goal of containing the Soviet bloc. But the Geneva provision for a delayed resolution of the status of the South created an opening that was quickly exploited by the president and his secretary of state, John Foster Dulles. They sponsored Ngo Dinh Diem as the leader of the South Vietnamese state created earlier by the French. To shore up this bulwark against further communist expansion, they also hastily constructed the Southeast Asia Treaty Organization (SEATO) to line up Britain, France, Pakistan, Thailand, Australia, New Zealand, and the Philippines behind the United States. SEATO proved nothing more than a talk shop, but the Eisenhower administration's backing for Diem did succeed in making Geneva's temporary division into something that looked permanent. Diem gradually consolidated his political control, rejected the national elections stipulated by the Geneva agreement, created the Republic of Vietnam to control the South, and set about eliminating potential rivals, including the former emperor, Bao Dai, and those recently associated with the Viet Minh during the anti-French war.

The emergence of a U.S.-sponsored South Vietnamese state in turn challenged Hanoi's commitment to national unity as part of the long-term liberation struggle. Ho had initially reacted to the half a loaf Geneva had given him with stoic acceptance. Hanoi's allies in Moscow and Beijing were not interested in a confrontation with Washington over Vietnam, so Ho agreed to put the southern question on hold for the moment, focusing instead on building a socialist state in the North. However, Diem rejected any national election to end the Geneva-imposed division and persisted in his repressive campaign against Hanoi's remaining organizational assets in the South.

Ho and his colleagues began to reassess their policy. In 1959 they shifted toward a more aggressive southern strategy, which involved opening a supply and communications line to the South (the Ho Chi Minh Trail). To safeguard the portion of the trail that ran through Laos, the DRV threw its support to Laotian Communist forces locked in conflict with the U.S.-backed royal army. The new southern strategy also involved the creation in 1960 of the NLF, a new version of the Viet Minh. Its main task was to mobilize a wide spectrum of southern society against the Diem regime. Finally, Hanoi sought the support of Moscow and Beijing, a goal complicated by the rising discord between the two Communist powers. Nikita Khrushchev's Soviet Union held back, restrained by its commitment to peaceful coexistence with the United States. Mao Zedong's China offered considerably more help. Post-Geneva aid to the DRV substantially exceeded Soviet grants, and by 1962 it included a major transfer of weapons. In 1963, with Hanoi tilting ideologically toward Beijing, military staffs began discussing a coordinated response to a possible U.S. invasion.

In the course of these developments, Le Duan emerged as an influential voice and Ho's successor as party leader. A native of central Vietnam, he had a genuine working-class background. Both he and his father had been railway workers. Le Duan had participated in the founding of the Indochinese Communist Party and spent a good part of the 1930s and early 1940s in French prisons. During the French war he served in the South, heading up the party's Central Office for South Vietnam (COSVN). Directing the struggle in the South gave him unusual insight on, as well as an emotional investment in, that contested region.

By the early 1960s, as the struggle for the South began to heat up, four sorts of Vietnamese (all southerners) played prominent roles. The first were the Viet Minh activists in the South who had gone north in 1954 as part of the disentangling of hostile forces (and thus were known as regroupees). They now returned home, marching along the newly inaugurated and still quite rudimentary Ho Chi Minh Trail through Laos and Cambodia. They reinforced a second group—the stay-behind members of the Viet Minh who had survived the Diem repression and who had been desperately calling for support from the North. Easily lost to sight was a third group, peasants on whom activists depended as they built the NLF's village network. Peasant political engagement, important in frustrating the French, would help undermine the regime of Ngo Dinh Diem just as it would in time make the war difficult for the Americans. Finally, on the other side of the conflict was an assortment of anti-Communist southerners who had aligned with Diem. They included, notably, Catholics who had fled Communist rule in 1954, officers and administrators who had thrown in their lot with the French, and landlords who were wedded to the rural status quo.

By 1963 the struggle among these groups of South Vietnamese backed by either Hanoi or Washington had become intense and posed choices for the patrons that carried major long-term consequences. President John Kennedy had continued his predecessor's support for the Diem regime. But the U.S. nation-building project was in serious trouble. Diem was threatened not only by the NLF but also by other southerners antagonized by his autocratic style. Kennedy could not stomach an NLF victory and thus an embarrassing defeat for his policy, and so he decided that Diem should go. The DRV's leaders watched the crisis in the South for hints of U.S. intentions; Diem's overthrow confirmed that U.S. leaders were sticking to the same interventionist script even if they varied the way they delivered their lines.

The following materials on the deepening Vietnamese-American antagonism push to the fore classic questions about how countries maneuver themselves into unwanted conflicts:

- What made the fate of South Vietnam such a difficult issue in relations between Vietnamese and American leaders?
- By what stages did leaders in Hanoi and Washington advance toward a showdown? Who made the key decisions at each stage?
- How did the emerging struggle for South Vietnam look from the perspective of ordinary Vietnamese?

A COUNTRY DIVIDED OR UNITED?
JULY 1954–DECEMBER 1960

Both the Vietnamese Communist Party and the Eisenhower administration bowed to the Geneva conference arrangements, but neither did so gladly. Geneva thus represented a truce, not an end to conflict.

2.1 Ho Chi Minh, report to the Communist Party Central Committee, 15 July 1954

With a compromise agreement taking shape at the Geneva conference, Ho sought to dispel the discontent within the party about settling short of victory. He called for a conciliatory postwar policy while pointing to the danger posed by U.S. policy and maintaining the ultimate goal of a united Vietnam.

[N]ow the French are having talks with us while the American imperialists are becoming our main and direct enemy; so our spearhead must be directed at the latter. . . . US policy is to expand and internationalize the Indochina war. Ours is to struggle for peace and oppose the US war policy. . . .

. . . We must take firm hold of the banner of peace to oppose the US imperialists' policy of direct interference in, and prolongation and expansion of, the war in Indochina. Our policy must change in consequence: formerly we confiscated the French imperialists' properties; now, as negotiations are going on, we may, in accordance with the principle of equality and mutual benefit, allow French economic and cultural interests to be preserved in Indochina. . . . In the past, our aim was to wipe out the puppet administration and army with a view to national reunification; now we practice a policy of leniency and seek reunification of the country through nation-wide elections.

Peace calls for an end to the war; and to end the war one must agree on a cease-fire. A cease-fire requires regrouping zones, that is, enemy troops should be regrouped in a zone with a view to their gradual withdrawal, and ours in another. We must secure a vast area where we would have ample means for building, consolidating and developing our forces so as to exert influence over other regions and thereby advance towards reunification. The setting up of regrouping zones does not mean partition of the country; it is a temporary measure leading to reunification. Owing to the delimitation and exchange of zones, some previously free areas will be temporarily occupied by the enemy; their inhabitants will be dissatisfied; some people might fall prey to discouragement and to enemy deception. We should make it clear to our compatriots that the trials they are going to endure for the sake of the interests of the whole country, for the sake of our long-range interests, will be a cause for glory and will earn them the gratitude of the whole nation. We should keep everyone free from pessimism and negativism and urge all to continue a vigorous struggle for the complete withdrawal of French forces and for independence.

2.2 "Final Declaration of the Geneva Conference on the Problem of Restoring Peace in Indo-China," 21 July 1954

The Geneva settlement brought an end to the fighting between the French and the Viet Minh and secured the independence of Vietnam as well as Cambodia and Laos. No less important, it became a prime point of reference for all parties in the coming struggle over South Vietnam. It represented variously a set of restrictions to circumvent, a precedent or model for a new peace agreement, and a source of lessons for any future diplomacy. The most pertinent provisions — five in all — thus deserve reproducing exactly as they emerged from the conference proceedings.

4. The Conference takes note of the clauses . . . prohibiting the introduction into Viet-Nam of foreign troops and military personnel as well as of all kinds of arms and munitions. . . .

5. The Conference takes note of the clauses . . . to the effect that no military base under the control of a foreign State may be established

[in Vietnam] in the regrouping zones of the two parties [Hanoi and Saigon]. . . .

6. The Conference recognizes . . . that the military demarcation line is provisional and should not in any way be interpreted as constituting a political or territorial boundary. . . .

7. The Conference declares that, so far as Viet-Nam is concerned, the settlement of political problems, effected on the basis of respect for the principles of independence, unity and territorial integrity, shall permit the Viet-Namese people to enjoy the fundamental freedoms, guaranteed by democratic institutions established as a result of free general elections by secret ballot. . . . [G]eneral elections shall be held in July 1956, under the supervision of an international commission. . . .

12. In their relations with Cambodia, Laos and Viet-Nam, each member of the Geneva Conference undertakes to respect the sovereignty, the independence, the unity and the territorial integrity of the above-mentioned states, and to refrain from any interference in their internal affairs.

2.3 The Eisenhower administration's reaction to the Geneva accords, July and October 1954

With the ink on the Geneva accords hardly dry, the U.S. president and his senior advisers sought new ways to contain communism in Vietnam. This determination became immediately clear in public and private reactions to the Geneva settlement and resulted by the fall in a commitment to build a client state in southern Vietnam under the leadership of Ngo Dinh Diem with an army reshaped along American lines.

a. President Dwight Eisenhower, press conference statement, 21 July 1954

[T]he United States has not itself been party to or bound by the decisions taken by the [Geneva] Conference, but it is our hope that it will lead to the establishment of peace consistent with the rights and the needs of the countries concerned. The agreement contains features which we do not like, but a great deal depends on how they work in practice.

The United States is issuing at Geneva a statement to the effect that it is not prepared to join in the Conference declaration but, as loyal members of the United Nations, we also say that . . . the United States will not use force to disturb the settlement. We also say that any renewal of Communist aggression would be viewed by us as a matter of grave concern.

[Response to a reporter's question:] I think that when the freedom of a man in Viet-Nam or in China is taken away from him, I think our freedom has lost a little. I just don't believe that we can continue to exist in the world, geographically isolated as we are, if we just don't find a concerted, positive plan of keeping these free nations so tightly bound together that none of them will give up; and if they are not weakened internally by these other methods [communist propaganda, deceit, subversion, and coups], I just don't believe they will give up. I believe we can hold them.

b. National Security Council discussion of the Geneva settlement, 22 July 1954

[Secretary of State John Foster Dulles noted that] [t]he great problem from now on out was whether we could salvage what the Communists had ostensibly left out of their grasp in Indochina. . . . Secretary Dulles thought that the real danger to be anticipated came not primarily from overt Communist military aggression but from subversion and disintegration. In view of this, he said that he would almost rather see the French get completely out of the rest of Indochina and thus permit the United States to work directly with the native leadership in these states. . . .

. . . Of course, continued Secretary Dulles, it was not possible to say at this moment precisely how much money should be spent in any one of the free countries of Southeast Asia, but all of them in general must be built up if the dike against Communism is to be held. Accordingly, Secretary Dulles appealed to all the members of the Council to stand fast on this position. The President in turn called on all those present to support the views expressed by Secretary Dulles on these funds.

c. National Security Council discussion of support for Diem, 22 October 1954

Speaking with conviction, the President observed that in the lands of the blind, one-eyed men are kings. What we wanted, continued the President, was a Vietnamese force which would support Diem. Therefore let's get busy and get one, but certainly not at a cost of $400 million a year. The President said that he knew something from personal experience about doing this kind of job in this kind of area. He therefore was sure that something could be done and done quickly if we could simply decide on what to tell General [John] O'Daniel [head of the U.S. Military Assistance Advisory Group] to do.

Admiral Radford replied that there were 342 U.S. military personnel now in Vietnam for the purpose of training the native forces. This was much too small a number for carrying out a large-scale training program. Perhaps, therefore, the smart thing was to tell O'Daniel to go to Diem and tell him that the MAAG would try to organize an effective constabulary that would take its orders from Diem rather than from the Army. Admiral Radford also added his belief that the French were not really supporting Diem. . . .

The President then asked why we did not "get rough with the French". If we didn't do something very quickly, Diem would be down the drain with no replacement in sight. Accordingly, we ought to lay down the law to the French. It is true that we have to cajole the French with regard to the European area, but we certainly didn't have to in Indochina. . . .

The President then said that the obvious thing to do was simply to authorize General O'Daniel to use up to X millions of dollars — say, five, six or seven — to produce the maximum number of Vietnamese military units on which Prime Minister Diem could depend to sustain himself in power. . . .

[The president authorized] an urgent program to improve the loyalty and effectiveness of the Free Vietnamese forces.

2.4 President Ngo Dinh Diem, speech to the Council on Foreign Relations in New York, 13 May 1957, reflecting on the success of state building in South Vietnam

By 1957 Diem had consolidated his position in South Vietnam. His idiosyncratic brand of politics — shaped by his elite family's Confucian and Catholic outlook, by his own nationalism sharpened by his earlier work for the French, and by the advice and support of his influential siblings — seemed to be working. In May Diem took a victory lap in the United States, meeting with the president and appearing before Congress and influential foreign affairs groups. His public addresses reflected his newfound confidence while promoting his reputation as a firm anticommunist and dependable U.S. ally.

Our country inherited a bankrupt political system, a disorganized administration, a crumbling economy, an empty treasury. The country was plagued with politico-religious armed sects. . . . Our army was shapeless and under the command of foreigners. Nearly one million refugees — a tenth of the population — had to be received [from the North] and resettled. Moreover, Viet-Nam had to wrest back her sovereignty from France, who maintained over 150,000 troops in our country. We had to make of Viet-Nam, partitioned by the Geneva diktat, an independent and modern state, capable of governing and defending itself against colonialism, political and economic feudalism and, above all, against absorption by Communism, implanted in North Viet-Nam by the Geneva Accords. The task seemed almost hopeless and beyond our means. . . .

Events have belied those apprehensions. We have achieved independence without being engulfed by anarchy. We have preserved the peace without sacrificing our reconquered independence. We are now building a free economy. . . . In the same fashion, we shall achieve unification without abandoning freedom.

We have restored political stability, internal and external security, thanks to the sense of unity, the sound judgment and the energy of our people, as well as to the moral and material support of the American people. . . .

. . . American aid has met a complete success in Viet-Nam. . . .

The importation into China of a doctrine and of methods alien to Asia is a danger for its neighbours and especially for Viet-Nam. For Communism is organically interventionist.

It is only natural that Viet-Nam, which is the country most threatened by this new form of Colonialism, should seek to defend herself. For this reason we can only congratulate ourselves for our alliance with the United States, which is for us, like for other countries, a fundamental element of our legitimate defense.

2.5 Hanoi goes on the offensive, 1959–1960

Le Duan took the lead in making the case for stepping up action against the Diem government. After a quick inspection tour of the South in late 1958, he returned to Hanoi to make the case for answering the Diem repression with military as well as political action. He persuaded the Communist Party's governing Politburo, and its Central Committee agreed in principle at its January 1959 meeting. The following May, the party sent out formal instructions to implement this new, more forceful approach. In a September 1960 meet-

ing, party leaders raised the stakes in South Vietnam and also made Le Duan the permanent party leader. That meeting called for the creation of a united-front organization, modeled on the Viet Minh, with the task not simply of preserving the party's position in the South but of creating a broad popular movement to overthrow the U.S.-backed southern regime. In December the new organization, the NLF, dutifully sprang to life.

a. Politburo report to the Communist Party Central Committee, "On the Situation in South Vietnam," January 1959

The process of the establishment of the U.S.-Diem government clearly reveals that it is not a government that was born out of any national anti-communist struggle, but instead it is just a government that has accepted another master. The American imperialists and the Ngo family feudalists have replaced the French imperialists and the Bao Dai feudalists. This government is the result of the military and political failure of the French in their war of aggression against our nation, and it is also the result of the French imperialists' surrender to the American imperialists. It is a concrete representation on our nation of American aggression and neo-colonialist policy. It is also the result of the desperate struggle between the side representing socialism, national independence, peace, and democracy, and the side representing the colonial imperialist warmongers in Southeast Asia and the Pacific. . . .

In order to sustain this government, the U.S. and Diem have had to use armed force to terrorize and repress the mass movement demanding independence, democracy, peace, and reunification. During the past four years, the enemy's basic policy has been "denouncing communists" [*to cong*]. They have launched a series of "denounce communists" campaigns, using armed forces to conduct sweeps, arrest, murder, and torture the people and trying to pursue and destroy mass revolutionary organizations and the Party's organizational infrastructure. For this reason the situation in the rural countryside has remained constantly tense and unstable. At some times and in some places the situation is almost the same as it was during the war [against France]. The enemy's henchmen exploit their power by taking vengeance, by stealing property, by extorting money, and by shooting and murdering people without trial, ignoring the law. . . .

. . . [T]he U.S.-Diem regime in South Vietnam is fundamentally weak politically. But then why has it managed to survive over the past several years? It has survived because, following the ceasefire, we regrouped our armed forces, moving them up to North Vietnam. This meant that in the balance of forces between our side and the enemy, in South Vietnam the enemy is stronger than us. At the same time, we have a completely liberated North Vietnam that we can build into a large, solid revolutionary base area to continue pursuit of the revolutionary cause of our entire nation.

The U.S.-Diem forces rely on the military. They use military force to attack us and to strive to suppress and destroy our movement in South Vietnam. As for our side, we moved from armed struggle to political struggle. That means that we lowered our form of struggle, retreating from an offensive to a defensive posture.

b. Communist Party Central Committee resolution 15, January 1959

Because the South Vietnamese regime is an extremely reactionary and brutal colonialist and semi-feudal regime and because the South Vietnamese government is a dictatorial, warmongering imperialist and feudalist government, the people have no recourse other than revolution to liberate themselves from the shackles of slavery. Only the victory of the revolution can end the suffering of the South Vietnamese people and completely eliminate the [harmful] policies of the American imperialists and their lackeys in South Vietnam. . . . [The path of the Vietnamese revolution in South Vietnam] *is to use the power of the [civilian] masses, relying primarily on the political forces of the masses and supported by armed forces, to overthrow the imperialist and feudalist ruling authority and set up a people's revolutionary government.* That is the current goal of the people of South Vietnam. Because the U.S.-Diem ruling regime relies on armed force for its survival while we must rely on [civilian] mass forces and must use the masses to overthrow the enemy, if we want to achieve this goal, *only through a protracted and difficult process of struggle in which we actively build, consolidate, and develop revolutionary forces will we be able to create the necessary conditions for us to be able to seize favorable opportunities and secure final victory.* . . .

The process of carrying out a popular national democratic revolution in South Vietnam at the present time will be a process of building, consolidating, and developing mass struggle movements in the political, economic, and cultural arenas and ensuring that these movements follow the Party line. The process will advance from using lower struggle forms, pushing the enemy government back a step at a time, to the use of higher forms involving transformational changes that shake the government to its very foundations. Finally, the process will involve mobilizing the masses to rise up in insurrection to overthrow the US-Diem [regime] when the opportunity and timing, both domestically and internationally, is favorable. The amount of bloodshed that will result from this uprising will depend on the level of enemy resistance to the revolution and on the balance of forces between our side and the enemy. . . . During the course of this process, we must combine and coordinate the use of legal, semi-legal, and illegal forms of struggle. We must closely coordinate the activities of our urban movement with those of our movement in the rural countryside and in our base areas.

During this protracted, bitter, arduous, and complex . . . process, political struggle will play the primary role. . . . [I]n certain, limited areas armed self-defense forces and armed propaganda forces have grown up to support the political struggle. This has been a necessary development. However, when we use armed self-defense forces and armed propaganda forces, we must fully understand the principle that these forces are only to be used to support the political struggle and to support the interests of the political struggle. We must ensure that our cadre and our people . . . clearly understand that proselyting operations and organizing political forces from among the civilian masses is our basic and fundamental principle. Elimination of enemy thugs and officials [by assassination] must serve the interests of the political struggle and it must serve the interests of the movement. It must be conducted in a focused and extremely careful manner, and we must take the greatest precautions to conceal our forces and to preserve our organizations and agents. We must resolutely overcome the tendency to use terrorism against individuals instead of conducting a mass struggle.

c. National Liberation Front of South Vietnam, manifesto, December 1960

[T]he American imperialists, who had in the past helped the French colonialists to massacre our people, have now replaced the French in enslaving the southern part of our country through a disguised colonial regime. They have been using their stooge — the Ngo Dinh Diem administration — in their downright repression and exploitation of our compatriots, in their manoeuvres to permanently divide our country and to turn its southern part into a military base in preparation for war in Southeast Asia.

The aggressors and traitors, working hand in glove with each other, have set up an extremely cruel dictatorial rule. They persecute and massacre democratic and patriotic people, and abolish all human liberties. They ruthlessly exploit the workers, peasants and other labouring people, strangle the local industry and trade, poison the minds of our people with a depraved foreign culture, thus degrading our national culture, traditions and ethics. They feverishly increase their military forces, build military bases, use the army as an instrument for repressing the people and serving the US imperialists' scheme to prepare an aggressive war....

At present, our people are urgently demanding an end to the cruel dictatorial rule; they are demanding independence and democracy, enough food and clothing, and peaceful reunification of the country.

To meet the aspirations of our compatriots, the *South Viet Nam National Front for Liberation* came into being, pledging itself to shoulder the historic task of liberating our people from the present yoke of slavery.

The *South Viet Nam National Front for Liberation* undertakes to unite all sections of the people, all social classes, nationalities, political parties, organizations, religious communities and patriotic personalities, without distinction of their political tendencies, in order to struggle for the overthrow of the rule of the US imperialists and their stooges — the Ngo Dinh Diem clique — and for the realization of independence, democracy, peace and neutrality pending the peaceful reunification of the fatherland.

THE PERSPECTIVE OF NLF ACTIVISTS

Hanoi's decision in favor of a more active southern policy had a profound and immediate impact on two types of revolutionary activists who were to play a critical part in the rise of the NLF as a political and military force in South Vietnam. One group consisted of the "stay behinds" who had survived the Diem repression. The other was made up of veteran Viet Minh who had regrouped in the DRV after the Geneva division.

2.6 Le Van Chan (former Communist cadre), interview on rural organizing during the late 1950s

Le Van Chan (a pseudonym) provides a sense of the experience of Viet Minh activists who stayed behind and endured the Diem repression. This account reveals the appeal of the NLF to ordinary peasants with a sense of grievance.

Chan had been a party member since 1947 and had climbed into the upper echelon of the southern branch of the party organization. He was captured in 1962 and subsequently interviewed by Jeffrey Race, a discerning student of the southern insurgency.

[On Communist forces put on the defensive by Diem:] [T]he years 1954–1956 were a period of faith in the general elections, but toward the end of 1956 the communists were most pessimistic. . . .

During 1957 and 1958 the Party was able to recover its apparatus and its mass organizations, and it counted on contradictions within the government to produce a coup. Thus it emphasized troop proselytizing activities with the hope that in the event of a coup it could seize power. Because the Party judged that it had a sufficient chance to seize power in a coup through its mass organizations and its apparatus, it did not allow the armed forces it was still maintaining in the South to appear.

However, by 1959 the situation in the South had passed into a stage the communists considered the darkest in their lives: almost all their apparatus had been smashed [by the Diem government], the population no longer dared to provide support, families no longer dared to communicate with their relatives in the movement, and village chapters which previously had had one or two hundred members were now reduced to five or ten who had to flee into the jungle. Because of this situation Party members were angry at the Central Committee, and demanded armed action. The southern branch of the Party demanded of the Central Committee a reasonable policy in dealing with the southern regime, in order to preserve its own existence. If not, it would be completely destroyed.

In the face of this situation the Central Committee saw that it was no longer possible to seize power in the South by means of a peaceful struggle line, since the southern regime, with American assistance, was becoming stronger and not collapsing as had been predicted. Not only had the southern regime not been destroyed, it was instead destroying the Party. . . . As a result, the Fifteenth Conference of the Central Committee developed a decision [in January 1959] permitting the southern organization . . . to develop armed forces with the mission of supporting the political struggle line. These forces were not to fight a conventional war, nor were they intended merely for a guerrilla conflict. Their mission was to sap the strength of the government's village and hamlet forces, or what they called the "tyrannical elements." They were only to attack such units as entered their own base areas, in order to preserve the existence of the apparatus and to develop forces for a new line which the Central Committee would develop. Only in November of 1959 did this policy reach the village level, and it was from this decision that the guerrilla movement and the current armed forces in the South sprang into existence.

[On peasant reaction to Diem's policy of restoring to landlords parcels previously redistributed by the Viet Minh:] The peasants felt that they had spilled their blood to drive the French from the country, while the landlords sided with the French and fought against the peasants. Thus at the very least the peasants' rights to the land should have been confirmed. Instead, they were forced to buy the land, and thus they felt they were being victimized by the government. At the same time the Party apparatus took advantage of this situation to propagandize on how bad the government was, how it was the government of the landlords, stealing the land from the peasants. Added to this were the issues of corruption and abuses by officials. These things all made the people agree with the Party's propaganda on the land issue. After all, the peasants are 90 percent of the population of Vietnam, and land is their life-blood. If Diem took their land away, how could they be free, no matter how else he helped them? . . .

The peasants in the rural areas have a very limited outlook. Some have never in their lives left their village to visit Saigon or even their own provincial capital. They live close to the land and are concerned with nothing else. . . . Their concern is to see that their immediate interests are protected, and that they are treated reasonably and fairly.

In this situation, the communists are extremely clever. They never propagandize communism, which teaches that the land must be collectivized. If they did, how would the peasantry ever listen to them? Instead, they say: the peasants are the main force of the revolution; if they follow the Party, they will become masters of the countryside and owners of their land, and that scratches the peasants right where they itch. . . .

. . . Previously the peasantry felt that it was the most despised class, with no standing at all, particularly the landless and the poor peasants. For example, at a celebration they could just stand in a corner and look, not sit at the table like the village notables. Now the communists have returned and the peasants have power. The land has been taken from the landlords and turned over to the peasants, just as have all the local offices. Now the peasants can open their eyes and look up to the sky:

they have prestige and social position. The landlords and other classes must fear them because they have power: most of the cadres are peasants, most of the Party members are peasants, most of the military commanders are peasants. Only now do the peasants feel that they have proper rights: materially they have land and are no longer oppressed by the landlords; spiritually they have a position in society, ruling the landlords instead of being ruled by them. This the peasants like. But if the communists were to go and the government to come back, the peasants would return to their former status as slaves. Consequently they must fight to preserve their interests and their lives, as well as their political power.

2.7 Regroupees interviewed on returning to the South in the early 1960s

Between August 1964 and September 1965, Joseph Zasloff, working for the Rand Corporation (a think tank that did work for the Defense Department), conducted interviews with a large sample of regroupees who had either been captured or had defected to the Saigon side. The three whose views are excerpted below were from northern provinces of South Vietnam (Quang Nam and Quang Ngai). Typical of regroupees, they were Communist Party members who had earned their stripes fighting with the Viet Minh against the French. Hanoi regarded them as invaluable assets. The regroupees' comments reveal their frustration following the failure of elections in 1956 and the party's dilatory response to the Diem repression. (One regroupee described the pervasive homesickness of the late 1950s as "Northern days, Southern nights.")[1] They greeted with joy their orders in the early 1960s to return home. But they soon faced the challenges of traversing the still rudimentary Ho Chi Minh Trail and then rebuilding the devastated revolutionary organization in the South in the face of U.S.-inspired opposition.

a. NLF political cadre from a poor peasant family who joined the Viet Minh in 1945 (at age twenty-five), infiltrated the South in June 1961, and was captured in June 1964 (in his mid-forties)

[On dogged devotion to the revolutionary cause:] After the revolution of August '45, I thought we were getting very near our objective. But no, we

1. Quoted in J. J. Zasloff, *Political Motivation of the Viet Cong: The Vietminh Regroupees* (Rand memorandum RM-4703/2-ISA/ARPA, May 1968), 61.

had to fight in those nine years of Resistance [against the French] to get half the country. It was such a long struggle. Then I thought I was just going to regroup to the North to stay there two years [until the election], but I had to remain in the North seven years and then join the Liberation Front for three more years, and we still haven't got what we have been fighting and struggling for. But if I have to struggle all my life for these objectives, I will do it. If I cannot attain them in my lifetime, my children will continue my struggle; and if my children still do not achieve these goals, then my grandchildren will. There is a great solidarity among us. I cannot get discouraged.

[On eagerness to return south:] In 1957, when the unrest among the regroupees was strong, the [DRV] authorities had to do something about them. Diem was heard to be quite barbaric in oppressing the people in the South, especially the former Resistants. The regroupees could not stand to let people in their native villages suffer under Diem's rule. Someone had to talk to them during a whole night to try to calm them down, and he did not succeed at all — or accomplished little. The regroupees wanted to go very desperately. . . . When they were finally allowed to go south, they were exuberant. . . . They wanted to go home to their district, to their villages very much. Some died on the way south. Some who were so sick that they could not be sent south were extremely disappointed. Sometimes the latter insisted on a trip south and gave up their lives in the mountains.

b. NLF *senior captain, political cadre, and party member from a poor peasant family who joined the Viet Minh in 1945 (at age eighteen), infiltrated the South in 1960, and defected in June 1964 (in his mid-thirties)*

[On hardship facing early NLF units:] We lacked many things. From 1960 to 1962, we were completely self-sufficient. In 1963, the organizations among the people developed and the people supplied us food; this lessened our hardships. [In mid-1964] the situation, relatively speaking, had improved, because our forces had grown considerably. However, the troops' morale was tense, because they never had a moment to rest: study sessions, production of food, and fighting all day long. We did not have enough medicine to care for the sick, nor blankets to warm ourselves when the weather was cold. Everybody was weary, but thanks to the ideological guidance, they still liked the Front.

*c. NLF lieutenant in military intelligence and party member
from a middle peasant family who joined the Viet Minh in 1947
(at age sixteen), infiltrated the South in February 1962, and was
captured in September 1964 (in his mid-thirties)*

[On confidence in popular support:] If this revolution did not originate from the people, how could it have survived until now? If it had no support from the people, how could it have been so widely known and progress to this point? The revolution started out very poorly armed in many areas; it was the people who armed their soldiers. We have the people's support, but the revolution has not yet come to its successful ending. Why? Because there are still mighty weapons and lots of prisons on [the Saigon government (GVN)] side. If it were the GVN that had the support of the people, you would not have to fear defeat, because you would possess every means to bring the revolution to an end. . . .

At the beginning, we had only guerrillas at the village level who carried troubles to the GVN; now we have regiment-sized forces. A few years ago we lived in the mountain areas. Now we come down to the delta.

The GVN had its officials at the village level to conduct its business; now they are no more. The government's machinery has broken down completely at the village level. There is no one to carry out its programs. . . . The areas under Front control expand every year.

[On the U.S. role:] [T]he United States Government wants to turn South Vietnam into its colony, a market or a military base. But this is only their immediate aim. What they want most is to use South Vietnam as the gate to enter Southeast Asia. South Vietnam is already an American colony.

REACTING TO NLF SUCCESS, 1961–1963

Following its creation in late 1960, the NLF managed to extend its control across a substantial part of the countryside and to best the Saigon army in a series of sharp encounters. The NLF threat to the survival of a U.S. client increasingly worried the Kennedy administration. As much as earlier, Cold War orthodoxy made Vietnam an important battleground. But at the same time, a variety of sources—from presidential advisers to intelligence analysts to foreign leaders—warned against deepening U.S. intervention.

2.8 The Kennedy administration wrestles with an insurgency, November 1961

Washington's worries about the NLF culminated late in Kennedy's first year in office when a report from his secretaries of defense and state landed on his desk. They recommended a much expanded U.S. commitment. This included, if necessary, the dispatch of U.S. troops. Though Kennedy had doubts about sending troops, he did agree to planning for the possible use of American forces and to greater advisory and material support to ensure Diem's survival. Along with more economic and military aid went helicopters and armored vehicles for the Army of the Republic of Vietnam (ARVN), a steadily increasing number of U.S. military advisers (from 800 in 1961 to over 16,000 by late 1963), and an upgrade of the U.S. military headquarters in Saigon (renamed in February 1962 the Military Assistance Command, Vietnam [MACV]).

a. Secretary of Defense Robert McNamara and Secretary of State Dean Rusk, recommendations to President John F. Kennedy, 11 November 1961

It seems, on the face of it, absurd to think that a nation of 20 million people can be subverted by 15–20 thousand active guerrillas if the Government and people of that country do not wish to be subverted. South Viet-Nam is not, however, a highly organized society with an effective governing apparatus and a population accustomed to carrying civic responsibility. Public apathy is encouraged by the inability of most citizens to act directly as well as by the tactics of terror employed by the guerrillas throughout the countryside. . . .

The United States should commit itself to the clear objective of preventing the fall of South Viet-Nam to Communism. The basic means for accomplishing this objective must be to put the Government of South Viet-Nam into a position to win its own war against the guerrillas. We must insist that that Government itself take the measures necessary for that purpose in exchange for large-scale United States assistance in the military, economic and political fields. At the same time we must recognize that it will probably not be possible for the GVN to win this war as long as the flow of men and supplies from North Viet-Nam continues unchecked and the guerrillas enjoy a safe sanctuary in neighboring territory.

We should be prepared to introduce United States combat forces if that should become necessary for success. Dependent upon the circumstances, it may also be necessary for United States forces to strike at the source of the aggression in North Viet-Nam.

b. Kennedy comments to senior advisers (including McNamara, Rusk, incoming Central Intelligence Agency head John McCone, national security adviser McGeorge Bundy, and military adviser Maxwell Taylor), 15 November 1961

The President expressed the fear of becoming involved simultaneously on two fronts on opposite sides of the world [Europe and Southeast Asia]. He questioned the wisdom of involvement in Viet Nam since the basis thereof is not completely clear. By comparison he noted that Korea was a case of clear aggression which was opposed by the United States and other members of the U.N. The conflict in Viet Nam is more obscure and less flagrant. The President then expressed his strong feeling that in such a situation the United States needs even more the support of allies in such an endeavor as Viet Nam in order to avoid sharp domestic partisan criticism as well as strong objections from other nations of the world. The President said that he could even make a rather strong case against intervening in an area 10,000 miles away against 16,000 guerrillas with a native army of 200,000, where millions have been spent for years with no success. The President repeated his apprehension concerning support, adding that none could be expected from the French. . . .

. . . He cautioned that the technique of U.S. actions should not have the effect of unilaterally violating Geneva accords. He felt that a technique and timing must be devised which will place the onus of breaking the accords on the other side and require them to defend their actions. Even so, he realized that it would take some time to achieve this condition and even more to build up world opinion against Viet Cong. . . .

The President asked what nations would possibly support the U.S. intervention in Viet Nam, listing Pakistan, Thailand, the Philippines, Australia, New Zealand (?). . . . He described [the conflict in Vietnam] as being more a political issue, of different magnitude and (again) less defined than the Korean War. . . .

The President stated the time had come for neutral nations as well as others to be in support of U.S. policy *publicly*. . . . The President . . . expressed apprehension on support of the proposed action by the Congress as well as by the American people.

2.9 Central Intelligence Agency, secret memo on NLF methods for winning peasant support, 29 November 1963

The president's own intelligence agency was well aware of the NLF's rural appeal. CIA director John McCone sent this memo to the attention of Secretary of State Rusk. It correctly grasped the NLF's methods of winning support through patient organizing within villages, especially among poor peasants, young people, and women. But insightful analysts seemed to live in a world apart from policy makers, so their warning that the looming battle for hearts and minds in the countryside would not be easily won had little effect. Policy makers clung to sweeping Cold War propositions and simple images of villagers rendered inert by communist terror.

[The Communist-led resistance forces] seek to win the voluntary support of the population by various activities of a welfare or civic-action nature. By example they try to show that they are more efficient, honest, and humane as administrators than the enemy regime. At the same time, they are concerned with exercising control and extracting support in the form of manpower, food and labor. . . .

In areas still not "secure" or not under strong Viet Cong influence, the guerrilla forces must live a hit-and-run existence and have little opportunity to act as the effective local administration. In these areas they must nonetheless rely upon support, shelter, and supply from the civilian populace, which is obtained not only by force but by positive steps to convince the population that its aspirations are those of the Viet Cong. . . .

. . . While force and terrorism remain a major Viet Cong instrument against local officials of the South Vietnamese Government and recalcitrant villagers, recently captured Viet Cong documents clearly show that Viet Cong troops and agents are ordered to provide assistance to peasants and to avoid antagonisms and abuses, such as looting or violation of churches and pagodas.

A Communist land reform program in South Vietnam, begun by the Viet Minh, is still being carried out under the Viet Cong. . . .

Current reports also indicate that the Viet Cong provide assistance to peasants in land clearance, seed distribution, and harvesting, and in turn persuade or force peasants to store rice in excess of their own needs for the use of guerrilla troops. Controls are apparently imposed in Viet Cong zones to prevent shipments for commercial marketing in Saigon, or to collect taxes on such shipments. The Viet Cong themselves often pay cash or give promissory notes for the food they acquire.

. . . Captured Viet Cong doctors or medical personnel indicate that dispensaries for treatment of Viet Cong wounded often are scattered inconspicuously among several peasant homes in a village, and that civilians are treated as facilities and supplies permit. . . .

There are also references to primary and adult education, much of it in the form of indoctrination, and to Viet Cong–run schools operating almost side by side with government schools. . . .

The Viet Cong also promote cultural activities — heavily flavored with propaganda — through press, radio and film media, as well as live drama and festivals. . . .

A Viet Cong document discussing the successful construction of a "combat hamlet" indicates that primary stress is laid on determining the basic wants and needs of the inhabitants — frequently their concern for their own land. Propaganda is directed at convincing them that the government is threatening their interests, that defensive measures must be taken, and finally that offensive actions against government officials and troops are needed. The peasants presumably come to regard the Viet Cong as their protectors and to cooperate voluntarily with the Viet Cong military effort.

THE DIEM REGIME IN CRISIS, JULY–NOVEMBER 1963

By mid-1963 Diem was in deep difficulty. In the countryside he had lost significant ground to the NLF, while in his urban strongholds he faced a rising tide of protest. Hanoi's task was to exploit this opportunity but also to imagine how the United States might respond to the prospective failure of its strategy of "special war" (meaning military operations by ARVN units backed with U.S. money and arms but U.S. combat involvement limited to advisers). What Hanoi sought to avoid was a "limited war" or "local war," a term used to describe a substantial direct involvement of U.S. units in the fighting.

2.10 John F. Kennedy, press conference comments, 17 July 1963

The Buddhist-led opposition to Diem in Saigon and other major cities deeply unsettled the Kennedy administration. Kennedy's public remarks suggest how his own sense of caution collided with the demands of the policy of containment and probably his fear of the domestic political costs of retreat.

[REPORTER:] [T]here has been a good deal of public concern about the political situation in South Viet-Nam, and I would like to ask you whether the difficulties between the Buddhist population there and the South Vietnamese Government [have] been an impediment to the effectiveness of American aid in the war against the Viet Cong?
[KENNEDY:] Yes, I think it has. . . .

. . . Viet-Nam has been in war for 20 years. The Japanese came in, the war with the French, the civil war which has gone on for 10 years, and this is very difficult for any society to stand. It is a country which has got a good many problems and it is divided, and there is guerrilla activity and murder and all of the rest. Compounding this, however, now is a religious dispute. I would hope this would be settled, because we want to see a stable government there, carrying on a struggle to maintain its national independence.

We believe strongly in that. We are not going to withdraw from that effort. In my opinion, for us to withdraw from that effort would mean a collapse not only of South Viet-Nam, but Southeast Asia. So we are going to stay there.

2.11 Diem, press interview comments, 26 July 1963

Diem responded publicly to his American critics. He underlined his firm commitment to national independence against outside (meaning U.S.) interference and also his sterling credentials as an anticommunist ally.

One of the key factors for [a] good relationship between the governments and troops of friendly countries [alluding to the United States] and a newly independent country [Diem's Vietnam] . . . is first the diligent respect for the spirit as well as the letter of the independence of this newly independent country—The newer is the independence, the dearer is the price at which it has been acquired, the more passionately are the people attached to it. . . . If ever there were Vietnamese politicians who would propose a kind of protectorate of the United States over Vietnam in exchange for a support to their intrigues, such actions would not fail to harm the friendship between our two peoples.

The second key factor is a penetrating knowledge of the Communist subversive war, a total and [multifaceted] war, war which refuses actual combat but seeks instead the moral attrition of the opponent, a war which is fought on all fronts, political, economic, social, cultural, diplomatic and military, a war which is waged on a world scale although the spear's head is aimed at a few specific points of the globe only. . . . [Americans and Vietnamese] are forging together in Vietnam the weapon capable of victoriously countering this Communist subversive war, not only for the sake of Vietnam but also for any other place where it may be waged. . . . [W]e have to deal with the best Communist guerrilla army which can exist in the present world, in terms of cleverness, experience and toughness.

2.12 Communist leaders gauge the vulnerability of the U.S. position in South Vietnam, summer and fall 1963

With Diem on the ropes, the party leaders sought to anticipate the U.S. government's reaction. Nguyen Chi Thanh, a member of the powerful Politburo close to Le Duan, saw a frustrated and divided United States that was vulnerable to defeat. From a poor peasant family in central Vietnam, Thanh had risen to prominence in Viet Minh forces during the French war and would, as head of COSVN, become his party's senior leader in the South in 1965. Ho Chi Minh's crystal ball offered an equally hopeful if quite different picture. His Marxist reading of the American ruling class suggested the possibility of a U.S. retreat. Ho's appraisal may have been wishful thinking; as events would demonstrate, it was considerably wide of the mark.

a. Nguyen Chi Thanh, published assessment, July 1963

Having full confidence in their weapons, their dollars, and their political and military experience, and being served by a zealous flunkey — Ngo Dinh Diem —, the U.S. imperialists thought that everything would be smooth sailing. But their hopes did not materialize.

Nine years have passed without the U.S. imperialists being able to bring their schemes of aggression to any bright conclusions.

U.S. opinion is at present quite divided. The politicians and the military, at one in their aggressive aims, are however at variance on the methods to be used. For instance, some are for liquidating Ngo Dinh Diem immediately so as to prevent him from polluting "fine American democracy"; others are against "[swapping] horses while crossing the stream". In the military field, U.S. generals are still far from concurring with each other in strategy and tactics.

b. Ho Chi Minh, remarks to a Polish diplomat, fall 1963

Neither you nor I . . . know the Americans well, but what we do know of them . . . suggests that they are more practical and clear-sighted than other capitalist nations. They will not pour their resources into Vietnam endlessly. One day they will take pencil in hand and begin figuring. Once they really begin to analyze our ideas seriously, they will come to the conclusion that it is possible and even worthwhile to live in peace with us. Weariness, disappointment, the knowledge that they cannot achieve the goal which the French pursued to their own discredit will lead to a new sobriety, new feelings and emotions.

2.13 The Kennedy administration contemplates a coup, August–November 1963

With Diem faltering, the advisers surrounding Kennedy divided over whether to back a military coup or to press Diem harder for reform and for the ouster of his politically influential brother, Ngo Dinh Nhu. In August the president began flirting privately with the idea of a coup. Under Secretary of State George Ball, working with other second-level officials in the State Department, got casual approval to send a cable to set the coup in motion from Kennedy while the president was on vacation at Hyannis Port, Massachusetts. On the receiving end of the cable was Henry Cabot Lodge Jr., a prominent Massachusetts Republican and sometimes contender for his party's presidential nomination, who had just taken charge of the Saigon embassy. After the White House got cold feet, coup plans drifted while a CIA operative in Saigon stayed in touch with dissident Vietnamese generals. On 1 November, just as the coup finally began to unfold, Lodge spoke over the phone to Diem one last time. By the next day, Diem, as well as his brother, would be dead. The following documents provide a rare, intimate glimpse into how Washington went about overthrowing a client. The consequences — continued political instability and the increasing need for U.S. combat troops to save the day — make this record all the more important.

a. Under Secretary of State George W. Ball, cable to Ambassador Henry Cabot Lodge Jr., 24 August 1963

US Government cannot tolerate situation in which power lies in [Ngo Dinh] Nhu's hands. Diem must be given chance to rid himself of Nhu and his coterie and replace them with best military and political personalities available.

If, in spite of all your efforts, Diem remains obdurate and refuses, then we must face the possibility that Diem himself cannot be preserved.

b. Kennedy comments (recorded by National Security Council staffer Bromley Smith) at a White House meeting with advisers, 28 August 1963

The President noted that both Ambassador Lodge and General [Paul] Harkins [head of the U.S. military mission in Saigon] had recommended that we go ahead. He did not believe we should take the position that we have to go ahead because we have gone so far already. If a coup is not in the cards, we could unload. The [ARVN] generals talking about a coup did not appear to be very enthusiastic. . . .

The President said we should decide what we can do here [in Washington] or suggest things that can be done in the field [Saigon] which would maximize the chances of the rebel generals. We should ask Ambassador Lodge and General Harkins how we can build up military forces which would carry out a coup. At present, it does not look as if the coup forces could defeat Diem. . . .

The President asked the Defense Department to come away with ways of building up the anti-Diem forces in Saigon.

c. Ambassador Lodge, cable to Secretary of State Rusk, 29 August 1963

We are launched on a course from which there is no respectable turning back: The overthrow of the Diem government. There is no turning back in part because U.S. prestige is already publicly committed to this end in large measure and will become more so as facts leak out. In a more fundamental sense, there is no turning back because there is no possibility, in my view, that the war can be won under a Diem administration, still less that Diem or any member of the family can govern the country in a way to gain the support of the people who count, i.e., the educated class in and out of government service, civil and military — not to mention the American people. In the last few months (and especially days), they have in fact positively alienated these people to an incalculable degree. . . .

I realize that this course involves a very substantial risk of losing Vietnam. It also involves some additional risk to American lives. I would never propose it if I felt there was a reasonable chance of holding Vietnam with Diem.

d. White House cable sent via the State Department to Lodge, 29 August 1963

The usg [U.S. government] will support a coup which has good chance of succeeding but plans no direct involvement of U.S. Armed Forces. Harkins should state that he is prepared to establish liaison with the coup planners and to review plans, but will not engage directly in joint coup planning. . . .

You are hereby authorized to announce suspension of aid through Diem Government at a time and under conditions of your choice.

e. White House cable drafted by McGeorge Bundy (Kennedy's special assistant for national security affairs) and sent via the State Department to Lodge, 17 September 1963

We see no good opportunity for action to remove present government in immediate future. Therefore . . . we must for the present apply such pressures as are available to secure whatever modest improvements on the scene may be possible.

f. Bundy, cable sent via the CIA to Lodge, 5 October 1963

President today approved recommendation that no initiative should now be taken to give any active covert encouragement to a coup. There should, however, be urgent covert effort with closest security under broad guidance of Ambassador to identify and build contacts with possible alternative leadership as and when it appears.

g. White House cable sent via the CIA to Lodge, 9 October 1963

We have following additional general thoughts which have been discussed with President. While we do not wish to stimulate coup, we also do not wish to leave impression that U.S. would thwart a change of government or deny economic and military assistance to a new regime if it appeared capable of increasing effectiveness of military effort, ensuring popular support to win war and improving working relations with U.S.

h. Lodge, telephone conversation with Diem (record prepared by John M. Dunn, Lodge's personal assistant), 1 November 1963

PRESIDENT DIEM: Some military units have begun a rebellion, and I want to know what the attitude of the U.S. is?

AMBASSADOR: . . . I do not feel well enough informed at this time to be able to tell you. . . .

PRESIDENT DIEM: You must have some idea. I am, after all, the Chief of State. . . .

AMBASSADOR: . . . Now I am very worried about your physical safety. It has been reported to me that those in charge of the current activity against you offer both you and your brother safe conduct out of the country if you resign. Had you heard this?

PRESIDENT DIEM: No. (And then after a pause.) You have my telephone number.

AMBASSADOR: Yes, and you have mine. If I can do anything at all to insure your personal safety, please call me at once.

From Proxy War to Direct Conflict, 1963–1965

As 1963 came to a close, the players in the battle for the South took stock and reached conclusions that would entrench them more deeply in their mutually irreconcilable positions. Saigon was in political turmoil following Diem's death at the hands of U.S.-backed generals. The NLF seized the chance to expand its influence. Leaders in Hanoi, thinking victory was within their grasp, committed in December to increased support for the insurgency. Kennedy's assassination just weeks after Diem's put Lyndon Johnson in the hot seat. He immediately signaled that he would follow an unyielding policy.

Johnson would gradually ratchet up U.S. military involvement. In August 1964, after what appeared to be a pair of attacks on U.S. Navy destroyers operating in the Gulf of Tonkin off the DRV coast, he ordered U.S. aircraft to hit facilities along that coast. He also secured open-ended congressional backing for the use of force. With his presidential reelection secured in a landslide victory in November, the president grew bolder. In February and March 1965, he began bombing the North on a broader, sustained basis and dispatched the first U.S. combat unit to South Vietnam. American patrols were soon moving aggressively into the surrounding countryside. Finally in June, the MACV commander, William Westmoreland, called for a major troop commitment. Close advisers both in the government and in the Democratic Party leadership warned the president of dangers. However doubtful Johnson himself may have been, he finally decided in late July on a major buildup (to climb within several years to half a million men). Americans would now fight the war that the Saigon government was losing.

Under the spur of a growing U.S. commitment, the Communist Party intensified preparations for the looming confrontation. At home the party moved to a war footing, expanding the army and diverting resources from domestic economic development to the military. To bolster NLF forces, Hanoi dispatched additional regroupees and the first

People's Army of Vietnam (PAVN) combat units. In early 1965 the first PAVN regiments reached the Central Highlands, the sparsely populated mountainous region in the central interior of South Vietnam.

Internationally, Le Duan and his colleagues looked for backing from the two major Communist powers. But their task was complicated by the increasingly virulent dispute between Moscow and Beijing over ideology and ultimately over the leadership of the socialist bloc. The Vietnamese party had already in late 1963 sided in principle with the Chinese, who were calling for confrontation with imperialism and criticizing the "revisionist" Soviet policy of peaceful coexistence. But at the same time, Hanoi had argued that ideological disputes should not disrupt common action by the bloc or diminish support for Vietnam as a major front in the international socialist struggle.

This measured stance secured from Chinese leaders renewed pledges of support and finally induced the Soviets to make their own aid commitment. This Soviet commitment, made by the Leonid Brezhnev–led group that had removed Nikita Khrushchev from power in October 1964, was prompted by a determination to defend Moscow's claim to bloc leadership against Beijing's challenge. By April 1965 Moscow had formally committed to supply advanced weaponry not in the Chinese arsenal (notably fighter aircraft and surface-to-air missiles) and to send advisers and support personnel to help with the new high-tech hardware. The allies that Hanoi had recruited even as Johnson was increasing the military pressure would serve to deter an all-out American attack on the North, raise the costs of any U.S. aerial campaign, and provide the resources Hanoi would need to sustain NLF and PAVN units fighting a protracted war in the South.

Over a year and a half, Vietnamese and American leaders made decisions that led to war. The question for historians is how they went about making their fateful commitments.

- When did Johnson effectively opt for war — as early as November 1963 or as late as July 1965?
- How did Communist Party leaders respond to the growing U.S. commitment to South Vietnam? How did they understand U.S. goals and staying power?
- At what point had Washington's and Hanoi's deliberations gone so far that they could not turn back from a direct military collision? What kept tipping the balance to the side of war?

The overthrow of Ngo Dinh Diem failed to create an effective instrument that the United States could wield against the NLF. Instead the coup introduced a year and a half of instability in Saigon politics. The generals who had toppled Diem vied for power while neglecting the NLF military challenge. These trends cheered Hanoi.

3.1 A new president faces an old problem, November–December 1963

In his first days in office, Johnson confronted the unhappy consequences of the Diem coup and the broader challenges of stabilizing and preserving the Saigon government. He met with U.S. ambassador to Vietnam Henry Cabot Lodge Jr., CIA head John McCone, Secretary of State Dean Rusk, and Under Secretary of State George Ball. The new president demanded that his "country team" in Vietnam begin to turn the situation around. But Robert McNamara, the official who was most deeply involved in Vietnam policy and a man whose judgment Johnson trusted, began warning of looming perils soon after a two-day visit to South Vietnam.

a. President Lyndon Johnson, meeting with advisers, 24 November 1963

Ambassador Lodge reported that the change in government [Diem's overthrow] had been an improvement. . . . Lodge said that we were in no way responsible for the death of Diem and Nhu, that had they followed his advice, they would be alive today. . . . The tone of Ambassador Lodge's statements were optimistic, hopeful, and left the President with the impression that we are on the road to victory.

At this point McCone stated that our [CIA] estimate of the situation was somewhat more serious. We had noted a continuing increase in Viet Cong activity since the first of November as evidenced by a larger number of Viet Cong attacks. . . . Furthermore I [McCone] stated that the military [who had seized power from Diem] were having considerable trouble in completing the political organization of the government. . . .

The President then stated that he approached the situation with some misgivings. He noted that a great many people throughout the country questioned our course of action in supporting the overthrow of the Diem regime. He also noted that strong voices in the Congress felt we should get out of Vietnam. Both of these facts give the President considerable concern. He stated that he was not at all sure we took the right course in upsetting the Diem regime. . . .

The President then stated he has never been happy with our operations in Vietnam. He said there had been serious dissension and divisions within the American community [U.S. agencies in Saigon] and he told the Ambassador that he was in total charge and he wanted the situation cleaned up. He wanted no more divisions of opinion, no more bickering and any person that did not conform to policy should be removed. . . .

The President then said that . . . he wanted to make it abundantly clear that he did not think we had to reform every Asian into our own image. He said that he felt all too often when we engaged in the affairs of a foreign country we wanted to immediately transform that country into our image and this, in his opinion, was a mistake. He was anxious to get along, win the war — he didn't want as much effort placed on so-called social reforms.

b. Secretary of Defense McNamara, memo to President Johnson, 21 December 1963

The situation is very disturbing. Current trends, unless reversed in the next 2–3 months, will lead to neutralization at best and more likely to a Communist-controlled state.

The new government is the greatest source of concern. It is indecisive and drifting. . . .

The [U.S.] Country Team is the second major weakness. It lacks leadership, has been poorly informed, and is not working to a common plan. . . . Lodge simply does not know how to conduct a coordinated administration. . . . [H]e has just operated as a loner all his life and cannot readily change now. . . .

Viet Cong progress has been great during the period since the coup, with my best guess being that the situation has in fact been deteriorating in the countryside since July to a far greater extent than we realized because of our undue dependence on distorted Vietnamese reporting. The Viet Cong now control very high proportions of the people in certain key provinces, particularly those directly south and west of Saigon. . . .

Infiltration of men and equipment from North Vietnam continues using (a) land corridors through Laos and Cambodia; (b) the Mekong River waterways from Cambodia; (c) some possible entry from the sea and the tip of the [Mekong] Delta. The best guess is that 1000–1500 Viet Cong cadres entered South Vietnam from Laos in the first nine months of 1963. The Mekong route (and also the possible sea entry) is apparently used for heavier weapons and ammunition and raw materials. . . .

Plans for Covert Action into North Vietnam were prepared as we had requested and were an excellent job. . . .

. . . We should watch the situation very carefully, running scared, hoping for the best, but preparing for more forceful moves if the situation does not show early signs of improvement.

3.2 Communist Party Central Committee, resolution 9, on strategy toward the South, December 1963

What was worrisome to Washington was a great opportunity for the Hanoi-backed NLF. It had gained wide rural influence and created an effective armed force, and it could now better than ever exploit the confusion in Saigon. In a major meeting in December 1963, the party leadership engaged in a spirited debate that ended with a secret statement expressing optimism about victory and eagerness to press ahead militarily, even in the face of the troubling prospect of a direct U.S. combat role.

We have sufficient conditions to quickly change the balance of forces in our favor. And whether the U.S. maintains its combat strength at the present level or increases it, she must still use her henchmen's army [ARVN] as a main force. However, this army becomes weaker day by day due to the serious decline of its quality, the demoralization of its troops and the disgust of the latter for the Americans and their lackeys. . . .

As for us, we become more confident in the victory of our armed forces. . . .

If the U.S. imperialists send more troops to Viet-Nam to save the situation after suffering a series of failures, *the Revolution in Viet-Nam will meet more difficulties, the struggle will be stronger and harder but it will certainly succeed in attaining the final victory.* . . . [T]he U.S. imperialists cannot win over 14 million Vietnamese people in the South who have taken arms to fight the imperialists for almost 20 years, and who, with all the compatriots throughout the country, have defeated the hundreds of thousands [of] troops of the French expeditionary force. . . .

Our people's revolutionary war in SVN [South Vietnam] is still a war in which our people use a small force to counter a large force. Our people must destroy and wear down the enemy's force while developing our force. We must fight the enemy in all fields in order to weaken his forces and demoralize his troops. . . .

The general guideline for our people's revolutionary war in SVN is to conduct a protracted war, relying mainly on our own forces, and to combine political struggle and armed struggle in accordance with each area and time. . . .

. . . [W]e are preparing for the General Offensive and Uprising by using military and political forces to disintegrate the pro-U.S. government's troops and provoke uprisings in the rural area and cities still under enemy occupation. . . .

Mountainous area: South Viet-Nam's mountainous area occupies an important strategic position. It offers many favorable conditions for us to conduct a protracted struggle even in the most difficult situations. This is the area where we can build up a large armed force and annihilate many enemy troops in large-scale attacks. We can also use the mountainous area as a stepping stone to expand our activities to the lowlands and, when the situation allows, to attack the key positions of the enemy. In case the enemy expands the war to a larger scale, the mountainous area together with the lowland will enable us to fight a protracted war against him. We should make every effort to control the mountainous areas and have the determination to build these areas into a solid base. . . .

The lowland and the rural area: These are rich and heavily populated areas. There, our revolutionary movement is active and our revolutionary base-level organizations are relatively widespread. . . . If we succeed in gaining control over the lowlands and rural areas, we will save the mountainous area from isolation. In doing so, we can also develop our forces in these areas and create an advantageous position for our troops to attack enemy key positions. . . .

Urban area: This is the area where leading agencies of the enemy, including organs of his central government, are located, where the enemy is concentrating his strong repressive forces and facilities. But this is also the area where the people live in great number and they have a high political enlightenment; they have risen up several times to struggle against the enemy. When the situation is favorable for us to conduct a General Offensive and Uprising, there is the possibility that the people in urban areas will also rise up and coordinate with the revolutionary troops coming from outside to overthrow the enemy's central government. Our principal guideline for operations in the urban areas consists of conducting *political struggle*, setting up a reserve force, and waiting for favorable conditions. . . . [I]f the situation develops to a point where the balance of forces between us and the enemy changes to our advantage, we can deal the enemy decisive blows right in the urban area. . . .

Though our armed forces are maturing and our regular forces are developing day after day, the type of war waged by our three forces [main, regional, and local] remains one of guerrilla warfare for a long time to come. *The main purpose of our campaigns and combat activities is to destroy the enemy's forces.* It is necessary for us to attack where the enemy is most vulnerable. Therefore, at present, *we must attack the enemy troops while they are out of their fortifications*, or moving on roads, waterways, or in the air. *Our major combat tactics to be adopted are to lay ambushes, conduct raids, or gradually advance toward mobile warfare*, when conditions permit. . . .

We must strive to consolidate and broaden the Liberation Front of South Viet-Nam based on the workers-peasants alliance and led by the Party, so as to give it the ability to motivate the people on a wider scale, to accomplish its new political missions prescribed by the Party, and *to assume part of the responsibilities as a revolutionary administration in the liberated areas*. . . .

The Mission of North Viet-Nam:

. . . [I]t is time for the North to increase aid to the South, the North must bring into fuller play its role as the revolutionary base for the whole nation. . . .

We should plan to aid the South to meet the requirements of the Revolution, and because of this aid, we must revise properly our plan for building North Viet-Nam.

. . . [W]e must increase our economic and defensive strength in North Viet-Nam. We should increase our vigilance at all times and be ready to face the enemy['s] new schemes. At the same time, we should be prepared to cope with the eventuality of the expansion of the war into North Viet-Nam. . . .

. . . [W]e will certainly win the final victory. The most important thing at the present time is that the entire Party, the entire people from North to South must have full determination and make outstanding efforts to bring success to the revolution of our Southern compatriots and achieve peace and unification of the country, to win total victory, to build a peaceful, unified, independent, democratic, prosperous and strong Viet-Nam.

3.3 PAVN officer, interview on the intensified military effort, 1963–1964

This PAVN officer, a veteran of the French war and a party member, provides insight on the role of the first purely North Vietnamese units to go south. He had been wounded in action in mid-1964, captured by ARVN forces, and interviewed by employees of the Rand Corporation. The resulting transcript, in which the prisoner is not identified by name, has been reordered along chronological lines to make it easier to follow.

The aim of my unit was to form, together with already existing units in Central Vietnam, a Main Force Regional unit to liberate the plains region, and to enlarge the liberated area, so that the rear could supply manpower and materiel. If this could be achieved, it would end to a large extent the reliance of Front units in the area on supplies from the North . . . each company received 30,000 piasters to buy rice from the people in case we were ambushed or got lost on our way South. . . .

My first combat experience in the South was an ambush near the route leading from Tam Ky to Duc Phu. We destroyed two ARVN companies; we captured 24 ARVN soldiers; the rest fled in the mountains or were killed in the fighting. After this attack we rested and consolidated our ranks. . . . We were told that we would have to behave nicely toward the people, that we would have to observe the "three togetherness rules": help the people, educate, and indoctrinate them, and that we should not threaten them. . . . Through my experiences I observed that the morale of the ARVN was rather low and that their fighting capability was not good. . . . When we captured 24 ARVN, we tied them and brought them back to our area to interrogate them. . . . When we were through with our interrogation we gathered the people for a meeting and then released them. . . . We didn't mistreat them. They ate the same food as we. We tore our hammocks in half to give to them. . . .

The people were very happy over our victory, because from then on they could work in peace. After the attack they gave us eggs, and chickens, and milk to the wounded. . . . Six fighters were killed and eleven were wounded. . . . Since our first combat experience was a success, we were all very enthusiastic. . . .

. . . To replace the losses we recruit the youths in the areas which we liberate. . . . We only recruit the people who volunteer to join our ranks. After we liberate an area, we explain to the people the aim of our struggle. Those who want to join are accepted into our ranks. . . .

At first the people in the countryside didn't understand our policy and they were very afraid of us. But as we stayed in their villages they got to understand us more through our daily activities, and their fear disappeared. They became closer to us, and confided in us. . . . Even if Hanoi stopped sending arms, supplies, and men to the Front, the Front would still be able to win because the Front responds to the aspirations of the people. I admit that the GVN is stronger than the Front militarily, but the GVN doesn't have the support of the people. . . .

. . . We are confident that we will win. No matter how rich and powerful the Americans are, they will not be able to defeat the Revolution because we will drag out this war. We are not going to fall in their trap and conduct a big and swift offensive.

3.4 James B. Lincoln (army captain advising the ARVN), letter to Clark Lincoln, 14 August 1965, comparing NLF and Saigon forces

The military advisory mission of which James Lincoln was an important part had taken shape in the late 1950s with the objective of creating a South Vietnamese army that could contain the DRV. Despite a dramatic increase in the advisory effort during the Kennedy years, the ARVN had not become an effective fighting force. Here Captain Lincoln sums up his impressions based on six months of on-the-job experience. He remained an adviser until October 1966.

The large [ARVN] combat operation . . . is a very common occurrence. I would say that less than 1/3 of all planned operations made any contact with the VC [Viet Cong]. There are various reasons—first, the VC have their own very efficient intelligence nets. There are probably VC sympathizers in every major Hq. of the Vietnam Army. . . . Next, the VC are extremely good at slipping out of an area, or hiding in an area where there is an operation. An example—near my area four Battalions entered an area to look for a VC company that was reported in the area. There was not a shot fired, and nobody could figure out how the VC slipped out of the area, all escape routes were covered with blocking positions. About a week later they went back into the same area and found out why. The VC had a fantastic underground network of caves to hit [hide] the entire Company, and all the entrances were next to impossible to find. . . . Everywhere is vulnerable—if the VC want to make an attack, they have the upper hand. We can only fight them as best we can and wait for help to arrive. However, they always plan and execute very carefully. There is usually only one or two roads or entrances into an area they plan to attack. Quite often they will drop a few mortar rounds into a location, with no intention of making a ground attack. They realize, however, that the camp under attack will call for reinforcements, and they will come by truck since it will be nighttime. The main VC force simply waits along the road into the area and ambushes the relief force — it's all very simple. As soon as you think you have them figured out, they *will* make a ground attack, but so sorry you told the relief forces not to come because of suspected ambush. Another thing that has amazed me is the accuracy of the mortar. It is very difficult for them to carry the ammo., so it is precious and every round [must count]. In almost all cases where they have mortared a location, all rounds hit right on target, including the first round. I guess they have one of their boys pace off the distance beforehand. . . .

. . . The [ARVN] soldiers themselves are good fighters, but they are very underpaid, and poorly led. . . . Their morale is poor, and this brings about the biggest problem in the Army — AWOLs [soldiers absent without leave] and deserters. . . . The Gov. just doesn't look after their soldiers well enough to keep them happy. All soldiers' housing is terrible, dependents are not thought of in the least — they have no provisions for getting pay home when the husband is off on a big operation, maybe for over a month. . . . Next — poor leadership. The commanders of the Army units are usually inexperienced, and only worried about staying alive, and getting a soft job back in Saigon somewhere. The high level commanders are more worried about political things than military considerations. District chiefs are the same way — they usually plan and go out on as few operations as possible, mostly worried about keeping the province chief happy from a political viewpoint. . . . Nobody is really sure who to support — maybe tomorrow there will be another coup and the guy they supported will be thrown out. It's all highly confusing, but one thing is sure — it really hurts the military effort.

JOHNSON ESCALATES, AUGUST 1964–APRIL 1965

The steady erosion of Saigon's political authority and military effectiveness presented the Johnson administration with a choice between accepting defeat and raising the U.S. commitment. Johnson's own can-do spirit and the preferences of his advisers (all Kennedy holdovers) prevailed.

3.5 Gulf of Tonkin resolution approved by Congress, 10 August 1964

Johnson sought to delay any major decision on Vietnam until after the November 1964 presidential election, which would make him president in his own right. But reports of attacks on U.S. destroyers in the Gulf of Tonkin disrupted that plan. Considerable confusion long surrounded this incident. As it turns out, the first attack (on 2 August) did occur, apparently on the decision of a local commander alarmed by a U.S.-supported coastal raid by South Vietnamese forces. The second attack appears to have been the figment of overanxious U.S. sonar operators during poor weather. Johnson in any case ordered retaliatory air strikes against DRV coastal facilities and then asked Congress for support in the form of a resolution drafted in the White House giving the president broad powers to act in Southeast Asia. This measure, which in effect substituted for the constitutionally mandated declaration of war, passed the Senate by a vote of 98–2 and the House unanimously.

Whereas naval units of the Communist regime in Vietnam, in violation of the principles of the Charter of the United Nations and of international law, have deliberately and repeatedly attacked United States naval vessels lawfully present in international waters, and have thereby created a serious threat to international peace; and

Whereas these attacks are part of a deliberate and systematic campaign of aggression that the Communist regime in North Vietnam has been waging against its neighbors and the nations joined with them in the collective defense of their freedom; and

Whereas the United States is assisting the peoples of southeast Asia to protect their freedom and has no territorial, military or political ambitions in that area, but desires only that these people should be left in peace to work out their own destinies in their own way: Now, therefore, be it

Resolved by the Senate and House of Representatives of the United States of America in Congress assembled, That the Congress approves and supports the determination of the President, as Commander in Chief, to take all necessary measures to repel any armed attack against the forces of the United States and to prevent further aggression.

3.6 McGeorge Bundy to Lyndon Johnson, arguing for a bombing campaign, 7 February 1965

With the election over and Congress formally behind him, Johnson seemed disposed to raise the pressure on Hanoi. An attack on U.S. bases in the South in early 1965 prompted McGeorge Bundy, then in Vietnam, to call for retaliation in the form of a bombing campaign against the DRV. One of the influential Kennedy holdovers, Bundy argued on his return to Washington that gradual escalation could intimidate Hanoi and buoy flagging spirits in Saigon.

[T]he best available way of increasing our chance of success in Vietnam is the development and execution of a policy of *sustained reprisal* against North Vietnam — a policy in which air and naval action against the North is justified by and related to the whole Viet Cong campaign of violence and terror in the South.

While we believe that the risks of such a policy are acceptable, we emphasize that its costs are real. It implies significant U.S. air losses even if no full air war is joined, and it seems likely that it would eventually require an extensive and costly effort against the whole air defense system of North Vietnam. U.S. casualties would be higher — and more visible to American feelings — than those sustained in the struggle in South Vietnam. . . .

. . . We must keep it clear at every stage both to Hanoi and to the world, that our reprisals will be reduced or stopped when outrages in the South are reduced or stopped — and that we are *not* attempting to destroy or conquer North Vietnam. . . .

We emphasize that our primary target in advocating a reprisal policy is the improvement of the situation in *South* Vietnam. . . .

The [anti-Communist] Vietnamese increase in hope could well increase the readiness of Vietnamese factions themselves to join together in forming a more effective government.

We think it plausible that effective and sustained reprisals, even in a low key, would have a substantial depressing effect upon the morale of Viet Cong cadres in South Vietnam. . . .

. . . [I]t is of great importance that the level of reprisal be adjusted rapidly and visibly to both upward and downward shifts in the level of Viet Cong offenses. We want to keep before Hanoi the carrot of our desisting as well as the stick of continued pressure. We also need to conduct the application of the force so that there is always a prospect of worse to come.

. . . At a minimum [a policy of sustained reprisal] will damp down the charge that we did not do all that we could have done, and this charge will be important in many countries, including our own. Beyond that, a reprisal policy — to the extent that it demonstrates U.S. willingness to employ this new norm in counter-insurgency — will set a higher price for the future upon all adventures of guerrilla warfare, and it should therefore somewhat increase our ability to deter such adventures. We must recognize, however, that that ability will be gravely weakened if there is failure for any reason in Vietnam.

3.7 Johnson, speech at Johns Hopkins University, Baltimore, 7 April 1965

The president agreed to the bombing campaign (which would become known as Rolling Thunder) and quickly followed by dispatching the first U.S. combat units to secure the Da Nang air base from which the bombing was conducted. In a major speech in April, which Johnson had helped to write, he sought to explain decisions that left the United States and the DRV just short of war.

Why must this Nation hazard its ease, and its interest, and its power for the sake of a people so far away?

We fight because we must fight if we are to live in a world where every country can shape its own destiny. And only in such a world will our own freedom be finally secure. . . .

. . . North Viet-Nam has attacked the independent nation of South Viet-Nam. Its object is total conquest.

Of course, some of the people of South Viet-Nam are participating in [an] attack on their own government. But trained men and supplies, orders and arms, flow in a constant stream from north to south.

This support is the heartbeat of the war.

And it is a war of unparalleled brutality. Simple farmers are the targets of assassination and kidnapping. Women and children are strangled in the night because their men are loyal to their government. And helpless villages are ravaged by sneak attacks. Large-scale raids are conducted on towns, and terror strikes in the heart of cities. . . .

Over this war — and all Asia — is another reality: the deepening shadow of Communist China. The rulers in Hanoi are urged on by Peking. This is a regime which has destroyed freedom in Tibet, which has attacked India, and has been condemned by the United Nations for aggression in Korea. It is a nation which is helping the forces of violence in almost every continent. The contest in Viet-Nam is part of a wider pattern of aggressive purposes.

Why are these realities our concern? Why are we in South Viet-Nam?

We are there because we have a promise to keep. Since 1954 every American President has offered support to the people of South Viet-Nam. . . .

We are also there to strengthen world order. Around the globe, from Berlin to Thailand, are people whose well-being rests, in part, on the belief that they can count on us if they are attacked. To leave Viet-Nam to its fate would shake the confidence of all these people in the value of an American commitment and in the value of America's word. The result would be increased unrest and instability, and even wider war.

We are also there because there are great stakes in the balance. Let no one think for a moment that retreat from Viet-Nam would bring an end to conflict. The battle would be renewed in one country and then another. The central lesson of our time is that the appetite of aggression is never satisfied. To withdraw from one battlefield means only to prepare for the next. . . .

In recent months attacks on South Viet-Nam were stepped up. Thus, it became necessary for us to increase our response and to make attacks by air. This is not a change of purpose. It is a change in what we believe that purpose requires.

We do this in order to slow down aggression.

We do this to increase the confidence of the brave people of South Viet-Nam who have bravely borne this brutal battle for so many years with so many casualties.

And we do this to convince the leaders of North Viet-Nam — and all who seek to share their conquest — of a very simple fact:

We will not be defeated. [applause]

We will not grow tired.

We will not withdraw, either openly or under the cloak of a meaningless agreement. . . .

. . . We have no desire to see thousands die in battle — Asians or Americans. We have no desire to devastate that which the people of North Viet-Nam have built with toil and sacrifice. We will use our power with restraint and with all the wisdom that we can command.

But we will use it. . . .

. . . [O]ur generation has a dream. It is a very old dream. But we have the power and now we have the opportunity to make that dream come true.

For centuries nations have struggled among each other. But we dream of a world where disputes are settled by law and reason. And we will try to make it so. [applause]

For most of history men have hated and killed one another in battle. But we dream of an end to war. And we will try to make it so.

For all existence most men have lived in poverty, threatened by hunger. But we dream of a world where all are fed and charged with hope. And we will help to make it so. [applause] . . .

This generation of the world must choose: destroy or build, kill or aid, hate or understand.

We can do all these things on a scale that's never [been] dreamed of before.

Well, we will choose life. And so doing we will prevail over the enemies within man, and over the natural enemies of all mankind.

HANOI PREPARES FOR WAR, OCTOBER 1964–MAY 1965

Party leaders met in August and September — in the immediate wake of the Gulf of Tonkin incident — to decide on countermeasures to what seemed a U.S. escalation of the conflict. Le Duan, as Communist Party head and the leading voice on policy toward the South, presided over this effort. Aiding him was Pham Van Dong. From a gentry family in central Vietnam, Dong had embraced communism in the mid-1920s and had, for his party activities, done time in a French prison (1931–1937). He helped Ho organize the Viet Minh and went on to become a mainstay in the government of the DRV, serving as premier from 1955 to 1986.

3.8 Conversations between Vietnamese and Chinese leaders, October 1964 and April 1965

On one key front, the party leadership proceeded confident of continued Chinese support. The Tonkin Gulf incident had caused Mao Zedong, the chair of China's Communist Party, to reiterate his commitment to resist a U.S. invasion and convinced him to beef up air defenses along the DRV border and base some aircraft in the DRV itself. By December China had agreed to a major troop commitment, mainly engineer and antiaircraft units to be stationed in the northern provinces of the DRV to free PAVN forces to go south. The first of these Chinese deployments arrived in June 1965. Together senior Viet-

namese and Chinese representatives worked out this program of assistance while also trying to gauge the Johnson administration's likely course. In this Chinese record of two meetings, Pham Van Dong and Le Duan spoke for the Vietnamese side. They addressed Mao and Liu Shaoqi, the number two figure in the party.

a. Pham Van Dong and Mao Zedong, conversation in Beijing, 5 October 1964

[MAO ZEDONG:] Whether or not the United States will attack the North, it has not yet made the decision. Now, it [the United States] is not even in a position to resolve the problem in South Vietnam. If it attacks the North, [it may need to] fight for one hundred years, and its legs will be trapped there. Therefore, it needs to consider carefully. The Americans have made all kinds of scary statements. . . .

PHAM VAN DONG: This is also our thinking. The United States is facing many difficulties, and it is not easy for it to expand the war. Therefore, our consideration is that we should try to restrict the war in South Vietnam to the sphere of special war [directed against the U.S.-backed ARVN], and should try to defeat the enemy within the sphere of special war. We should try our best not to let the U.S. imperialists turn the war in South Vietnam into a limited war [involving a substantial and direct U.S. role in the fighting], and try our best not to let the war be expanded to North Vietnam. We must adopt a very skillful strategy, and should not provoke it [the United States]. Our Politburo has made a decision on this matter, and today I am reporting it to Chairman Mao. We believe that this is workable.

MAO ZEDONG: Yes.

PHAM VAN DONG: If the United States dares to start a limited war, we will fight it, and will win it.

MAO ZEDONG: Yes, you can win it.

b. Le Duan and Liu Shaoqi, conversation in Beijing, 8 April 1965

LE DUAN: We want some volunteer pilots, volunteer soldiers . . . and other volunteers, including road and bridge engineering units.

LIU SHAOQI: It is our policy that we will do our best to support you. We will offer whatever you are in need of and we are in a position to offer. . . . If you do not invite us, we will not come; and if you invite one unit of our troops, we will send that unit to you. The initiative will be completely yours.

3.9 Premier Pham Van Dong, statement on terms for a settlement, 8 April 1965

Hanoi's second front was public diplomacy, offering to reactivate the 1954 Geneva accords, including notably its provision for a nonaligned South Vietnam (document 2.2). This carefully constructed offer, made publicly by the DRV's premier, was meant to give the Americans a way out with a minimum loss of face while also impressing on the international community the reasonableness of Hanoi's position.

1. Recognition of the basic national rights of the Vietnamese people: peace, independence, sovereignty, unity and territorial integrity. According to the Geneva Agreements, the U.S. government must withdraw from South Vietnam all U.S. troops, military personnel and weapons of all kinds, dismantle all U.S. military bases there, [and] cancel its "military alliance" with South Vietnam. It must end its policy of intervention and aggression in South Vietnam. According to the Geneva Agreements, the U.S. government must stop its acts of war against North Vietnam, [and] completely cease all encroachments on the territory and sovereignty of the Democratic Republic of Vietnam.

2. Pending the peaceful reunification of Vietnam, while Vietnam is still temporarily divided into two zones[,] the military provisions of the 1954 Geneva Agreements on Vietnam must be strictly respected: the two zones must refrain from joining any military alliance with foreign countries, there must be no foreign military bases, troops and military personnel in their respective territory.

3. The internal affairs of South Vietnam must be settled by the South Vietnamese people themselves, in accordance with the programme of the South Vietnam National Front for Liberation without any foreign interference.

4. The peaceful reunification of Vietnam is to be settled by the Vietnamese people in both zones, without any foreign interference.

3.10 Le Duan, letter to Nguyen Chi Thanh and other comrades, May 1965, reacting to the U.S. military escalation

Hanoi's third front was military, as rising U.S. troop levels threatened to turn special war in the South into a local or limited war. Here Le Duan urged his COSVN colleagues to try to head off deeper American involvement. But even

*in the worst case, southern forces could, he argued, directly confront and ul-
timately overcome the world's most potent military power by exploiting its
many vulnerabilities.*

To prevent the US from turning the "special war" into a "local war" in the
South or carrying the land war to the North, the best counter-measure
is for us to strike harder and more accurately in the South, causing the
rapid disintegration of the puppet army, the US mainstay. We must step
up military and political struggles and rapidly create the opportunity to
move toward generalized attacks and general insurrection, catching the
Americans napping, and preventing them from plunging into new military adventures. . . .

. . . From 1,000 armed people [before 1959], today we have tens of thousands of troops capable of mounting attacks to destroy enemy troops by
the thousands. If the Americans switch over to "local war" in the South
with from 250,000 to 300,000 troops, they will be confronted with our
protracted war of resistance. To have to fight a long-drawn-out war is the
US Achilles' heel. . . .

. . . [S]ince the US was bogged down in the Vietnam war, its economy
has been in a critical state with its gold reserve diminishing rapidly.

Taking this opportunity, the Japanese, West German, British and
French capitalists began to scramble for lucrative US-controlled markets
in the world. Thus judging from its economic interests, the US is also
afraid of fighting a prolonged war.

In contrast, our economy basically remains an agricultural economy,
with major industrial centres still non-existent and with 80% of consumer
goods being supplied by handicrafts. Therefore, with sufficient rice and
sweet potatoes to eat, we can fight the Americans five, ten years or longer. . . . Moreover, we enjoy the assistance of fraternal socialist countries
and thus are more confident in waging a long war of resistance. . . .

Within the US ruling circles, the "doves" and the "hawks" are at log-
gerheads with one another. . . . Contradictions between the US and its
client regimes and those among the different groups of US lackeys . . .
also are growing acute. The enemy is being divided. Thus, militarily, we
are not yet in a position to prevail over the enemy, but politically we can
get the upper hand and capitalize on the enemy's inner contradictions to
split his ranks and weaken him to the point of disintegration.

. . . We believe in our final victory because we firmly hold the following
points in our favour:

a) *The will to fight and to win* of our entire people from South to North, from Party members to the popular masses. This will stems from our nation's tradition of dauntlessness in its history of protracted struggle against foreign aggression [from defeating the Mongol invaders to driving out the French]. . . .

b) *The leadership of our Party, a party experienced in revolutionary struggle and firmly grasping the laws governing people's war.* . . .

c) *The approval, support and assistance of brothers and friends all over the world.* . . .

Although in our camp there are [Sino-Soviet] divergencies over many issues, yet in our people's struggle against US aggression, for national salvation, the fraternal countries in the main approve our line and give us whole-hearted assistance. The national liberation movement and the international communist and workers' movement are on our side. Peace- and justice-loving people in the world support our just cause. . . .

. . . [I]f the US is still rash enough to make a test of strength with the Vietnamese nation in a protracted war, then it will find us combat-ready and determined to fight and defeat the US aggressors in whatever type of war.

Here, in the North, *we already are prepared for the worst*, the fraternal countries are ready to give us aid. If the US is foolish enough to move land forces to the North, here we will also fight and win. Even if we have to sacrifice hundreds of thousands of lives, even if Hanoi is reduced to rubble, the North will always join the South in its determination to figh[t] and defeat the US aggressors, to save the nation and reunify the country.

"GOING OFF THE DIVING BOARD," JUNE–JULY 1965

Johnson finally had to face the choice that he and his predecessors had sought to avoid. In early June General William Westmoreland reported that only a major U.S. combat commitment could save the ARVN from defeat, "successfully take the fight to the VC," and convince the enemy that "they cannot win."[1] The president now had to act decisively or face the loss of South Vietnam.

1. William Westmoreland, telegram to the Joint Chiefs of Staff, 7 June 1965, in U.S. Department of State, *Foreign Relations of the United States, 1964–1968*, vol. 2 (Washington, D.C.: U.S. Government Printing Office, 1996), 735.

3.11 Johnson, comments to Robert McNamara, 21 June 1965

Remarkably Johnson himself harbored deep doubts about a large-scale U.S. military intervention. The following selection, taken from a telephone conversation that Johnson had secretly recorded, enumerates most of the weaknesses in the U.S. position that historians today would list.

I think that in time it's going to be like the Yale professor [antiwar historian Staughton Lynd] said — that it's going to be difficult for us to very long prosecute effectively a war that far away from home with the divisions that we have here, particularly the potential divisions. And it's really had me concerned for a month, and I'm very depressed about it 'cause I see no program from either [the Department of] Defense or State that gives me much hope of doing anything except just prayin' and gasping to hold on during the monsoon [season of heavy rains] and hope they'll quit. I don't believe they [are] ever goin' to quit. I don't see how, that we have any way of either a plan for victory militarily or diplomatically. And I think that's something that you and [Secretary of State] Dean [Rusk] got to sit down and try to see if there's any people that we have in those departments that can give us any program or plan or hope; or, if not, we got to see if we have you go out there or somebody else go out there and take one good look at it and say to these new people [the newly installed government headed by Generals Nguyen Cao Ky and Nguyen Van Thieu], "Now, you've changed your government about the last time and this is it." Call the Buddhists and the Catholics and the generals and everybody together and say, "We're going to do our best." And be sure they're willing to let new troops come in and be sure they're not gonna resent us. "If not, why y'all can run over us and have a government of your own choosing. But we just can't take these changes all the time." That's the Russell plan. [Richard] Russell [a Democratic senator from Georgia, the influential conservative chair of the Senate Armed Services Committee, and a former Johnson mentor] thinks we ought to take one of these changes [in the Saigon government] to get out of there. I don't think we can get out of there with our treaty [under SEATO?] like it is and with what all we've said. And I think it would just lose us face in the world, and I shudder to think what all of 'em would say.

3.12 Under Secretary of State George Ball argues against a major troop commitment, June–July 1965

Of those in the Johnson inner circle, this senior State Department official argued most persistently against the expanded U.S. military role. On the one hand, Ball offered a rationale for disengagement, and on the other, he drew on his understanding of the troubled French war to suggest that the long odds against military success made a diplomatic settlement the wiser course. His reference in the second document to "white foreign (U.S.) troops" raises the interesting question of whether he was warning about cultural differences, about possible racial antagonism, or about the dangers of assuming the French imperial role.

a. Memo to Rusk, McNamara, Bundy, and others, 29 June 1965, proposing "re-education" on the U.S. Vietnam commitment

It should by now be apparent that we have to a large extent created our own predicament. In our determination to rally support, we have tended to give the South Vietnamese struggle an exaggerated and symbolic significance (Mea culpa, since I personally participated in this effort).

The problem for us now — if we determine not to broaden and deepen our commitments — is to re-educate the American people and our friends and allies that:

(a) The phasing out of American power in South Vietnam should not be regarded as a major defeat — either military or political — but a tactical redeployment to more favorable terrain in the overall cold war struggle;

(b) The loss of South Vietnam does not mean the loss of all of Southeast Asia to the Communist power . . . ;

(c) We have more than met our commitments to the South Vietnamese people. We have poured men and equipment into the area, and run risks and taken casualties, and have been prepared to continue the struggle provided the South Vietnamese leaders met even the most rudimentary standards of political performance;

(d) The Viet Cong — while supported and guided from the North — is largely an indigenous movement. Although we have emphasized its cold war aspects, the conflict in South Vietnam is essentially a civil war within that country;

(e) Our commitment to the South Vietnamese people is of a wholly different order from our major commitments elsewhere. . . . We have *never* had a treaty commitment obligating us to the South Vietnamese people or to a South Vietnamese government. Our only treaty commitment in that area is to our SEATO partners, and they have—without exception—viewed the situation in South Vietnam as not calling a treaty into play. To be sure, we *did* make a promise to the South Vietnamese people. But that promise is conditioned on their own performance, and they have not performed.

b. Memo to Johnson, "A Compromise Solution in Vietnam," 1 July 1965

The South Vietnamese are losing the war to the Viet Cong. No one can assure you that we can beat the Viet Cong or even force them to the conference table on our terms no matter how many hundred thousand *white foreign* (U.S.) troops we deploy.

No one has demonstrated that a white ground force of whatever size can win a guerrilla war—which is at the same time a civil war between Asians—in jungle terrain in the midst of a population that refuses cooperation to the white forces (and the SVN[ese]) and thus provides a great intelligence advantage to the other side. Three recent incidents vividly illustrate this point:

(a) The sneak attack on the Danang Air Base which involved penetration of a defense perimeter guarded by 9,000 Marines. *This raid was possible only because of the cooperation of the local inhabitants.*

(b) The B-52 raid that failed to hit the Viet Cong *who had obviously been tipped off.*

(c) The search-and-destroy mission of the 173rd Airborne Brigade which spent three days looking for the Viet Cong, suffered 23 casualties, and never made contact with the enemy *who had obviously gotten advance word of their assignment.* . . .

. . . So long as our forces are restricted to advising and assisting the South Vietnamese, the struggle will remain a civil war between Asian peoples. Once we deploy substantial numbers of troops in combat it will become a war between the United States and a large part of the population of South Viet-Nam, organized and directed from North Viet-Nam and backed by the resources of both Moscow and Peiping.

The decision you face now, therefore, is crucial. Once large numbers of US troops are committed to direct combat they will begin to take heavy casualties in a war they are ill-equipped to fight in a non-cooperative if not downright hostile countryside.

Once we suffer large casualties we will have started a well-nigh irreversible process. Our involvement will be so great that we cannot — without national humiliation — stop short of achieving our complete objectives. *Of the two possibilities I think humiliation would be more likely than the achievement of our objectives — even after we had paid terrible costs.*

... Should we commit US manpower and prestige to a terrain so unfavorable as to give a very large advantage to the enemy — or should we seek a compromise settlement which achieves less than our stated objectives and thus cut our losses while we still have the freedom of maneuver to do so?

... In my judgment, if we act before we commit substantial US forces to combat in South Viet-Nam we can, by accepting some short-term costs, avoid what may well be a long-term catastrophe.

3.13 McNamara, memo to Johnson on a sharp increase in U.S. forces in Vietnam, 20 July 1965

In response to Westmoreland's request for more troops, the influential secretary of defense made one of his hurried visits to Vietnam. On his return he gave his formal endorsement as well as a grim appraisal of the U.S. prospects.

The situation in South Vietnam is worse than a year ago (when it was worse than a year before that). After a few months of stalemate, the tempo of the war has quickened. A hard VC push is now on to dismember the nation and to maul the army. The VC main and local forces, reinforced by militia and guerrillas, have the initiative and, with large attacks (some in regimental strength), are hurting ARVN forces badly. . . . The central highlands could well be lost to the National Liberation Front during this monsoon season. . . . [The Saigon] government is able to provide security to fewer and fewer people in less and less territory as terrorism increases. . . .

. . . Nor have our air attacks in North Vietnam produced tangible evidence of willingness on the part of Hanoi to come to the conference table in a reasonable mood. The DRV/VC seem to believe that South Vietnam is on the run and near collapse; they show no signs of settling for less than a complete take-over. . . .

. . . There are now 15 US (and 1 Australian) combat battalions in Vietnam; they, together with other combat personnel and non-combat personnel, bring the total US personnel in Vietnam to approximately 75,000.

I recommend that the deployment of US ground troops in Vietnam be increased by October to 34 maneuver battalions. . . . The battalions—together with increases in helicopter lift, air squadrons, naval units, air defense, combat support and miscellaneous log[istical] support and advisory personnel which I also recommend—would bring the total US personnel in Vietnam to approximately 175,000. . . . It should be understood that the deployment of more men (an additional perhaps 100,000) may be necessary in early 1966, and that the deployment of additional forces thereafter is possible but will depend on developments. . . .

. . . The DRV, on the other hand, may well send up to several divisions of regular forces in South Vietnam to assist the VC if they see the tide turning and victory, once so near, being snatched away. This possible DRV action is the most ominous one, since it would lead to increased pressures on us to "counter-invade" North Vietnam and to extend air strikes to population targets in the North; acceding to these pressures could bring the Soviets and the Chinese in. The Viet Cong, especially if they continue to take high losses, can be expected to depend increasingly upon the PAVN forces as the war moves into a more conventional phase; but they may find ways to continue almost indefinitely their present intensive military, guerrilla and terror activities, particularly if reinforced by some regular PAVN units.

––––––––––

3.14 Johnson, meetings with advisers, 21–25 July 1965

In late July the president discussed with his chief advisers a large increase in U.S. forces. His first two meetings, held on 21 and 22 July, were formal, and each lasted over three hours. A third, informal gathering took place on 25 July at the presidential retreat at Camp David. Clark Clifford, Robert McNamara, and the ambassador to the United Nations, Arthur Goldberg, were present. Clifford, a senior statesman in the Democratic Party, was one of a number of party leaders who were warning Johnson of the difficulty of sustaining public support for war over the long term. Was the point of all this talk in late July to help the president make a decision or to confirm a decision he had already made?

a. White House meeting, 21 July 1965

BALL: Isn't it possible that the VC will do what they did against the French—stay away from confrontation and not accommodate us?

[Chair of the Joint Chiefs of Staff (JCS) EARLE G.] WHEELER: Yes, but by constantly harassing them, they will have to fight somewhere.

MCNAMARA: If VC doesn't fight in large units, it will give ARVN a chance to re-secure hostile areas. . . .

PRESIDENT [to Wheeler]: What makes you think if we put in 100,000 men Ho Chi Minh won't put in another 100,000?

WHEELER: This means greater bodies of men—which will allow us to cream them. . . .

BALL: I think we have all underestimated the seriousness of this situation. Like giving cobalt treatment to a terminal cancer case. I think a long protracted war will disclose our weakness, not our strength.

The least harmful way to cut losses in SVN is to let the government decide it doesn't want us to stay there. Therefore, put such proposals to SVN government that they can't accept, then it would move into a neutralist position—and I have no illusions that after we were asked to leave, SVN would be under Hanoi control. . . .

PRESIDENT: . . . [W]ouldn't we lose credibility breaking the word of three presidents[?] . . .

BALL: The worse blow would be that the mightiest power in the world is unable to defeat guerrillas.

PRESIDENT: Then you are not basically troubled by what the world would say about pulling out?

BALL: If we were actively helping a country with a stable, viable government, it would be a vastly different story. Western Europeans look at us as if we got ourselves into an imprudent [situation].

PRESIDENT: But I believe that these people [the Vietnamese] are trying to fight. They're like Republicans who try to stay in power, but don't stay there long.

(aside—amid laughter—"excuse me, [Henry] Cabot [Lodge]") . . .

PRESIDENT: Two basic troublings:

1. That Westerners can ever win in Asia.

2. Don't see how you can fight a war under direction of other people whose government changes every month. . . .

RUSK: If the Communist world finds out we will not pursue our commitment to the end, I don't know where they will stay their hand.

I am more optimistic than some of my colleagues. I don't believe the VC have made large advances among the VN [Vietnamese] people.

. . . I don't see great casualties unless the Chinese come in.

LODGE: There is a greater threat to [bringing on] World War III if we don't go in. Similarity to our indolence at Munich [referring to the appeasement of Hitler in a failed attempt to avert World War II].

I can't be as pessimistic as Ball. We have great seaports in Vietnam. We don't need to fight on roads. We have the sea. Visualize our meeting vc on our own terms. We don't have to spend all our time in the jungles.

b. Meeting at the White House, 22 July 1965

PRESIDENT: Doesn't it really mean if we follow Westmoreland's requests [for more troops] we are in a new war—this is going off the diving board[?]

MCNAMARA: This is a major change in US policy. We have relied on SVN to carry the brunt. Now we would be responsible for satisfactory military outcome. . . .

MCNAMARA [on dominoes to fall as a result of abandoning Vietnam]: Laos, Cambodia, Thailand, Burma, surely affect Malaysia. In 2–3 years Communist domination would stop there, but ripple effect would be great—Japan, India. We would have to give up some bases. [Pakistani president] Ayub [Khan] would move closer to China. Greece, Turkey would move to neutralist position. Communist agitation would increase in Africa. . . .

PRESIDENT: If we come in with hundreds of thousands of men and billions of dollars, won't this cause them to come in (China and Russia)?

[Army Chief of Staff General HAROLD] JOHNSON: No, I don't think they will.

PRESIDENT: MacArthur [U.S. commander during the Korean War who was caught off guard by Chinese intervention] didn't think they would come in either.

[General] JOHNSON: Yes, but this is not comparable to Korea. . . .

PRESIDENT: But China has plenty of divisions to move in, don't they?

[General] JOHNSON: Yes, they do.

PRESIDENT: Then what would we do?

[General] JOHNSON: (long silence) If so, we have another ball game.

PRESIDENT: But I have to take into account they will. . . .

PRESIDENT: Do all of you think the Congress and the people will go along with 600,000 people and billions of dollars 10,000 miles away?

[Army Secretary STANLEY] RESOR: Gallup Poll shows people are basically behind our commitment.

PRESIDENT: But if you make a commitment to jump off a building, and you find out how high it is, you may withdraw the commitment.

PRESIDENT: I judge though that the big problem is one of national security. Is that right?

(murmured assent)

c. Clark Clifford, comments to Johnson at a Camp David meeting, 25 July 1965

Don't believe we can win in SVN. If we send in 100,000 more, the [DRV] will meet us. If the [DRV] run[s] out of men, the Chinese will send in volunteers. Russia and China don't intend for us to win the war. If we don't win, it is a catastrophe. If we lose 50,000+ it will ruin us. Five years, billions of dollars, 50,000 men, it is not for us.

At end of monsoon, quietly probe and search out with other countries—by moderating our position—to allow us to get out. Can't see anything but catastrophe for my country. . . .

————

3.15 Johnson, press conference statement, 28 July 1965

Setting aside doubts, Johnson announced at a low-key White House press conference that he was sending 50,000 fresh troops to Vietnam. Like his Johns Hopkins speech almost four months earlier (document 3.7), this announcement mingled Cold War platitudes with deeply personal reflections and with deep regret. The war was for Americans now on in earnest but not with enthusiasm.

We did not choose to be the guardians at the gate, but there is no one else.

Nor would surrender in Viet-Nam bring peace, because we learned from Hitler at Munich that success only feeds the appetite of aggression. The battle would be renewed in one country and then another country, bringing with it perhaps even larger and crueler conflict, as we have learned from the lessons of history.

Moreover, we are in Viet-Nam to fulfill one of the most solemn pledges of the American Nation. Three Presidents — President Eisenhower, President Kennedy, and your present President — over 11 years have committed themselves and have promised to help defend this small and valiant nation.

Strengthened by that promise, the people of South Viet-Nam have fought for many long years. Thousands of them have died. Thousands more have been crippled and scarred by war. We just cannot now dishonor our word, or abandon our commitment, or leave those who believed us and who trusted us to the terror and repression and murder that would follow....

Let me also add now a personal note. I do not find it easy to send the flower of our youth, our finest young men, into battle. . . . I have seen them in a thousand streets, of a hundred towns, in every State in this Union — working and laughing and building, and filled with hope and life. I think I know, too, how their mothers weep, and how their families sorrow.

This is the most agonizing and the most painful duty of your President.

. . . I have now been in public life 35 years, more than three decades, and in each of those 35 years I have seen good men, and wise leaders, struggle to bring the blessings of this land to all of our people. . . .

But I also know, as a realistic public servant, that as long as there are men who hate and destroy, we must have the courage to resist, or we will see it all, all that we have built, all that we hope to build, all of our dreams for freedom — all, *all* will be swept away on the flood of conquest.

So, too, this shall not happen. We will stand in Viet-Nam.

The Lords
of War,
1965–1973

Americans and Vietnamese began a brutal and prolonged exchange of blows in the latter part of 1965. In this slugging match, PAVN and NLF forces had inferior resources but a clear strategy that had proven effective against the French and the Diem regime. As in the past, success depended on popular commitment, above all in villages, from which the NLF drew recruits, moral support, food, intelligence, and shelter. It also depended on the organizational strength of the Vietnamese Communist Party and the state it controlled and on the backing of Soviet and Chinese allies.

On the American side, General William Westmoreland opted for a strategy of attrition. U.S. combat units would probe for the enemy and, once they had located their foes, batter them with massive firepower. This approach in effect took the conduct of the war from the hands of the Saigon military government—even as it gained a degree of stability under Generals Nguyen Van Thieu and Nguyen Cao Ky—and put the initiative in the hands of a U.S. expeditionary force with better equipment, discipline, and organization. Defying Westmoreland, the enemy remained in the field fighting while American forces suffered from their own form of attrition as ambushes, snipers, and mines took their toll on men and morale.

This trial by arms reached its climax with the Tet Offensive. In late January 1968 (during Tet, the lunar new year celebration), the NLF seized major population centers with the hope that the attacks would precipitate the collapse of the Saigon government, demoralize the Americans, and thus end the war. The gamble failed on the ground in Vietnam, but it set off shock waves in Washington and throughout the U.S. political system. Lyndon Johnson renounced his claim to another term in the White House and halted the bombing of the North beyond the twentieth parallel in order to initiate negotiations. The slugfest had reached a turning point. Both sides had thrown their best punches, yet both were still standing and still defiant.

What followed the Tet Offensive is familiar to historians of war once the knot of conflict is tightly tied: the spasms of violence that engulf the lives of millions, the great passions that bloodshed requires and reinforces, and the social fissures that open up under the steady demands of sacrifice. But every war must end once exhaustion drains away the will if not the capacity to continue the fight. As Vietnamese and American leaders took stock in the wake of the Tet Offensive, they recognized that the knot of their war was tightly tied. How to untie it was by no means clear.

Richard Nixon took direction of the war in 1969 determined to avoid anything that resembled a humiliating retreat. His search for an honorable way out began almost from the moment he became president, and it would consume and ultimately doom his presidency. To buck up the American public, Nixon embraced "Vietnamization"—a gradual shift of the ground war from American troops to the ARVN. At the same time, he sought to compel the enemy to settle on terms that gave the U.S.-backed government in Saigon a good chance of survival. To that end he made sure that the ARVN was better armed and that it enjoyed the full support of American airpower. He also dramatically extended the fighting into the areas of Cambodia and Laos that the enemy used for supply lines and refuge.

The party leadership under Le Duan had its own substantial set of problems. Hanoi had to worry about Chinese patrons who had been unhappy in 1968 with the prospect of the DRV's opening talks with the Johnson administration. To compound tensions, Mao Zedong began his own conversation with the Nixon administration in 1971. Rising contention over their relative influence over Cambodia would by degrees create yet a third and still more difficult layer to the relationship. On top of all this, Hanoi had to make sure that the intense rivalry between Beijing and Moscow (culminating in armed border clashes in early 1969) did not compromise the commitment both those Communist powers had made to the struggle in Vietnam. Morale in the North was beginning to sag. The General Offensive, which had begun in January 1968 and continued through September, ate up scarce resources yet showed no signs of producing a dramatic turn in the war. The NLF was badly hurt, and recovery was slow.

Stubborn but chastened, each side started to probe for enemy weaknesses and to dribble out concessions in intermittent secret talks, which began in August 1969 in Paris. There Henry Kissinger, Nixon's close White House adviser, faced a DRV delegation headed by Xuan Thuy and reinforced by special adviser Le Duc Tho, who shuttled between Paris and Hanoi. Tho was a senior party leader with close ties to Le Duan. He had helped found Vietnam's Communist Party and endured six years in French prisons. He later played a prominent role in the southern resistance, against first the French and then the Americans.

Not until October 1972 had both sides suffered enough failures on the battlefield and delivered enough concessions that they could reach a deal. The Nixon administration, already well on its way to liquidating the U.S. combat presence in Vietnam, pledged a total withdrawal and dropped long-standing demands for the elimination of northern forces from the South. Hanoi made its own concessions, promising the return of all U.S. prisoners and setting aside its insistence on the overthrow of the "illegitimate" Saigon government as a precondition for peace. The October agreement envisioned Saigon and Hanoi seeking reconciliation through a peaceful political process.

President Thieu flatly rejected these terms, stoutly resisting pressure from his American patrons to sign on. Nixon resorted to what appears to have been a bout of symbolic bombing of Hanoi in December. He hoped to demonstrate to Thieu, to domestic critics on the right, and perhaps even to himself a readiness to act ruthlessly in defense of the South. Having made that point, Nixon proceeded to accept in January 1973 an agreement virtually indistinguishable from the one negotiated the previous October.

The documents that follow raise some basic question about how Washington and Hanoi directed their respective war efforts:

- How well did leaders on each side think through their strategies, including the nature of the battlefield, the attitude of the enemy, the availability of weapons and supplies, the support of allies, and the definition of victory?
- What problems began to erode the U.S. war effort? Did Nixon devise a war strategy that actually addressed those problems, or was he simply playing for time and a lucky break?
- What were the major turning points in the conduct of the war?

STRATEGIES FOR VICTORY, SEPTEMBER–NOVEMBER 1965

The steady DRV buildup of PAVN and NLF forces in South Vietnam followed by Johnson's major troop commitment in mid-1965 left the two sides poised for war and assessing their military options in anticipation of a long struggle.

4.1 Le Duan, letter to comrades in COSVN, November 1965

Le Duan's guidance here to the party leaders heading COSVN confirmed his earlier confidence (document 3.10) that it was possible to handle the worst case — a U.S. decision to shift to a limited war waged by a substantial U.S. combat force.

[If several hundred thousand American troops reinforce half a million puppet troops,] we still have the possibility of winning a decisive victory in a relatively short time.

. . . [S]hould the US bring in half a million or so GIs, . . . we are firmly confident that *the US cannot fight a long-drawn-out war and defeat us; on the contrary our protracted resistance will surely end in victory. . . .*

From the military point of view, it is easier to destroy puppet troops than US forces, for the latter are newcomers and consequently more self-complacent, reliant on their weapons and somewhat motivated by national pride. As for the puppet troops, they are reeling from past setbacks, bewildered, and their fighting will is sagging. Therefore, we should uphold our determination to destroy them and rapidly bring about their large-scale disintegration. On the other hand, . . . we should carefully study [the] most appropriate tactical forms and operational ways to wipe out US troops. . . .

Although inferior in number to the puppet army, the US forces have strong firepower, huge bases with many modern war means, fuel and ammunition right in our country. Therefore, it is important to wear down big US bases, airports, stores, as well as bearing down on big puppet and US units. . . .

Together with military struggle, utmost attention should be paid to organizing and leading the masses around US bases to carry out political struggle, agitprop [agitation and propaganda] work among US troops so as to limit the enemy's sweeps and raids, and protect the people's lives and properties.

In the coming spring–summer period we should try and put out of action about ten thousand US troops as planned, and in some year to come, about forty or fifty thousand — which is a new requirement to win a decisive victory in this war.

4.2 General William Westmoreland, directive to U.S. commanders, 17 September 1965

Unlike his foes, who had a tested strategy, the U.S. commander on the ground had to work out his approach. Westmoreland's thinking on how to achieve victory finally emerged with clarity in September. This directive assumed that technological superiority would allow U.S. forces to grind the enemy down. It also assumed that these operations would do limited harm to civilians and unfold in close coordination with Saigon officials.

The war in Vietnam is a political as well as a military war. It is political because the ultimate goal is to regain the loyalty and cooperation of the people, and to create conditions which permit the people to go about their normal lives in peace and security.

At the present time, large geographical areas of Vietnam are dominated by the VC. Some areas are completely controlled, while in others the people live under the shadow of VC military forces and terrorists. Although the VC is the enemy, it does not follow that the people who live in the areas which he dominates are also the enemy. Eventually, the GVN must reestablish control over these same areas and these same people, many of whom currently have no alternative to VC control because the GVN has been unable to give them the protection they want and deserve.

Because of the situation described above, the application of U.S. military force in Vietnam and the conduct of U.S. troops must be carefully controlled at all times. On the one hand, maximum effectiveness must be achieved in operations against the VC; on the other hand, a conscious effort must be made to minimize battle casualties among those non-combatants who must be brought back into the fold in the course of time. This requires an extremely high caliber of leadership plus the exercise of judgment and restraint not formerly expected of soldiers. . . .

Thus, the ultimate aim is to pacify the Republic of Vietnam by destroying the VC — his forces, organization, terrorists, agents, and propagandists — while at the same time reestablishing the government apparatus, strengthening GVN military forces, rebuilding the administrative machinery, and re-instituting the services of the Government. During this process security must be provided to all of the people on a progressive basis. . . .

Operations against VC base areas should be repetitive based on a carefully designed campaign of sustained actions which ultimately will dominate the bases and render them useless. By driving the VC from the base, he is forced to reconstitute his supplies, rearrange his liaison and communications system, rebuild his shelters, redig his tunnels, reestablish his security and warning system, and thus consume much time and energy. Furthermore, if his new base must be situated farther back in remote areas, his threat to population centers is diminished proportionately.

Limited operations against vc bases will be effective in keeping the enemy off balance, denying him free utilization of safe areas, and forcing him either to move frequently or to withhold forces for the defense of base complexes. Long range artillery, naval gunfire, fighter bombers, strategic bombers and land and amphibious raids will hamper his operations, reduce his forces, destroy his morale and materially detract from his ability to prosecute the war effectively. . . .

The US unit commander should establish close liaison with the [GVN] province chief immediately, and plan his operations in cooperation with and in support of province officials and their plans. . . .

. . . Even when an area is occupied by securing forces, the vc may be expected to remain active with his political and subversive infra-structure and clandestine agents. An area cannot be considered pacified until these vc activities have been identified and either destroyed or removed, and until the services and activities of the GVN have been fully reinstated.

4.3 McNamara's deepening doubts, November 1965 and May 1967

Robert McNamara quickly recognized the difficulties facing Westmoreland's attrition strategy. He visited Vietnam in the immediate aftermath of the first major encounter between U.S. and PAVN forces, at Ia Drang between 14 and 17 November 1965. Westmoreland publicly described the outcome as a brilliant victory, but what McNamara learned led him to raise a warning flag for the president. A second appraisal, prepared a year and a half later in response to Westmoreland's request for an additional 200,000 troops and JCS plans for expanding the war, was even less hopeful. As impresario of the war, McNamara cautioned his boss against a military escalation but could hold out no surefire alternative road to victory. Johnson, himself doubtful, refused to expand the war and agreed to only 55,000 more men.

a. Report to President Johnson after a two-day visit to Vietnam, 30 November 1965

[The Ky-Thieu] "government of generals" is surviving, but not acquiring wide support . . . ; pacification is thoroughly stalled, with no guarantee that security anywhere is permanent and no indications that able and willing leadership will emerge in the absence of that permanent security. . . .

The dramatic recent changes in the situation are on the military side. They are the increased infiltration from the North and the increased willingness of the Communist forces to stand and fight, even in large-scale engagements. The Ia Drang River Campaign of early November is an example. The Communists appear to have decided to increase their forces in South Vietnam both by heavy recruitment in the South (especially in the [Mekong] Delta) and by infiltration of regular North Vietnamese forces from the North. . . .

. . . We have but two options, it seems to me. One is to go now for a compromise solution . . . and hold further deployments to a minimum. The other is to stick with our stated objectives and with the war, and provide what it takes in men and matériel. If it is decided not to move now toward a compromise, I recommend that the United States both send a substantial number of additional troops [raising the U.S. total to about 400,000 by the end of 1966 and perhaps adding another 200,000 in 1967] and very gradually intensify the bombing of North Vietnam. . . .

. . . We should be aware that deployments of the kind I have recommended will not guarantee success. US killed-in-action can be expected to reach 1000 a month, and the odds are even that we will be faced in early 1967 with a "no-decision" at an even higher level [a stalemate with even more troops involved].

b. Draft memo to Johnson (read by the president), 19 May 1967

This memorandum is written at a time when there appears to be no attractive course of action. . . .

The Vietnam war is unpopular in this country. It is becoming increasingly unpopular as it escalates — causing more American casualties, more fear of its growing into a wider war, more privation of the domestic sector, and more distress at the amount of suffering being visited on the non-combatants in Vietnam, South and North. Most Americans do not know how we got where we are, and most, without knowing why, but taking advantage of hindsight, are convinced that somehow we should not have gotten this deeply in. All want the war ended and expect their President to end it. Successfully. Or else.

This state of mind in the US generates impatience in the political structure of the United States. It unfortunately also generates patience in Hanoi. (It is commonly supposed that Hanoi will not give anything away pending the trial of the US elections in November 1968.)

The "big war" in the South between the US and the North Vietnamese military units [PAVN] is going well. We staved off military defeat in 1965; we gained the military initiative in 1966; and since then we have been hurting the enemy badly, spoiling some of his ability to strike. . . .

All things considered, there is consensus that we are no longer in danger of losing this war militarily.

Regrettably, the "other war" against the VC is still not going well. Corruption [on the Saigon government side] is widespread. Real government control is confined to enclaves. There is rot in the fabric. Our efforts to enliven the moribund political infrastructure have been matched by VC efforts. . . . In the Delta, because of the redeployment of some VC/[PAVN] troops to the area north of Saigon, the VC have lost their momentum and appear to be conducting essentially a holding operation. On the government side there, the tempo of operations has been correspondingly low. The population remains apathetic, and many local government officials seem to have working arrangements with the VC which they are reluctant to disturb.

The National Liberation Front (NLF) continues to control large parts of South Vietnam, and there is little evidence that the [GVN's] revolutionary development program is gaining any momentum. The Army of South Vietnam (ARVN) is tired, passive and accommodation-prone, and is moving too slowly if at all into pacification work. . . .

. . . Hanoi's attitude currently is hard and rigid. They seem uninterested in a political settlement and determined to match US military expansion of the conflict. . . . There continues to be no sign that the bombing has reduced Hanoi's will to resist or her ability to ship the necessary supplies south. Hanoi shows no signs of ending the large war and advising the VC to melt into the jungles. The North Vietnamese believe they are right; they consider the Ky regime to be puppets; they believe the world is with them and that the American public will not have staying power against them. . . .

. . . [T]he Soviets apparently have been unwilling to use whatever influence they may have in Hanoi to persuade North Vietnam to come to the conference table while the bombing continues. . . .

. . . The Peking Government continues to advise Hanoi not to negotiate. . . . There is no reason to doubt that China would honor its commitment to intervene at Hanoi's request, and it remains likely that Peking would intervene on her own initiative if she believed that the existence of the Hanoi regime was at stake. . . .

The war in Vietnam is acquiring a momentum of its own that must be stopped. Dramatic increases in US troop deployments, in attacks on the North, or in ground actions in Laos or Cambodia are not necessary and are not the answer. The enemy can absorb them or counter them, bogging us down further and risking even more serious escalation of the war.

THE TET OFFENSIVE GAMBLE, JULY 1967–MARCH 1968

Beginning in early 1967, party leaders desperately sought a way to break the stalemate in the war with the Americans. Only by achieving a battlefield success could they hope to force the Americans into negotiations, bring an end to the bombing of the North, and secure the withdrawal of U.S. forces from the South. Complicating matters, Nguyen Chi Thanh, the Communist commander in the South responsible for the conduct of any offensive, died in Hanoi in early July during a working visit. At this point Le Duan took the initiative. Working with Vo Nguyen Giap's associate General Van Tien Dung, he devised an audacious plan for "a general offensive and a general uprising," a strategic concept for ultimate victory in the South that had been on the minds of party leaders at least since late 1963 (document 3.2). Also known as the Tet Offensive, this attack envisioned all-out assaults by the NLF, backed by PAVN units, on both the enemy military and major cities. Inflicting heavy casualties on U.S. and ARVN units and seizing the enemy's urban strongholds were sure to break the battlefield stalemate and shake the Johnson administration and deepen public dissent at the very start of a presidential election year.

4.4 Hanoi's difficult strategic decision, July 1967 and January 1968

Le Duan's plan deeply divided the top party leadership. Defense Minister Giap, the architect of the Dien Bien Phu victory, warned that the success of any major offensive depended on first crippling ARVN and U.S. forces. Also doubtful was the old and ailing Ho Chi Minh. The following meeting notes taken by General Dung record Ho's doubts and offer a rare glimpse into inner-party debate. Le Duan pressed ahead, elaborating his plan over the second half of 1967 and securing final Central Committee approval (with Ho abstaining) in January. Immediately after the meeting, Le Duan offered last-minute guidance to COSVN (now headed by Pham Hung, Thanh's successor), including an optimistic reading of the situation and an outline of the strategic concept behind the military campaign scheduled to begin the night of 30–31 January.

a. Ho Chi Minh's objections, Politburo meeting, 18–19 July 1967

1. This [Le Duan–Van Tien Dung] draft is good, comprehensive, and optimistic, but *we need to consider whether the report . . . is subjective* [unrealistic].
2. We may strive to win a quick victory, but *we must pay attention to the need to be able to fight a protracted war.*
3. We have many advantages, but *we also must recognize our difficulties*, such as in the area of rear services [logistics] and support.
4. The draft talks about winning a military victory, but *we must also pay attention to the need to preserve the strength of our people. If our people and our resources become exhausted, then we will not be able to fight, no matter how many troops we have.*
5. We must pay attention to the need to expand guerrilla warfare and to provide additional equipment to our guerrillas.
6. We must make sure that we grow stronger as we fight, that we fight continuously, and that we are able to fight for a long time [i.e., that we are able to fight a protracted war].

b. Le Duan, letter to COSVN comrades, 18 January 1968

After repeated setbacks, the US and satellite troops cannot "search and destroy" successfully; the puppet troops have not enough forces to "pacify". The enemy forces are stretched over the battlefields and encircled by our people's armed and political forces. The strategic position of the US-puppets is being upset; their troops' morale is sagging; their internal contradictions are increasing. US imperialism had to cope with very great political, military and financial difficulties not only in the South but even in the USA. In the world US imperialism is isolated and the US position is also weakening. . . .

Our armed forces have matured by leaps and bounds. Applying flexible combat methods, they have wiped out large enemy forces, struck at a number of towns, a series of US–puppet airfields, stores and strategic communication lines, and won resounding victories. The masses in all enemy-held areas and in a number of towns have risen up in various ways; hundreds of thousands of people seething with revolutionary fervour have risen up to wrest back independence, freedom, peace, food and clothing. . . .

The above-mentioned situation enables us to shift the revolutionary war to a *period of winning a decisive victory*. This is a great strategic opportunity to launch a general offensive and a general uprising. . . .

. . . Our policy is to stretch the enemy throughout the Southern battlefield, drive his main force to battlefields advantageous to us and deal it crushing blows; or counter-attack in big annihilation battles breaking his "search and destroy" operations. *This is the main thrust of our general offensive, an orientation for attack by our main force.*

On the other hand, *another main thrust must be aimed at the towns.* Here we have to use a crack military force and the political force of the revolutionary masses, combine the spearheads of the shock force with the uprisings of the masses in the towns and the adjacent rural areas, while mobilizing enemy troops to mutiny or give up fighting so as to wipe out many of these forces, strike at the US–puppet nerve centres, destroy their bases, stores, signal centres and means of transport and communication; encircle the enemy in the towns and expand rural areas under our control. Thus we will strike at the enemy's brain, heart and arteries. . . .

. . . *The orientation for our offensive and uprising is aimed at the towns but we should bear in mind that the greatest and most important result is to conquer and keep the countryside.* When the enemy is compelled to withdraw into the towns, we will have the conditions to mobilize the masses in the countryside to rise up, co-ordinate their action with the people's armed forces to liquidate and cause puppet troops to disintegrate, break the ruling apparatus in the hamlets and communes [and] expand our control in vast rural areas. . . .

. . . I eagerly wish that together with our Southern fighters and fellow-countrymen you will apply all your energy and strength to this strategic battle and win the greatest victory to welcome Uncle Ho in the South.

4.5 The impact of the Tet Offensive on the Johnson administration, March 1968

The Tet gamble succeeded. It overran most major urban areas and shook the Americans. In late February General Westmoreland called for an additional 207,000 troops, setting off a debate within the Johnson administration. Clark Clifford, newly installed as secretary of defense and earlier an opponent of a major troop commitment (document 3.14c), was skeptical about sending more troops. He argued instead for putting more of the burden of combat on the Saigon forces and at the same time giving them more resources to fight with (what would become known as Vietnamization). He laid out his views in a pair of two-hour White House meetings with the president and other advisers (including Secretary of State Rusk, JCS chair Wheeler, CIA head Richard Helms, and presidential aides Maxwell Taylor and Walt Rostow). After extensive consultation within the administration and with senior policy specialists on the outside ("the wise men"), Johnson appeared before television cameras in late March to announce that he was ready to deescalate the conflict, effectively paving the way for negotiations. In a surprise move, he also announced that he was withdrawing from the presidential race.

a. Secretary of Defense Clark Clifford and Johnson, discussions with Johnson's advisers, 4–5 March 1968

[CLARK CLIFFORD:] Frankly, it came as a shock that the Vietcong-North Vietnamese had the strength of force and skill to mount the Tet offensive—as they did. They struck 34 cities, made strong inroads in Saigon and in Hue. There have been very definite effects felt in the countryside. . . .

There are grave doubts that we have made the type of progress we had hoped to have made by this time. As we build up our forces, they build up theirs. We continue to fight at a higher level of intensity. . . .

Under the present situation, there is a good deal of talk about what the ARVN "will do" but when the crunch is on, when the crunch comes, they look to us for more. When they got into the Tet offensive, Thieu's statement wasn't what more they could do but that "it is time for more U.S. troops." . . .

The reserve forces in North Vietnam are a cause for concern as well. They have a very substantial population from which to draw. They have no trouble whatever organizing, equipping, and training their forces.

We seem to have a sinkhole. We put in more — they match it. We put in more — they match it. . . .

The Soviets and the Chinese have agreed to keep the North Vietnamese well armed and well supplied.

The Vietcong are now better armed than the ARVN. They have:

— better rifles

— better training

— more sophisticated weapons (mortars, artillery, rockets).

I see more and more fighting with more and more casualties on the U.S. side and no end in sight to the action. . . .

We should tell the South Vietnamese that the General [Westmoreland] has asked for 200,000 more troops, but we are giving only 25,000. We should let them know that you [Johnson] are delaying your decision until you know what the GVN will do about:

— removal of the poor unit commanders

— meaningful steps to eliminate corruption

— meeting their own leadership responsibilities

— not only saying they will do something, but meaning it as well.

If they are not, we should know it now. . . .

[THE PRESIDENT:] . . . [I]t appears we are about to make a rather basic change in the strategy of this war, if:

— we tell the ARVN to do more fighting.

— we tell them we will give 20,000 men; no more.

— we tell them we will do no more until they do more.

— we tell them we will be *prepared* to make additional troop contributions but not unless they "get with it."

I frankly doubt you will get much out of them unless they have a good coach, the right plays, and the best equipment. . . .

. . . Let's . . . give the South Vietnamese the best equipment we can.

b. President Johnson, address from the White House, 31 March 1968

[The Tet attack] failed to achieve its principal objectives.

It did not collapse the elected government of South Vietnam or shatter its army — as the Communists had hoped.

It did not produce a "general uprising" among the people of the cities as they had predicted.

The Communists were unable to maintain control of any of the more than 30 cities that they attacked. And they took very heavy casualties.

But they did compel the South Vietnamese and their allies to move certain forces from the countryside into the cities.

They caused widespread disruption and suffering. Their attacks, and the battles that followed, made refugees of half a million human beings. . . .

We are prepared to move immediately toward peace through negotiations.

So, tonight, in the hope that this action will lead to early talks, I am taking the first step to deescalate the conflict. We are reducing—substantially reducing—the present level of hostilities.

And we are doing so unilaterally, and at once.

Tonight, I have ordered our aircraft and our naval vessels to make no attacks on North Vietnam, except in the area north of the demilitarized zone where the continuing enemy buildup directly threatens allied forward positions and where the movements of their troops and supplies are clearly related to that threat. . . .

. . . [W]e are prepared to withdraw our forces from South Vietnam as the other side withdraws its forces to the north, stops the infiltration, and the level of violence thus subsides. . . .

With America's sons in the fields far away, with America's future under challenge right here at home, with our hopes and the world's hopes for peace in the balance every day, I do not believe that I should devote an hour or a day of my time to any personal partisan causes or to any duties other than the awesome duties of this office — the Presidency of your country.

Accordingly, I shall not seek, and I will not accept, the nomination of my party for another term as your President.

4.6 The Communist Party's southern office, assessment of the Tet Offensive, March 1968

The Tet gamble also failed. It shook the NLF as much as it did Johnson. Exposed militarily and politically, cadres suffered heavy losses, units were put out of action, and supply lines were disrupted. Nevertheless, party strategists put a positive spin on the results and planned two additional offensive blows in the months ahead. The following COSVN assessment from March notes the achievements and the areas for improvement but gives little sense of how well the U.S. and ARVN forces had fought, how little urban support the NLF had received, how much rural control the NLF was having to cede to Saigon, and how much of the burden of the fighting PAVN forces would thereafter carry. Despite his earlier doubts about the Tet Offensive, Giap assumed responsibility for directing PAVN operations.

[A]fter a month of continuous offensives and simultaneous uprisings conducted on all battlefields in the South, we have recorded great and unprecedented victories in all fields, inflicting on the enemy heavier losses than those he had suffered in any previous period.

1) We wore down, annihilated and disintegrated almost one-third of the puppet [Saigon] troops' strength, wore down and annihilated about one-fifth of U.S. combat forces . . . : destroyed and forced to surrender or withdrawal one-third of the enemy military posts, driving the enemy into an unprecedentedly awkward situation. . . .

2) We attacked all U.S.-puppet nerve centers, occupied and exerted our control for a definite period and at varying degrees over almost all towns, cities and municipalities in the South. . . .

3) We liberated additional wide areas in the countryside containing a population of 1.5 million inhabitants. . . .

. . . [These successes] have . . . inspired a strong confidence in final victory among compatriots in both the North and South. These successes have moreover won the sympathy and support of the socialist countries and the world's progressive people (including the U.S. progressive people) for our people's revolutionary cause, seriously isolated the U.S. imperialists and their lackeys, deepened their internal contradictions and thereby weakened the U.S. will of aggression. . . .

We have won great successes but still have many deficiencies and weak points:

1) In the military field — From the beginning, we have not been able to annihilate much of the enemy's live force and much of the reactionary clique. . . .

2) In the political field — Organized popular forces were not broad and strong enough. . . .

3) The puppet troops proselyting failed to create a military revolt movement in which the troops would arise and return to the people's side. . . .

The above-mentioned deficiencies and weak points have limited our successes and are, at the same time, difficulties which we must resolutely overcome.

The U.S. strategy of attrition had no more succeeded than had the DRV's strategy of dealing a fatal blow to the Americans. With the war still in stalemate, both sides began to make adjustments. Richard Nixon came into the White House with Vietnam an albatross around his neck and with big plans to pursue overtures to the Soviet Union and China. Better relations with Moscow and Beijing were for him goals in their own right, but he also hoped that they would press Hanoi on peace terms Washington could live with. On the other side, Le Duan and his colleagues could see that even though the Tet Offensive had fallen short of its military objectives, it had further shaken American resolve. But how to exploit U.S. vulnerability to achieve the liberation of the South?

4.7 High-level DRV delegation, meeting with Chinese leaders, Beijing, 17 November 1968

Vietnamese and Chinese leaders met shortly after Nixon's election to read his intentions and to devise an appropriate counterstrategy. Beneath the surface the Vietnamese were also trying to keep in good repair the alliance with the indispensable "elder brother." Beijing continued to deter a U.S. invasion of the DRV; maintained a stream of military supplies, agricultural goods, and machinery right down to the end of the fighting in 1975; and kept troops in the DRV until July 1970 (170,000 at peak) to help with air defense and transport. While the scale of Soviet help with advanced weaponry increased, Chinese backing remained critical to sustaining the war effort. The Chinese had advocated a patient strategy of protracted war and had opposed both the Tet gamble and the decision to open negotiations with Washington. But by the time of this gathering in Mao Zedong's residence, attended by the leading party and military leaders on the Chinese side, they had come around to the Vietnamese position. Pham Van Dong represented the Vietnamese side, seconded by Nguyen Van Linh (referred to here as Muoi Cuc). Linh was a northerner whose long service in COSVN gave him a southern perspective. After reunification in 1975, he administered South Vietnam and then, as general secretary of the Communist Party (1986–1991), implemented a major economic reform program.

[MAO ZEDONG:] The US has great difficulties in their undertaking. . . .
They already have been involved in Asia for 4 or 5 years now. . . . The
US capitalists who invested in Europe should be displeased and dis-
agree. . . . At present their allies in Europe are complaining a lot, saying
that [the United States] reduces the number of its troops [in Europe]
and withdraws its experienced troops and good equipment [from Eu-
rope], not to mention the troops withdrawn from South Korea and
Hawaii. The US has a population of 200 million people, but it cannot stand wars. If they want to mobilize some tens of thousand[s] of
troops, they must spend a lot of time and money. . . .

We agree with your slogan of fighting while negotiating. Some
comrades worry that the US will deceive you. But I tell them not to
[worry]. Negotiations are just like fighting. You have drawn experience, understood the rules. But sometimes they can deceive you. . . .

PHAM VAN DONG: . . . Sitting at the negotiating table does not mean
[we] stop fighting. On the contrary, fighting must be fiercer. In that
way, we can attain a higher position, adopt the voice of the victorious and strong, who knows how to fight to the end and knows that
the enemy will fail eventually. This is our attitude. If we think otherwise, we will not win. In this connection, the South must fight fiercely,
at the same time carry out the political struggle. At present, conditions in the South are very good. The convening of talks in Paris represents a new source of encouragement for our people in the South.
They say that if the US fails in the North, they will definitely fail in
the South.

MAO ZEDONG: Is it true that the American troops were happy when talks
were announced?

MUOI CUC: I would like to tell you, Chairman Mao, that the Americans
celebrate the news. Thousands of them gather to listen to radio coverage of the talks. When ordered to fight, some wrote on their hats: "I
am soon going back home, please do not kill me."

Saigon troops are very discouraged. Many of them openly oppose
Thieu. . . . The morale of the Saigon troops and government officials
is very low. . . .

. . . . Our victories gained in the South are due, to a great extent, to
the assistance, as well as the encouragement of the Chinese people
and your [encouragement], Chairman Mao.

MAO ZEDONG: My part is very small.

MUOI CUC: Very big, very important.

MAO ZEDONG: Mainly because of your efforts. Your country is unified, your Party is unified, your armed forces are unified, your people, regardless in the South or North, are unified, which is very good.

MUOI CUC: We hold that the spiritual support offered by China is most important. Even in the most difficult situations, we have the great rear area of China supporting us, which allows us to fight for as long as it takes. . . .

MAO ZEDONG: The US now respects the Party and Government in Vietnam led by President Ho, respects the NLF led by President Nguyen Huu Tho [a French-educated lawyer and secret member of Vietnam's Communist Party]. The US also does not think highly of the Thieu clique, considering them ineffective.

PHAM VAN DONG: That is correct.

MAO ZEDONG: The US gives Saigon a lot of money, but much has been embezzled.

PHAM VAN DONG: In Paris, Thieu's representatives verbally opposed the US. We then asked the American representatives why the US allowed Saigon to do so. [The president's personal representative W. Averell] Harriman replied that Saigon by so doing tried to show that they are not puppets. . . .

MAO ZEDONG: It is necessary to have political education for your troops. You should take advantage of the negotiations for political education. Before every big battle, it is always an imperative to spend time on political education. There should be only two or three, or four at most, big campaigns every year. The regular troops should spend the remaining time on political education.

PHAM VAN DONG: That is what we do. . . .

. . . . We think that what Chairman Mao has said is very correct, very suitable for the situation in our struggle against the US for national salvation.

MAO ZEDONG: Some [of my thinking] is not necessarily correct. We have to refer to the actual developments.

PHAM VAN DONG: Ultimately, it is we who make the decisions based on the actual situation in Vietnam and on how we understand the rules of the war. This is also what Chairman Mao has told President Ho and other Vietnamese comrades. Once again, we would like to reiterate before Chairman Mao and other leaders of the CCP [Chinese Communist Party] that we are determined to fight until the final and total victory is gained. It is the best way to express our gratitude for the support and aid provided to us by Chairman Mao and the CCP as well as the fraternal Chinese people.

4.8 President Richard Nixon plots a way out, March–May 1969

Once in office, Nixon worked out a Vietnam policy that built on the approach Johnson had devised after Tet. He quickly embraced Vietnamization—the plan to upgrade South Vietnamese forces so that they could take over the burden of fighting from the Americans. Nixon also continued the peace talks in Paris, hoping to secure the satisfactory settlement that U.S. prestige and commitments demanded. Critical to such a settlement were the survival of the Thieu regime and the withdrawal of PAVN forces along with U.S. troops from South Vietnam. Nixon assumed that tough talk, hard bargaining, and the occasional unleashing of U.S. military power would push Hanoi to terms he could live with. Though not mentioned in the documents here, the president and Kissinger were secretly laying the groundwork for diplomatic overtures to Moscow and Beijing that they hoped would in turn add to the pressure on Hanoi to make concessions. By April 1969 the president had worked out the details of his plan, and the next month he asked for patience from a public longing for a speedy conclusion to the war.

a. Nixon, meeting with the National Security Council, 28 March 1969

The President . . . asked, "how do we de-Americanize this thing in such a way as to influence negotiations and have them move along quicker?" . . .

. . . The President stated that timing is a problem. "We must move in a deliberate way, not to show panic. We cannot be stampeded by the likes of [Senator J. William] Fulbright [whose criticism of the war appears in document 6.3]." . . .

The President stated, "we need a plan. If we had no [U.S. midterm?] elections, it would be fine. . . . The reality is that we are working against a time clock. We are talking 6 to 8 months. We are going to play a strong public game but we must plan this. We must get a sense of urgency in the training of the South Vietnamese. We need improvement in terms of supplies and training."

Secretary of Defense [Melvin] Laird stated, "I agree, but not with your term de-Americanizing. What we need is a term Vietnamizing to put the emphasis on the right issue."

The President agreed. . . .

The President re-emphasized that the South Vietnamese must do more. . . .

The President stated, ["]in my view we should agree to total withdrawal of U.S. forces but include very strong conditions which we know may not be met.["] . . .

The President said there is no doubt that U.S. forces will be in Vietnam for some time, something like a large military assistance group, but our public posture must be another thing.

b. Nixon, address from the White House, 14 May 1969

When we assumed the burden of helping defend South Vietnam, millions of South Vietnamese men, women, and children placed their trust in us. To abandon them now would risk a massacre that would shock and dismay everyone in the world who values human life.

Abandoning the South Vietnamese people, however, would jeopardize more than lives in South Vietnam. It would threaten our long-term hopes for peace in the world. A great nation cannot renege on its pledges. A great nation must be worthy of trust. . . .

If Hanoi were to succeed in taking over South Vietnam by force — even after the power of the United States had been engaged — it would greatly strengthen those leaders who scorn negotiation, who advocate aggression, who minimize the risks of confrontation with the United States. It would bring peace now but it would enormously increase the danger of a bigger war later.

If we are to move successfully from an era of confrontation to an era of negotiation, then we have to demonstrate — at the point at which confrontation is being tested — that confrontation with the United States is costly and unrewarding. . . .

What kind of a settlement will permit the South Vietnamese people to determine freely their own political future? Such a settlement will require the withdrawal of all non–South Vietnamese forces, including our own, from South Vietnam, and procedures for political choice that give each significant group in South Vietnam a real opportunity to participate in the political life of the nation.

To implement these principles, I reaffirm now our willingness to withdraw our forces on a specified timetable. We ask only that North Vietnam withdraw its forces from South Vietnam, Cambodia, and Laos into North Vietnam, also in accordance with a timetable. . . .

The political settlement is an internal matter which ought to be decided among the South Vietnamese themselves, and not imposed by outsiders. . . .

Reports from Hanoi indicate that the enemy has given up hope for a military victory in South Vietnam, but is counting on a collapse of American will in the United States. There could be no greater error in judgment. . . .

Tonight, all I ask is . . . , whatever our differences, that you support a program which can lead to a peace we can live with and a peace we can be proud of. Nothing could have a greater effect in convincing the enemy that he should negotiate in good faith than to see the American people united behind a generous and reasonable peace offer.

4.9 Ninth COSVN conference, resolution on a shift in strategy, early July 1969

While Vietnamization and negotiations unfolded, Communist Party leaders undertook their own strategic reappraisal. By April 1969 Hanoi was ready to concede that an immediate and total victory was beyond reach. PAVN and NLF forces had suffered more than a year of offensive action and heavy casualties. General Creighton Abrams, Westmoreland's deputy, who took charge in mid-1968, had exploited their vulnerability to expand both territory and population under Saigon's control. Hanoi's new approach, intended to put the contest in the South on a basis that would be sustainable over the long term, envisioned more limited military action conducted on a more cautious basis with more attention given to the political dimensions of the resistance. As part of that shift, the NLF announced in June the creation of the Provisional Revolutionary Government as a formal rival to the Thieu government in Saigon. Although copies of the April discussions that led to this new approach are not available, we do have COSVN's July circular, marked "absolutely secret," which spells it out.

[The Americans] *have been forced to de-escalate the war step by step and adopt the policy of de-Americanizing the war,* beginning with the withdrawal of 25,000 U.S. troops, hoping to extricate themselves from their war of aggression in our country. This is the heaviest failure ever known in the U.S. imperialists' history of aggression. . . .

However, . . . we have *not yet produced any leaping development of decisive significance in our struggle* against the enemy. Beside the big victories and strong points, we still have many weak points, shortcomings and difficulties. At present, the obstacles which most impede the progress of the General Offensive and Uprising in our war theater are: We have failed to promote a *strong political high tide* suitable to the requirements of the General Offensive and Uprising phase and the great political opportunity now prevailing; our *military proselyting* spearhead is still weak and has not taken full advantage of our great opportunity to accelerate the collapse of the puppet army and administration; *guerrilla warfare* has developed slowly and unevenly; our territorial forces at provincial and district levels, and even some units of our main forces at region level did not fight in good directions and according to good methods, and their combat efficiency is still low; the replenishment of forces, especially for units at region level and even for many provincial units, is still beset with prolonged difficulties; the building of political forces, especially *Party Chapters, Youth Group Chapters and masses' associations at the infrastructure level* is making slow progress; the operations ensuring material support to the front lines are deficient and many areas still have difficulties [in getting supplies].

TALKING AND FIGHTING, APRIL 1970–JANUARY 1973

After more than a year marked by diplomatic deadlock, Nixon took a tougher line. He sought to punch Hanoi into submission. Le Duan proved Nixon's match in stubbornness, confident he could wear the enemy out. Through a process of military blows and counterblows punctuated by diplomatic concessions, Washington and Hanoi gradually moved toward terms that would bring their war to an end.

4.10 Richard Nixon, address from the White House on the invasion of Cambodia, 30 April 1970

A frustrated Nixon added to his strategy what he thought of as a madman gambit. He imagined that behaving like a madman — threatening to lash out with the full might of the U.S. military — might scare Hanoi or at least alarm its allies enough to bring concessions in the Paris talks. In his first exercise in intimidation, Nixon ordered U.S. and South Vietnamese forces into eastern Cambodia and then turned to a war-weary and deeply divided public to justify his decision.

In cooperation with the armed forces of South Vietnam, attacks are being launched this week to clean out major enemy sanctuaries on the Cambodian-Vietnam border. . . .

The action that I have announced tonight puts the leaders of North Vietnam on notice that we will be patient in working for peace; we will be conciliatory at the conference table, but we will not be humiliated. We will not be defeated. We will not allow American men by the thousands to be killed by an enemy from privileged sanctuaries. . . .

My fellow Americans, we live in an age of anarchy, both abroad and at home. We see mindless attacks on all the great institutions which have been created by free civilizations in the last 500 years. Even here in the United States, great universities are being systematically destroyed. . . .

If, when the chips are down, the world's most powerful nation, the United States of America, acts like a pitiful, helpless giant, the forces of totalitarianism and anarchy will threaten free nations and free institutions throughout the world.

I have rejected all political considerations in making this decision. . . .

Whether my party gains in November is nothing compared to the lives of 400,000 brave Americans fighting for our country and for the cause of peace and freedom in Vietnam. Whether I may be a one-term President is insignificant compared to whether by our failure to act in this crisis the United States proves itself to be unworthy to lead the forces of freedom in this critical period in world history. I would rather be a one-term President and do what I believe is right than to be a two-term President at the cost of seeing America become a second-rate power and to see this Nation accept the first defeat in its proud 190-year history.

4.11 Le Duan, letter to Pham Hung and other senior COSVN leaders on the U.S. push into Cambodia, July 1970

The Cambodian operation in April–May 1970 briefly disrupted PAVN's cross-border staging area, while Nixon's backing of a coup against Norodom Sihanouk led by one of his generals, Lon Nol, succeeded in putting the Cambodian government in the anticommunist camp. But the broader effects of these developments were, in Le Duan's estimate, positive. They gave impetus to the Kampuchean (Cambodian) Communist Party and created an Indochinawide revolutionary front unfavorable to the Americans and their Vietnamese allies. This view rested on a conception going back to the French era of Indo-

china as a single entity. The Communists imagined a regional federation of three revolutionary states in which Vietnam, as the most advanced of those states, would naturally playing a leading role. No less important in Le Duan's optimistic reading was his conviction that the U.S. position remained fundamentally weak.

[T]he Nixon Administration thinks that we lack the strength to endure more fighting, while the United States, with its abundant economic potential, its financial resources and its policy of using Vietnamese to fight Vietnamese, using Asians to fight Asians, will be able to create a strong position from which to negotiate with us and compel us to make concessions.

But so far what has occurred on the battlefront has not been in accordance with the desires of the United States. The enemy has continued to meet with heavy failure; for our part, our position on the whole battlefield has been maintained. The enemy has had to admit that the forces of the liberation army are still strong, with sufficient supplies and high morale. Our political forces from the countryside to the cities are undergoing further training. Recently, the political struggle movement has strongly developed in the cities, particularly in Saigon. We have gradually struck back at the enemy's "pacification" plan. The false optimism on the enemy's side is gradually giving way to increasing concern and pessimism. Some people in the Nixon Administration have begun to think that the "Vietnamization of the war" may fail.

The war in Vietnam has had a deep impact on the political, social, economic and financial situation in the United States. Forced to de-escalate the war but still trying to prolong it, Nixon has driven the opposition in the US to a bitter extreme. The anti-war movement has taken on a new quality. Not only has it involved students and other young people who do not want to enlist and get killed in Vietnam but it has also spread to part of the American GIs and officers' corps. More seriously still, it has drawn in even people of business and financial circles since the war has brought about irreparable inflation in the US and reduced the profits of US monopoly capital. . . . Following the Kampuchea events [the dispatch of U.S. forces across the border into Cambodia], the US Congress has become more opposed to the US president, which is unusual in this country during a war. Some figures in the US Administration have spoken out against Nixon. In the near future, this wave of opposition will gain further force, and no matter how stubborn he is, Nixon cannot help pulling a large part of the US forces out of South Vietnam. . . .

. . . Of late, [U.S. imperialists] have teamed up with the Lon Nol clique to overthrow Prince Sihanouk and send US troops to Kampuchea, widening the war to the whole of Indochina. This is a very serious and adventurist move, and is part of their attempt to gain a position of strength. They are nurturing the hope of destroying our logistic bases and cutting off one of our important supply routes while strengthening the Lon Nol puppet regime, thus forming an anti-Communist defence line running from South Vietnam through Kampuchea to Thailand and creating a new position of strength to force our liberation army to withdraw and limit its advance at the 17th Parallel.

These adventurous moves have only aggravated the US imperialists' defeat. . . . Their Lon Nol allies turn out to be weak in all fields, military, political and economic. On the other hand, a revolutionary tide has surged up in Kampuchea in quite a short time, winning extremely great successes and creating an unprecedented leap forward in the history of our fraternal Kampuchean people's revolution. . . .

. . . At present, Kampuchea is the weakest link in the whole chain of the enemy's force dispositions on the Indochinese peninsula. So, it is the main target for our attacks. Kampuchea is a battlefield favourable for the destruction and disintegration of not only the Lon Nol puppet army but also a large part of the South Vietnamese regular forces now being bogged down there. . . .

. . . [I]n our strategy for the coming period, beside the requirement of driving the US troops out of Vietnam, we lay emphasis on the destruction and disintegration of an important part of the Saigon army's regular forces. Moreover, our goals also include the winning of a fundamental victory for the Kampuchean revolution, completely ridding it of the US neo-colonialist regime. . . .

. . . [W]e should do our best to help our Kampuchean friends politicise their peasants, especially those living in important and populous areas, rich in resources, build people's administrations at the grassroots and vigorously develop their political and armed forces. We need to help them and even join forces with them in striving to build and strengthen their liberated areas. . . .

. . . At the present juncture of the war, we are controlling large mountain areas [roughly the broad region surrounding the Ho Chi Minh Trail, running from North to South Vietnam, including adjacent areas of Laos and Cambodia].... These areas hold a position of strategic importance. One task of extremely large dimensions, decisive for the whole war of resistance in the southern part of our country as well as in our fraternal Kampuchea and Laos, is to strive to build that large liberated area into a politically and militarily strong base, capable of self-sufficiency in food. By so doing, we can ensure our strategic corridor in the short run, and in the long run provide a firm foothold for the revolutionary forces of the three countries in any circumstance of the war....

... [O]ur revolution is now entering a new stage with favourable conditions and practical capabilities to defeat the imperialist ring-leader, liberate South Vietnam and the whole Indochinese peninsula, and fulfil our lofty international obligations toward the fraternal peoples of Kampuchea and Laos as well as the world revolution. That is the greatest pride of every Vietnamese of the Ho Chi Minh era.

4.12 Henry Kissinger and Xuan Thuy (head of the DRV delegation to the Paris talks), exchange on PAVN forces staying in South Vietnam, 7 September 1970

With little to show for his Cambodian gamble either on the battlefield or at the negotiating table, Nixon gave ground. In September he instructed Kissinger to agree to a withdrawal of U.S. troops on a fixed schedule without explicit reference to the long-standing U.S. insistence on the departure of North Vietnamese forces. The DRV delegate, Xuan Thuy, responded by focusing on the other outstanding issue, the status of the Saigon government. This issue would block progress in the talks for another two years.

[KISSINGER:] There are two fundamental points; first, we have accepted the principle of total withdrawal [covering 384,000 troops]; second, we have presented a schedule for total withdrawal [over twelve months]. We believe that our attitude, if reciprocated, can lead to a rapid end of the conflict.

Let me now turn to the political questions....

- First, our overriding objective is a political solution that reflects the will of the South Vietnamese people and allows them to determine their future without outside interference.
- Second, a fair political solution should reflect the existing relationship of political forces.

- Third, we will abide by the outcome of the political process which we have agreed upon. . . .

[THUY:] It is our view that the Saigon administration has been established by the U.S. It is not genuinely democratic, and it is not democratically elected by the South Vietnamese people.

So, in order to make clear the political relationships, we should let the South Vietnamese people decide themselves. . . .

But the main question is who will organize the elections. . . .

[KISSINGER:] We are prepared—I can say this on the highest authority—to have a political contest in *all* of South Vietnam, in areas controlled by the Saigon government as well as in other areas. . . .

How can you have such a political contest? Your proposal has been that the Saigon government must be replaced before such an election. . . . This we cannot do. . . . You have been very suspicious with the concept of mixed electoral commissions. I don't care what we call them. I think that the essential thing is to concentrate on how to organize elections rather than how to organize a government. . . .

THUY: . . . [W]ith the present Saigon administration with its army, how can fair elections be organized . . . ?

KISSINGER: . . . Either there will be free elections which we all accept, or there will not be free elections and you will continue fighting and you will be no worse off than you are now.

4.13 Nixon and Kissinger, taped Oval Office conversation, 2 June 1971, in the wake of failed ARVN operations in Laos

Still at odds with Hanoi on the disposition of the Saigon government, Nixon decided to gamble a second time. In February 1971 the bigger and better armed and trained ARVN moved with U.S. backing into southern Laos to disrupt the Ho Chi Minh Trail. Far from demonstrating its prowess, the cream of the Saigon military suffered heavy losses and retreated in disarray, dealing a serious blow to the hopes invested in Vietnamization. Nixon's outburst recorded here reveals the psychological pressure he was feeling in the face of a war that he could not bring to a satisfactory conclusion.

[NIXON:] [I]f we don't get . . . any Soviet [diplomatic] breakthrough, if we don't get the Chinese, . . . about November of this year, I'm going to take a goddam[n] hard look at the hole card. As long as we've still got the air force . . .

KISSINGER: —[unclear]—

NIXON: —I'm not talking about bombing passes, I'm, we're gonna take out the dikes [in the DRV], we're gonna take out the power plants, we're gonna take out Haiphong, we're gonna level that goddamn country! [Nixon is shouting and pounding his desk, while Kissinger is trying to speak.]

KISSINGER: Mr. President—

NIXON: Now that makes me shout.

KISSINGER: —Mr. President, I think, I think the American people would understand that.

NIXON: . . . The point is, we're not gonna go out whimpering, and we're not gonna go out losing. . . .

KISSINGER: Mr. President, I will enthusiastically support that, and I think it's the right thing to do—. . . .

NIXON: . . . [L]et 'em give me one more whack at it, I'm going to knock their goddamn brains out. . . .

. . . You know, this crap about morality—of course it's violent[?]—the biggest thing is, war is immoral because people are immoral, and they're aggressive all over the world. Hitler was a vicious son of a bitch, and somebody had to stop him. Right?

KISSINGER: Absolutely.

NIXON: That's exactly [unclear] the North Vietnamese are bastards. . . .

I do not intend to preside here and go out whimpering. . . . Right now there's not a goddamn thing to lose. Nothin' to lose. We['re] gonna turn Right. We're gonna hit 'em, bomb the livin' bejesus out of 'em.

———

4.14 Nixon and Kissinger, taped Oval Office conversations on the North Vietnamese spring offensive, April–May 1972

Hanoi decided to try its luck by launching a major conventional offensive in late March 1972. Nixon fulminated and then went into madman mode again. With the ARVN under intense pressure and with the U.S. combat presence sharply reduced, he unleashed American air power on the battlefield, where PAVN forces suffered heavy losses. He also struck Hanoi, Haiphong, and other major DRV cities in some of the most intense bombing of the war.

[25 April:]

NIXON: Will the [U.S. air] attack on the North help in any way [unclear]?
. . .

You see, the attack on the North that we have in mind: [unclear] power plants, uh, whatever is left of the POL [petroleum, oil, and lubricants], the docks—. . .

—docks, and, I still think we ought to take the dikes out now. . . .

Will that drown people?

KISSINGER: That will drown about 200,000 people [unclear]—[The volume of Kissinger's voice perceptibly drops at this point]

NIXON: Well, no, no, no, no, no, no. I'd rather use a nuclear bomb. Have you got that ready?

KISSINGER: Now that, I think, would just be, uh, too much, uh—

NIXON: A nuclear bomb, does that bother you?

[Kissinger response virtually inaudible]

NIXON: I just want you to think big, Henry, for Christ's sake! [Said in an animated, angry-sounding tone of voice]

KISSINGER: I think we're going to make it. [Now upbeat in tone]

[Comments by NIXON to Kissinger, Chief of Staff H. R. Haldeman, Secretary of the Treasury John Connally, and Kissinger aide Alexander Haig, 4 May:] Under no circumstances can I, with all the things I believe, fail to use the total power of this office—[pause] with the exception of nuclear weapons, [pause] that I cannot do, [pause] unless it's necessary [unclear] the power of this office to see that the United States does not lose. . . .

Now to do that there are two different plans. One is to bomb. The difficulty with bombing is that it's totally expected, totally expected, because we did it before. . . . They'll suffer some losses, but it isn't going to be effective. . . .

Now in my view there's only one way to finish North Vietnam. It is to blockade [sea access with mines] and bomb. Blockade first and follow with bombing. Bombing is essential for taking out the railways to China, the roads into China, and to destroy the POL and other supplies. . . .

. . . [F]or once we've got to use the maximum power of this country against a shit-asshole country to win the war.

4.15 Hanoi's instructions to Le Duc Tho and Xuan Thuy, May–October 1972, edging toward a compromise settlement

In the course of the spring and summer, Hanoi resolved to push toward a peace agreement. The calculations behind this decision were complex, as the guidance that party leaders in Hanoi sent their negotiating team in Paris makes clear. One critical element was the failure of the spring offensive, launched in March and maintained into the summer, to alter the situation on the battlefield. Another was the worrisome Soviet and Chinese contact with the United States, dramatically signaled by Nixon's visits to Beijing in February 1972 and to Moscow the following May (despite intense bombing of Hanoi and mining of the Haiphong harbor). Hanoi also faced growing tensions with Beijing over Soviet influence in the DRV and patronage of the Kampuchean Communist Party. Yet a third element was the lure of taking advantage of the electoral pressures and divisions that Nixon faced in his bid for a second term. To push talks ahead, Hanoi reluctantly put aside demands for the removal of the Thieu regime, accepting the Saigon government as a player in the post-ceasefire maneuvering for advantage. Hanoi also soft-pedaled demands for U.S. reparations.

a. 6 May 1972

We are recording big victories but not yet big enough to compel the US to give up Vietnam and Indochina. The US is striving to strengthen its forces in SVN and to intensify its attacks in North Vietnam to prevent us from launching offensives against Hue and Kontum [in the Central Highlands]. . . . or at least to delay them so that it may consolidate its defence as a bargaining card when the moment of settlement comes.

Diplomatically, the US is endeavouring to use the Soviet Union and China to limit our success on the battlefield and to make pressure for an early solution. . . .

There have been transactions between the US and the Soviet Union with regards to the Vietnam problem. . . . We should be vigilant of the scheme for undermining [direct U.S.-DRV talks] and finding another way to settle the Vietnam problem, for instance by convening an international conference [like the 1954 Geneva conference].

b. 22 July 1972

Internally, the US is torn by sharp contradictions between the US people and Nixon, and between the Republican Party and the Democratic Party regarding the Vietnam problem. In solving the problem, the relation of force on the battlefield is the principal factor, but taking advantage at present of the acute contradictions in the US election is very important.

c. Mid-August 1972

The spring–summer 1972 offensive by Vietnamese forces has achieved important strategic successes and has doomed Nixon's Vietnamization plan to a strategic failure. . . . However, the relation of forces between the revolutionary forces and the enemy in SVN is balanced. We have not yet secured predominance over the enemy. . . .

. . . The principle stand for the settlement of the Vietnam problem is:

— The US should completely and definitively end all its military involvement in SVN. . . .

— The keeping of our poli[t]ical and military forces in SVN and the preservation of our controlled areas in SVN will create conditions for the development of our strength and the weakening of the Saigon political and military forces, the setting up of a three-component government in SVN, and the guarantee of democratic freedoms to the people. . . .

— The payment of war reparations by the US for the reconstruction of North Vietnam is of great importance. . . .

In this struggle, we rely mainly on our own strength but we should pay utmost attention to taking advantage of the internal contradictions of the US. . . . We should negotiate and settle the problem with Nixon, but when the impossibility of settling with him becomes apparent, we should support the opposition and make Nixon lose the election. . . .

. . . [T]he support of the world's people is more important for us than ever. We should launch a strong movement in the world to win support for our people's struggle and position as well as to condemn Nixon's war of annihilation and his stubborn, deceitful stance.

d. 4 October 1972

We should endeavour to end the war before the US election. . . .

Our primary requirement at present is to end the US war in SVN. The US should withdraw all its forces, end its military involvement in SVN and stop its air and naval war and its mining in [the DRV]. The end of the US military involvement and the cease-fire in SVN will lead to the *de facto* recognition of the existence of two administrations, two armies, and two areas in SVN. If these objectives are reached, they will constitute an important victory . . . and create a new balance of forces to our great advantage. . . .

What we do not obtain in this agreement [particularly on the overthrow of the Thieu regime and a formal U.S. commitment on reparations] is due to the situation; even though we continue to negotiate until after the election we still cannot obtain it, unless there is a change in the balance of forces in SVN. However, if we succeed in ending the US military involvement in SVN, we will have conditions to obtain these objectives later in the struggle with the Saigon clique and win bigger victories.

4.16 Nixon on the Saigon government's survival after a peace agreement, October–November 1972

In August in the secret Paris talks, Le Duc Tho made a major concession: he accepted the Thieu government as one player in the transitional process following the end of fighting in the South. This concession made it possible for the two sides to reach mutually agreeable terms in October. The key elements were U.S. disengagement, the return of U.S. prisoners, and the continuation of the Thieu government. Nixon now found himself with a major headache. Privately he recognized that the emerging peace agreement would leave the Saigon government vulnerable. But at the same time he had to bring Thieu on board or face the politically embarrassing charge of abandoning a U.S. ally. In a string of personal letters to Thieu backed up by a parade of American emissaries, Nixon sought to present the peace terms in a positive light while offering assurances of continued support and highlighting the damage any refusal to cooperate would inflict on U.S.–South Vietnamese ties. Ultimately Nixon sought to placate his balky client by presenting Hanoi with a long list of changes to the October agreement and by threatening U.S. military action if Hanoi did not help Nixon out by making fresh concessions.

a. Nixon and Kissinger, taped conversation, 6 October 1972

[KISSINGER:] [S]omewhere down the road he'll [referring to Thieu] have no choice except to commit suicide. . . .

PRESIDENT NIXON: . . . . We don't want him to — him personally or the 17 million South Vietnamese collectively — to commit suicide.

KISSINGER: That's right.

PRESIDENT NIXON: Or, to be murdered. Now, that's all this thing is about.

KISSINGER: That is true.

PRESIDENT NIXON: And goddamn, if that isn't morality. . . .

KISSINGER: . . . I actually think we can settle it [an agreement with Hanoi]. On terms, however. [*Unclear*]—

PRESIDENT NIXON: On our terms [*unclear*] but not Thieu's.

KISSINGER: On . . . close to our terms. But—and I also think that Thieu is right, that our terms will eventually destroy him.

PRESIDENT NIXON: You're convinced of that, Henry?

KISSINGER: . . . [G]iven their weakness, their disunity, it will happen—

PRESIDENT NIXON: [*Unclear*] fear—they're scared to death of these people, the North. . . .

KISSINGER: . . . We can improve the situation in South Vietnam drastically [by military operations], but we can't get our prisoners back. And before they [*unclear*] they will offer us our prisoners for a withdrawal. And in that case, we've got, I think at this point, we have to take that. . . .

PRESIDENT NIXON: That's a deal we have to take, Henry.

KISSINGER: That's right, but that will also collapse the South Vietnamese, except we won't be so responsible for the whole settlement. . . .

PRESIDENT NIXON: Well, if they're that collapsible, maybe they just have to be collapsed. . . . [W]e cannot keep this child sucking at the tit when the child is four years old. You know what I mean? . . .

KISSINGER: . . . You may get it [a peace agreement] before the election. . . .

PRESIDENT NIXON: Well, I don't want it before the election with a Thieu blow-up.

KISSINGER: Right.

PRESIDENT NIXON: If we do, it's gonna hurt us very badly.

b. Nixon, message to Thieu, 16 October 1972

[W]e and Hanoi's negotiators have reached an essential agreement on a text. . . .

. . . [W]e have no reasonable alternative but to accept this agreement. It represents major movement by the other side, and it is my firm conviction that its implementation will leave you and your people with the ability to defend yourselves and decide the political destiny of South Vietnam.

. . . In the period following the cessation of hostilities you can be completely assured that we will continue to provide your Government with the fullest support, including continued economic aid and whatever military assistance is consistent with the ceasefire provisions of this government. . . .

. . . I can assure you that we will view any breach of faith on [Hanoi's] part with the utmost gravity; and it would have the most serious consequences.

c. Nixon, message to Thieu, 29 October 1972

Just as our unity has been the essential aspect of the success we have enjoyed thus far in the conduct of hostilities, it will also be the best guarantee of future success in a situation where the struggle continues within a more political framework. If the evident drift towards disagreement between the two of us continues, however, the essential base for U.S. support for you and your Government will be destroyed.

d. Nixon, message to Thieu, 14 November 1972

[W]hile we will do our very best to secure the changes in the agreement [requested by Thieu], we cannot expect to secure them all. . . .

But far more important than what we say in the agreement [regarding PAVN forces remaining in South Vietnam] is what we do in the event the enemy renews its aggression. You have my absolute assurance that if Hanoi fails to abide by the terms of this agreement it is my intention to take swift and severe retaliatory action. . . .

. . . I repeat my personal assurances to you that the United States will react very strongly and rapidly to any violations of the agreement. But in order to do this effectively it is essential that I have public support and that your Government does not emerge as the obstacle to a peace which American public opinion now universally desires.

4.17 Nguyen Van Thieu, address to the National Assembly, 12 December 1972, denouncing the terms of the Paris peace accords

In 1968, Thieu (by then the dominant figure in the Saigon government) had opposed Johnson's decision to halt the bombing and begin negotiations. His strong public stance then had slowed Johnson's efforts to begin peace talks on the eve of the election and helped Nixon defeat the Democratic presidential candidate, Hubert Humphrey. In 1972, with the Americans once more pushing toward peace, Thieu again resisted. He would not put his seal of approval on negotiations conducted behind his back and amounting in his view to a

sellout that would have fatal consequences for his government. He would not
hear of sharing power with the NLF, and he was justifiably worried about the
continued PAVN presence in his country. Playing the spoiler, he demanded
changes large and small in the settlement language. His defiance finally took
public form in December when he aimed his shafts mainly at the Commu-
nists. Hanoi and Washington soon adjourned the peace talks.

The Communists have carried out [their scheme to take over South Viet-
nam] through an armed and blatant aggression for the past 15 years.
Now, realizing that they do not succeed, they try to achieve the same objective by a false peace solution through the agreement which they are
struggling to obtain. When they succeed in forcing us to sign this agreement, and after they have supposedly chased all the Americans out of
Viet Nam [in] every form, with the 300,000 troops [the Communists] still
maintain in the South and [with] a disguised coalition government called
a tripartite "Government of National Reconciliation and Concord" and
with a secure North Viet Nam totally free to receive military aid from the
Communist powers[,] it would then be only a matter of a short period of
time before the Communists take-over South Viet Nam, either by military
or political means. . . .

The Communists put themselves in the position of masters engaged
in talks only with the United States, forcing the United States to sign
while considering the Republic of Viet Nam as only a puppet with the
obligation to carry out the Agreement. . . .

. . . [T]he main basis that we demand in any peace solution . . . is:

—North Vietnamese troops should totally withdraw to North Viet
Nam.

—Any political solution for South Viet Nam should be left to the people of South Viet Nam, and only the people in South Viet Nam will decide
by themselves. . . .

. . . [A]s long as North Vietnamese troops remain in the South, a political solution concerning South Viet Nam could not be achieved quickly
and adequately between the South Vietnamese parties because the NLF
itself cannot be free to decide on its course of action and the way to implement its political objective. It continues to remain an instrument to
serve the political objective of the Communist North Vietnamese and
only them.

4.18 "Agreement on Ending the War and Restoring Peace in Viet-Nam," signed in Paris by the representatives for the United States, the DRV, the Saigon government, and the NLF's Provisional Revolutionary Government, 27 January 1973

Caught between an implacable Vietnamese ally and an equally implacable Vietnamese foe, Nixon sought a way out by once more donning his madman mask. To appease Thieu and signal to the DRV that he meant business, Nixon ordered a bombing campaign during the Christmas season. The Communist leadership held firm on settlement terms while imposing heavy costs on attacking U.S. aircraft. Now out of options, Nixon proceeded to accept an agreement virtually identical to the one of the previous October. This agreement also followed the Geneva accords of two decades earlier and the plan offered by Pham Van Dong in 1965 (documents 2.2 and 3.9). Reluctantly, at the last minute, Thieu joined the United States, the DRV, and the NLF's provisional government in signing the accord.

Supplementing the formal commitment in article 21 on reconstruction aid, Nixon wrote to DRV prime minister Pham Van Dong on 1 February, promising around $3.25 billion over five years. Hanoi regarded the payment as reparation, while Nixon seems to have hoped it would guarantee Hanoi's good behavior during the transitional period.

[Article 1:] The United States and all other countries respect the independence, sovereignty, unity, and territorial integrity of Viet-Nam as recognized by the 1954 Geneva Agreements on Viet-Nam. . . .

[Article 2:] A cease-fire shall be observed throughout South Viet-Nam as of 2400 hours G.M.T., on January 27, 1973.

At the same hour, the United States will stop all its military activities against the territory of the Democratic Republic of Viet-Nam. . . .

[Article 4:] The United States will not continue its military involvement or intervene in the internal affairs of South Viet-Nam.

[Article 5:] Within sixty days of the signing of this Agreement, there will be a total withdrawal from South Viet-Nam of troops, military advisers, and military personnel, including technical military personnel and military personnel associated with the pacification program, armaments, munitions, and war material of the United States and those of the other foreign countries [allied with the United States]. Advisers from the above-mentioned countries to all paramilitary organizations and the police force will also be withdrawn within the same period of time.

[Article 6:] The dismantlement of all military bases in South Viet-Nam of the United States and of the other foreign countries . . . shall be completed within sixty days of the signing of this Agreement. . . .

[Article 8:] (a) The return of captured military personnel and foreign civilians of the parties shall be carried out simultaneously with and completed not later than the same day as the troop withdrawal mentioned in Article 5. . . .

(b) The parties shall help each other to get information about those military personnel and foreign civilians of the parties missing in action. . . .

[Article 15:] The reunification of Viet-Nam shall be carried out step by step through peaceful means on the basis of discussions and agreements between North and South Viet-Nam, without coercion or annexation by either party, and without foreign interference. . . .

Pending reunification:

(a) The military demarcation line between the two zones at the 17th parallel is only provisional and not a political or territorial boundary, as provided for in paragraph 6 of the Final Declaration of the 1954 Geneva Conference. . . .

(d) North and South Viet-Nam shall not join any military alliance or military bloc and shall not allow foreign powers to maintain military bases, troops, military advisers, and military personnel on their respective territories, as stipulated in the 1954 Geneva Agreements on Viet-Nam. . . .

[Article 21:] . . . [T]he United States will contribute to healing the wounds of war and to postwar reconstruction of the Democratic Republic of Viet-Nam and throughout Indochina.

The View
from the Ground,
1965–1971

The Vietnam War swept up millions of people during its grim progress. The numbers on the American side are known with fair precision. Of the 26.8 million men eligible to serve between 1964 and 1973, 3.1 million actually entered the military and saw service in Vietnam. Casualties totaled 321,000, of whom some 58,000 died. African Americans accounted for one in ten U.S. servicemen in Vietnam and slightly more than a tenth of those who died. (Both percentages were just below the proportion in the total U.S. population.) Only a quarter of those in Vietnam were draftees (compared to two-thirds during World War II), and most personnel who ended up in Vietnam played a supporting role. The ratio of "tooth to tail" (in the parlance of the military) was roughly one combatant in the field to seven in support.

The picture for Vietnamese participants is considerably less clear. In the DRV the eligible ultimately included everyone sixteen to forty-five years old; most called up were peasants. A partial mobilization in July 1966 raised the total PAVN force by the end of the year to 600,000. Those sent south together with NLF regulars and guerrillas numbered some 376,000 by that point.[1] In the post-1968 phase of the war, with the NLF much diminished, PAVN units bore the brunt of the fighting. PAVN and NLF units combined paid dearly between 1965 and 1975—at least 522,000 deaths (by some estimates), with an additional 300,000 missing in action. The ARVN forces numbered in the range of half a million in 1966–1967, rising thereafter as a result of Vietnamization to over 1 million. At least 254,000 of those fighting on the Saigon side lost their lives. The total number of Vietnamese fighters on both sides who died probably approached 1 million. An additional 65,000 city folk in the North were killed by American bombs.

1. Military History Institute of Vietnam, *Victory in Vietnam: The Official History of the People's Army of Vietnam, 1954–1975*, trans. Merle L. Pribbenow (Lawrence: University Press of Kansas, 2002), 182, 464 n. 12, 464 n. 14.

PAVN and NLF soldiers were in nearly the reverse position from that of the U.S. soldiers they were confronting. They had a cause in which most could believe. The multiple personal reasons to fight were reinforced by a steady, systematic party-directed effort at keeping morale high. But these same fighters had to confront a much greater likelihood of death than Americans ever did. They were in the struggle for the duration, not just twelve months, and they faced a foe with an overwhelming advantage in weaponry. They had to absorb the punishment the far more powerful Americans could throw at them, and then the survivors had to line up and take the punishment again.

In the DRV women played an unusually important role in the war effort. One estimate puts women who served in the military at one time or another at almost 1.5 million. Of these, 60,000 were in the regular forces, almost 1 million were in the local forces, and an unspecified additional number were part of professional teams assigned to special war-related tasks. In addition, at least 170,000 volunteer youths (70 to 80 percent women) were mobilized between 1965 and 1975 to keep the Ho Chi Minh Trail open. Women also played an expanded role in economic production, replacing men called up for service. The number of women in the workforce tripled between 1965 and 1969.[2]

No less important were the southerners pulled into the war. Unnumbered villagers fought as irregulars and otherwise supported the resistance. We can only guess their totals from the estimated deaths of civilians—in the range of 300,000. The war's impact on city dwellers was substantial. The U.S. presence added another foreign layer of cultural and economic influences to the preexisting French influence. Prostitution, a black market, and a thriving consumer culture were but the most obvious of these U.S. effects. At the same time, cities were inundated by peasants fleeing a dangerous, smoldering countryside. The refugee problem was enormous: something on the order of half of all South Vietnamese were forced to flee their homes at least once between 1954 and 1975. The U.S. policy of creating free-fire zones in NLF areas subjected civilians to indiscriminate bombing and artillery fire, destroyed villages, and drove many villagers to the safety of Saigon-controlled areas. Saigon officials struggled to meet refugee demands for housing, food, schooling, and medical care.

2. Karen G. Turner with Phan Thanh Hao, *Even the Women Must Fight: Memories of War from North Vietnam* (New York: Wiley, 1998), 20–21 (estimate of women in military service by military historian Nguyen Quoc Dung), 58 (women in the workforce).

The experience of these American and Vietnamese participants was enormously diverse. Much depended on time and place. Take the soldiers as an example. U.S. and PAVN regulars fighting in the Central Highlands saw a different war than did American patrols playing cat and mouse with NLF guerrillas in Mekong Delta villages. Their wars differed in turn from that of a marine platoon locked in deadly confrontation with main force NLF soldiers along the narrow coastal plains.

The post–Tet Offensive stage of the war was an especially trying time for virtually all participants. Among U.S. troops the losses continued unabated in 1969 and 1970 until Nixon's steady, phased withdrawal began reducing their combat role. During that time morale suffered and discipline declined. Men in the field wore peace symbols, hippie beads, and long hair. They anxiously wondered if they would be the last to die in what more and more saw as a pointless war. NLF and PAVN forces had suffered heavy casualties during the Tet Offensive and the follow-on attempts to wring victory from the initial surprise. PAVN soldiers knew they faced a meat grinder with slim chances of return. ("Born in the North to die in the South" was the telling way recruits described their fate.) Well-connected young North Vietnamese schemed to avoid service just as privileged young Americans had been doing. Troops inducted and sent south fought dutifully but against heavy odds. Even southern city folks, who were relatively insulated from the destruction, succumbed to war weariness, especially after the Americans started shifting the fighting to the ARVN.

For NLF organizers the time after the Tet Offensive proved especially trying. They had suffered heavy losses in early 1968. Their urban networks, activated during the Tet Offensive, were afterward easily rolled up. Hard-won territorial gains in the countryside were lost as U.S. and ARVN troops took the offensive against a decimated NLF presence. Surviving NLF activists were isolated and vulnerable. Only as U.S. forces began to withdraw did rural organizing become easier again.

The final phase of the Vietnam War prompts questions that are worth keeping in mind while reading the documents to follow:

- What single feature above all others defined the experience of the American soldiers and Vietnamese fighters and organizers engaged directly in this conflict?
- How did those at war imagine the cause they were fighting for?
- How did soldiers view the enemy and the civilian population caught in the conflict?

- How do the various kinds of participant accounts assembled here — diaries, letters, wartime interrogations, and postwar recollections — differ from each other as sources?

TO THE RESCUE, 1965–1967

The U.S. units that arrived in 1965 and 1966 as part of Johnson's buildup were full of confidence. Soldiers soon, however, began to grasp the challenge of defeating an enemy who chose the time and place of battle and who enjoyed substantial popular support. Eating away at their confidence was the strain of daily patrolling, the frustration over Johnson's limited war policy, irritation over growing protest at home, and deepening dislike for the Vietnamese they were there to save.

5.1 Jack S. Swender (enlisted man in the First Marine Division), letter to "Uncle and Aunt," 20 September 1965

This Kansas City native arrived in Vietnam in July 1965. He was proud of the cause he was fighting for — and he died for it. He was killed in action the following December. He was twenty-two years old.

Some people wonder why Americans are in Vietnam. The way I see the situation, I would rather fight to stop communism in South Vietnam than in Kincaid, Humbolt, Blue Mound, or Kansas City, and that is just about what it would end up being. Except for the fact that by that time I would be old and gray and my children would be fighting the war. The price for victory is high when life cannot be replaced, but I think it is far better to fight and die for freedom than to live under oppression and fear.

. . . [C]ommunism cannot thrive in a society of people who know the whole truth. This war is not going to be won in a day or even a year. This war and others like it will only be won when the children of that nation are educated and can grow in freedom to rule themselves. Last year alone 4,700 teachers and priests in South Vietnam were killed. This we are trying to *stop* — this is our objective.

Well, enough soothing my own conscience and guilt.

5.2 George R. Bassett (sergeant in the 101st Airborne Division), letter to "Mom, Dad, and Kids," 28 March 1966

This native of Portland, Maine, began his first tour of duty in July 1965, and he returned as a volunteer for a second tour in 1967. Here he offers an optimistic reading of operations against PAVN forces in Tuy Hoa province (along the central coast south of Qui Nhon).

We are succeeding in our mission here. We have beaten the famous 95th [PAVN] Regiment down to their knees. We learned from prisoners we took when we captured one of their hospitals that the regiment was below 50% strength, and that they were hunting for food because we guarded the harvest and they couldn't get any of it. . . .

. . . This war isn't by the Geneva Convention. Charlie [short for "Victor Charlie," or "VC"] doesn't take any prisoners nor do we. Only when the CO [commanding officer] sees them first. We shoot the wounded. We only keep a prisoner if there is an LZ (landing zone) near where a chopper can come in and get him out. Charlie has no facilities for keeping prisoners nor any use for them.

Therefore surrender is not even considered in a hopeless situation. He has only got about five men from our brigade. We found two of them that had their privates in their mouth, sewn shut, hanging by their ankles from a tree.

That's when they gave us hatchets and we lifted a couple heads. Also tied bodies on the fenders of 2 1/2 ton trucks and drove through the village as a warning. We haven't had any mutilations since then that we know about.

Guess I told you they took our hatchets away.

5.3 John Dabonka (army soldier), letter to "Mom and Dad," 23 December 1966

Dabonka wrote this letter just after his arrival in the Mekong Delta. He was killed in action five weeks later near My Tho. He was twenty years old. (For the views of an NLF fighter operating in the same area at about the same time, see document 5.10.)

Everything is just fine — in fact it's better than I thought it would be. They have us in a big base camp. We're going to be staying here for a month. This area is perfectly safe. . . .

Besides the platoon leader, I'm the next most important man in the platoon. All the talk I hear from the guys who have been here awhile make it sound pretty easy over here. We eat three hot meals a day. I heard when we go to the field, they fly hot meals to us in the morning and night, and for lunch you eat C-rations, and you're allowed two canteens of water a day. When you're in home base you drink all you want, plus while you're in the field you get a beer and soda free every other day.

. . . All in all things look pretty good. They have PX's where you can buy whatever you want or need. . . .

The people live like pigs. They don't know how to use soap. When they have to go to the bathroom, they go wherever they're standing, they don't care who is looking. Kids not even six [years old] run up to you and ask for a cig. The houses they live in are like rundown shacks. You can see everything — they have no doors, curtains. I'm real glad I have what I have. It seems poor to you maybe, and you want new things because you think our house doesn't look good, but after seeing the way these people live, there's no comparison. We are more than millionaires to these people — they have nothing. I can't see how people can live like this. . . .

Right now our big guns are going off and it sounds good knowing it's yours and they don't have any.

5.4 Carl Burns (junior officer in the Twenty-fifth Infantry Division) describing the dawning doubts about the war effort, 1966–1967

Carl Burns became a helicopter pilot following graduation from Rutgers in 1964 with an officer's commission. He served in Vietnam from spring 1966 to spring 1967 in the heavily contested region northwest of Saigon.

At least in the area of the country I was in, Americans always took the brunt of the battle, always. Sometimes I think we had the . . . wrong Vietnamese group fighting with us. If we had the Vietcong fighting with us, we probably would have gotten out of there. They were better trained, more committed . . . [T]hese Vietnamese people [in villages] had no idea what democracy is, they had no idea what their government was, they knew nothing, other than . . . their village chief. . . . So, there was no reason for them to be committed to anything besides their village. . . .

. . . I was pretty bullish about the effort in the beginning, and then, it got to a point where many of us said to ourselves, you know, "What are we accomplishing?" It's not that we weren't protecting each other or doing what we were supposed to do, but they really came to the realization, . . . "All we're doing is killing each other," and . . . it's not like World War II, where you gain[ed] twelve miles one day and lost a mile the next day. . . . Philosophically, at least amongst most of the officers I knew, we . . . just started [asking], you know, "What's going on?" . . . [A]ll you see was, you know, dead bodies, on your side, dead bodies, on the other side, and then, nothing happening and some filtering in of what's going on [with antiwar protests] back home. . . .

. . . I had no problem with my leaders or the people I served with. It became, you know, "What the hell are the politicians back home [doing]? Why do they constrain us?" . . . [T]hey're not letting us do what we should be doing here to win . . . this thing.

———

5.5 Richard S. Johnson Jr. (second lieutenant in the First Marine Division), letters to "Penny," February–March 1967

For this University of North Carolina graduate, 1966 was a big year. He finished college, got his commission as a marine officer, went through basic officer training, and married Elizabeth Penfield Scovil (Penny). He arrived in Vietnam in early February. Like many junior officers in the field, he did not live long enough to learn his job. About two weeks after assuming command of his platoon, he was killed in action in the Duc Pho area (where Ha Xuan Dai of document 5.7 and Dang Thuy Tram of document 5.19 also operated). His letters reveal the tedium, excitement, anxiety, and longing for home that characterized the combat experience.

[postmarked 22 February:] I am sitting on a hill about 6 miles south of Chu Lai, killing leeches and hoping a V. C. will walk by so we can shoot at it or them. . . . [T]here isn't much happening.

We got shot at this morning from about 500 yards and called in [an] air strike. About $10,000 of bombs for 1 V. C. we aren't sure of. . . .

[Later entry:] I am back safe now. . . . I saw my 1st V. C. today. I was in a tree with field glasses. We were about to call artillery in on them when I got really shot at. We had two marines WIA [wounded in action]— they were shot out of a tree. I jumped down and grabbed my rifle. We never saw them but sort of shot it out. We broke contact and made it to an L Z for emergency extraction.

[1 March:] Got back from my second Patrol yesterday to some bad news.

Ron Benoit's patrol, the one I went out with last time, was landed on a booby trapped hill. Sgt. Barnes, [the platoon sergeant] who had been my instructor and was a real nice South Carolina country boy, was blown to pieces by a 500 pound bomb that was booby trapped—it also injured their corpsman who is now on the U. S. S. Repose in intensive care. Sgt Barnes literally disappeared from the face of the earth. (They took 8 WIA and 1 KIA [killed in action] in 3 minutes.) . . .

The patrol was very educational. I saw the jungle for the first time. It requires very slow and patient walking, in fact so slow and patient I thought I would go nuts. Then we got lost or thought we were. . . . We saw 6 V. C. but we were too strung out to fight so we hid. Then the last 3 days—it turned to cold rain and mud.

In case you wonder what the jungle is like. . . . It is sort of like a nightmare where everything is closing in around you and you sort of want to scream.

[24 March:] I'll spend Easter out in the bush. . . .

I think of you day and night and how our house looks and how nice Chapel Hill is this time of year. Then I get happy and think of how I'll be there this time next year. I guess Mother and Daddy will be up there about the time you get this letter.

[a second letter dated 24 March, two days before Johnson's death:] Just another note to say hello as I return to my waiting game before going on patrol. Next time out we split up and my new [platoon sergeant] takes out 1/2 the patrol and I, the other 1/2. . . .

It looks like this will be a hot patrol—weatherwise. It is primarily to O. P. [observation post] and stay hidden. Boy I hate to go out with so many people—too much noise.

. . . I guess I can really only say again I love you. That is really the only reason I write.

IN THE SHADOW OF THE GIANT, 1965–1968

Vietnamese got swept up in an increasingly destructive war for a variety of reasons—duress, a quest for revenge, patriotism, happenstance, the call of adventure, and land hunger. And they maintained varying levels of commitment. Many would die; some would reach their limits and defect or desert; a lucky and hardy few managed to stay in the bloody struggle year after year. Conventional PAVN forces, which played an increasingly important role in the escalating conflict in the South, and conventional units fielded by the NLF are represented in the documents here. But so too are those on the Saigon side who cheered the arrival of the Americans. At the end of this section, another important element in the southern struggle is represented—one of the women who helped sustain the NLF in the countryside.

5.6 Two Saigon loyalists between a rock and a hard place, 1965

Two interviews conducted by the Rand Corporation provide a sense of the Saigon government's difficulty in asserting rural control and the disruptive effects of intervention by U.S. forces. The two loyalists were quite ordinary youths from adjacent villages located about seventy-five miles northeast of Saigon. The villages came under NLF sway in late February 1965, were retaken by the ARVN in April, and then returned to NLF control in June. The GVN had lost out despite the gratitude some, perhaps many, villagers felt for a government resettlement program that had helped the poor improve their lives. To restore GVN control to the area and to keep the rice harvest out of NLF hands, elements of the recently arrived U.S. 173rd Airborne Brigade and the First Infantry Division intervened in late November and early December as part of Operation New Life. Our interviewees were arrested two days apart in late November by these U.S. forces and handed over to the ARVN. Particularly striking here is the degree to which the ARVN, not to mention U.S. forces, failed to take advantage of two favorably disposed villagers. Whatever its relative military weakness, the NLF had demonstrated at the rice-roots level the power of organization and relentless education.

a. Young man from the village of Vo Dat (described by his interviewer as "intelligent," "fairly well-educated," and "very sincere")

I was a member of the Village Notables Council, therefore I was a GVN civil servant. I was afraid of the VC coming. . . .

[After the February NLF takeover, everyone] who worked or had worked for the GVN [was] arrested. We were about 20. . . .

We were all taken to the mountains to attend a re-education course for a month. . . .

The cadre started to teach us how, since 1945, the whole nation has revolted against the French colonialists and rich reactionary landlords for the right to work and earn their living. Now the Revolution goes on in the South. The Front fights against the GVN and drives the Americans out of the country in order to bring the Revolution to a successful stage and bring happiness to the people. We were all traitors since we were all farmers and we worked for the GVN and made ourselves American eyes and ears. . . . Finally the cadre ordered each one of us to write a declaration telling all our activities since 1954, all our positions in the GVN administration, how many underground cadres we had helped the GVN to arrest, and how many Front secret organizations we had helped the GVN to discover. We also had to tell what our parents, brothers, and sisters did. The cadre told us to write the truth in our declaration. Only with this condition could we benefit from the Front's generosity and be set free. When we finished our declarations, the cadre took us back to our villages. We had spent almost one month in the mountains. . . .

. . . As soon as we returned from the course, the cadres gathered all the villagers in a meeting to judge us. . . . Finally, the cadres declared those who had been obliged to attend the re-education course were condemned to live under house arrest from 6 to 14 months. . . .

At the beginning of October, the cadre launched a campaign called "Enemy Spies Extermination Campaign". . . . [T]hey urged the villagers to denounce those who had worked for the GVN. . . . Our punishment didn't get any worse, but the cadres were satisfied because they could watch us closely, and *soil us in front of the villagers*. . . .

. . . [A]t first most of the villagers thought the Front forces were strong. Besides, the propaganda was very effective. Therefore, there were some villagers who had confidence in the Front and sympathized with the cadres. But later on, things changed. Contributions became heavier and heavier each day, the loss of freedom of movement, and trade, sorrow, fatigue, the loss of time and expenses due to forced labor made them see clearly. The real face of the Front appeared. The cadres lost the villagers' confidence and sympathy, some of us even hated them. . . .

On November 24, the Americans came and occupied [the village] next to mine. During the night of November 25, cadres, guerrillas and most of those who worked for the Front left my village. The next day, at 4:30 A.M. we heard gunfires, and at 6 A.M. American soldiers came into the village. . . .

. . . *I knew long ago that some day, GVN soldiers would come and reoccupy the village.* In order to help the GVN authorities to get rid of the VC that we hated, *my friend and I set up secretly a list of men who were entirely for the Front.* At the pagoda, we gave this list to the [ARVN] Chaplain Captain.

The latter as well as the Venerable Bonze [monk], advised us to leave the village as soon as possible for Vo Dat Village, because we might be kidnapped by the VC. Therefore, at 4 P.M. I left my village on my bicycle for Vo Dat Village. . . . As soon as I reached the entrance of Vo Dat Village, *the Americans arrested me without a word.* . . .

. . . I think most of the villagers considered the *Americans to be liberators.* But unfortunately, later on they found out that they had been mistaken in having confidence in the Americans. After I had left the village, the *Americans started to arrest people for no good reason.* . . .

The Americans who arrested me didn't say anything, they didn't ask any questions. They only tied up my hands, and bound my eyes. A few hours later, a car brought me to an airport where I had to sit on the open ground the whole night. The next day, at noon they took me into a tent, took off the blindfold, and a Vietnamese second-lieutenant interrogated me. He started by asking *whether I wanted to live or die.* I told him I would like to live. He asked me what I had done for the VC. I told him I never worked for the VC. He said I was lying and *he beat me. I was bleeding all over.* I tried to tell him the truth about VC control over my village. But he didn't believe me. *He kept beating me and telling me I lied.* That night I was allowed to sleep under a tent. The next day, I again had to sit under the sun the whole day, and stay there the whole night. The next morning . . . once again a Vietnamese lieutenant interrogated me. I told him the truth, but *like the other officer he said I lied, and beat me.* He didn't believe that I was a GVN civil servant, even when I told him about the Province Chief's decision which made me a member of the Council of Notables in my village. . . . He didn't even believe that I was the secretary of the Buddhist Association in my village although I showed him a certificate. . . . *Like the other officer, he kept beating me more and more and saying that I lied.* Really, I didn't know what I had to tell him. Finally, *they sent me to this prison.* . . .

. . . I hate the VC, and I am entirely for the GVN. And they arrested me without reason, beat me, maltreated me, put me in jail, and considered me as the worst of criminals. I really don't understand it. What can I do? What road should I take? *There are now 150 of us from my village in this prison.* I know almost all of them. *I know they didn't like the VC, they weren't for the Front, except for two or three.* I know they waited for the GVN soldiers to come, and they were happy to see the American soldiers come, like I was. But American soldiers arrested them and put them in jail. They don't know why and don't understand anything, just like me.

Now the paddy [rice in the field] is ripe, the harvest season is close. We should all be home to reap the paddy that we all need badly. I left my wife in my village and my old grand-mother who was very sick, and was ready to die. I hope the GVN will take our situation into account, consider our case justly and set us free soon. We only ask to be able to work quietly, in peace.

b. Young man from the village of Vo Xu

Since many youths from my village were joining the [GVN] Civil Guard at that time (February 1962) I decided to do likewise. I stayed with the Civil Guard until February, 1964. . . .

I wasn't demobilized. I deserted. While I was stationed in the various posts, my wife was always with me. In February 1964 I was designated to attend a driving course in Saigon. Since I couldn't take my wife with me to Saigon, I told her to return to my parents'. But she refused to do so. She told me that if I didn't take her with me, she would return to her parents'. But I didn't want her to return to her home. Besides, just as that moment my father fell ill and could no longer take care of his ricefields. Since I missed my parents a lot, I decided to desert. I left the post and came back to the village to live with my parents. . . .

. . . I think that the GVN officials in the village knew that I had deserted but they didn't say anything about it. . . .

[Following the NLF takeover in late February 1965, all the villagers] were frightened. Nobody dared say anything. Everybody did what he was told by the VC. Especially I who had been a GVN soldier, I was petrified. It was exactly like that for all those who had worked for the GVN. . . .

They didn't kill anybody. But they arrested some twenty people, and led them to the mountains to attend re-education sessions. . . .

At that time I was ill, so I was allowed to stay home. But my parents and my wife had to take the courses. . . .

At the beginning [of the NLF control], because the cadres talked well, and the sudden arrival of VC soldiers gave the impression that the Front forces were really very powerful, many people liked the cadres. But as time went by, the cadres became more and more demanding [labor details, taxes, guard duty, travel restrictions] and harder and harder, and life became more and more difficult. . . . This is why no one liked the cadres any longer, with the exception perhaps of a small number with relatives or children working for the VC. . . .

. . . [After ARVN forces drove the NLF from the village in April] I decided to present myself to the GVN military authorities. When I arrived at the market place, I met an old friend who had been in the Civil Guard with me. In the course of the conversation he confessed that he himself had deserted. While we were talking, a GVN sergeant who was behind us overheard what we said. So he arrested us as deserters. . . .

I was detained in the GVN soldiers' barracks . . . for seven days. During this time many sergeants advised me to join the Special Forces. They told me that it was the only way for me to avoid imprisonment because I was a deserter. So I agreed to join. . . .

I had to go on patrol in the forests constantly. It was very dangerous and I ran the risk of being killed at any moment. I was afraid to die. Besides, my village was once more under Front control at that time. If I had stayed in the Special Forces, I would have run the risk of never seeing my parents again. . . .

I had intended to give up my life as a soldier a long time ago. . . .

[My wife] agreed that I should resume my work as a farmer because the military profession was dangerous. . . .

Upon my return [to Vo Xu village], I had to present myself to the VC cadres to tell them the truth about my desertion. Then, to punish me for having joined the ARVN . . . the second time, they sent me to a re-education course . . . for seven days. . . .

The VC cadres forced me to become a hamlet guerrilla in August '65. But I wasn't the only one. All the men between the ages of eighteen and thirty in my hamlet were forced to join the hamlet guerrillas like me. Like them all, I was neither a VC nor a VC sympathizer. My village was under Front control. So we had to obey the cadres' orders. . . .

On November 25, artillery shells suddenly exploded near my village. . . . The village cadres and the guerrillas left the village right away. . . . I decided to take my family to Vo Dat to take refuge. . . . I met a group of American soldiers. One of them came to help me by pulling the bicycle.

. . . [A]n American came out. When he saw me wearing a shirt for soldiers, he asked me in Vietnamese if I was a soldier. I replied that I had been a soldier. So he began to search through my things and found a belt used by soldiers. He made me go inside the pagoda. . . . This is how I was arrested. . . .

I was a prisoner of the Americans in Vo Dat. An American came there to interrogate me. I have always been well treated. The Americans gave me adequate food. . . .

. . . [T]here is one thing that I don't understand. There are many people from my village in this prison right now. They told me that they all had been arrested by the Americans. I don't speak of myself because, being a deserter, I'm to blame. But the majority of these people have never done anything reprehensible. I don't understand why the Americans have thrown them in jail.

5.7 Ha Xuan Dai (PAVN medical corpsman), diary entries, November 1965

According to information in this diary, Dai had enlisted in the army in February 1961 at age nineteen, completed his training as a corpsman the next year, and headed south in late June 1965. In November his regiment collided with the U.S. First Cavalry Division in the battle of Ia Drang. (See document 4.3a for McNamara's reaction to that battle.) As the matter-of-fact entries here make clear, this fresh PAVN force faced trying conditions. Dai's fate is not known. His diary was captured by U.S. forces.

[16 November:] At 1300 hrs we gathered . . . to study the battlefield on a sand table, assign mission, establish a signal organization and military hospital. Tonight, combat orders will be given throughout D [Battalion].

[17 November:] Early in the morning, [enemy] observation planes and helicopters were roaring in the sky. F102 and 105 fighters bombed the Mo Duc and Duc Pho districts in Quang Ngai province. Then the [ARVN] troops landed by helicopters. After lunch, I went to E [Regiment] to get milk. This afternoon we marched to staging area 2. Tonight it was raining hard.

[18 November:] This morning, I sterilized medical instruments, syringes and vaccination needles. By 2300 hrs tonight, we will attack the Post of A.54. It will be my first battle to exterminate the enemy. It is a long wait until the firing time.

[19 November:] Last night, we would have attacked Post 7 of A.54, had the enemy not withdrawn from it at 1500 hrs on 18 November. Today I had nothing to do.

[21 November:] The whole [Quyet Tam Regiment] attacked a post located at the crossroads of Route 5 and National Route 1, near the railroad. . . . We were marching the whole day. It rained and was very cold. Everything was wet, including medicine. . . . We continued to fight until early in the morning on the 22nd. Then we retreated at 0400 hrs.

[22 November:] Enemy aircraft bombed us. There were many wounded. Company comrade Thanh of C [Company] 2 and Anh of C [Company] 4 were killed. Tonight, we moved into the jungle.

[23 November:] I stayed at the foot of the mountain, about two kilometers from an enemy post, to take care of our wounded. M.113 APC's [enemy armored personnel carriers] began to sweep near the foot of the mountain. Only 100 meters separated them from our shelter; it seemed as if we would be captured.

Helicopters, observation planes and F-105's bombed near us throughout the day. We could not eat or drink.

[24 November:] At Nui Hon where we assembled our wounded, one comrade died due to hunger and cold. I had to go back to our base to ask for personnel to carry the wounded soldiers. We have had no food since 22 [November]. There was only a bowl of fried rice for three men. I thought of having to eat tasteless wet rice. The first battle has been most difficult and complicated.

[26–28 November:] I spent three days in the Nui Lon forest (of the Mo Duc district). I had two attacks of fever. I was very tired and could taste nothing. It rained and rained, for three days. I thought of everything. I missed my mother, my grandmother and the family and was homesick. I felt like crying. I was miserable beyond expectation.

5.8 Nguyen Van Hoang (PAVN second lieutenant), interview on his determination to go into the army in 1967

This PAVN voice is that of an officer from Hanoi. He related to military interrogators his story of volunteering for military service.

During one of the air strikes in Haiphong my fiancée was killed by an American bomb. Immediately afterwards I decided that I had to go South to fight. At the time — this was in the summer of 1967 — I thought that the Liberation Army was riding the crest of a wave. If I didn't join up right away I'd miss my chance to take revenge. I reasoned that the Americans must be bombing the North in retaliation for their defeat in the South. I thought the NLF was on the verge of winning the decisive battle and that they would take Saigon in the very near future. I desperately wanted to go and kill a couple of Americans to relieve the bitterness I felt.

When my family learned that I had volunteered they were very unhappy about it. My mother cried for several days and nights straight. My father [a party member working in a government ministry] didn't cry, but he was obviously in distress. The day I left, my mother told me that both of them had been up the entire night, and that my father had been weeping along with her. When I said goodbye, my father told me, "You have to look after yourself, son, and try to return safely. For myself, I'm just trying to think of this as a study trip abroad for you. But be careful. Try to follow discipline and not get punished. And don't be too daring in the fighting. Don't make yourself a useless sacrifice. You are an educated man. It's not your vocation to be a soldier. That's a career that anyone can follow who knows how to pull a trigger. I'm unhappy that you're going. I want to see you back again." . . .

. . . One of my uncles was . . . the deputy chief of the Central Cadres Organizing Office in Hanoi. When he heard that I had volunteered he said, "Why are you joining? Don't you know the war in the South is a colossal sacrifice of troops? They're sending soldiers to the South to be killed at a merciless rate. They've taken most of the young men from Hanoi and from all over already, and they'll keep taking them. In war there has to be death. But this war isn't like when I fought against the French. Now the losses are in the thousands and tens of thousands. If you go now there's only one fate— unbearable hardship and possibly death— a meaningless death."

5.9 Huong Van Ba (NLF artillery captain), oral history of fighting, 1965–1968

Ba was one of the Viet Minh veterans who had regrouped to North Vietnam after the 1954 partition. He returned in 1964 via the Ho Chi Minh Trail. Here he relates his experience with B-52 bombing and with battle in the hotly contested area northwest of Saigon where Carl Burns (document 5.4) also served.

The first time I was attacked [by B-52s] was in Ben Cat. We were eating in our bunkers when they came, two groups five minutes apart, three planes in a group. It was like a giant earthquake. The whole area was filled with fire and smoke. Trees were falling all around. My shelter collapsed on me, although it hadn't been hit—I felt as if I were sitting in a metal case which someone was pounding on with a hammer. I was sure I was dying. An image passed through my mind quickly—of my mother giving me a checkered scarf the day I first joined the army. It was terrifying.

Up through 1966 I was in a lot of battles against the ARVN. . . . After that we were mostly engaged against U.S. forces from Cu Chi to Trang Bang. The Americans fought better than the ARVN. But you can't fight really well without hatred. . . .

. . . [I]n order to fight the Americans, you had to get close to them. You couldn't fight them from a distance. The best way was to attack them while they were on the move, or at night when they were stationed together. So our tactics were different from theirs. Their idea was to surround us with ground forces, then destroy us with artillery and rockets, rather than by attacking directly with infantry.

Usually we could get away from that, even when they used helicopters to try and surround us, because we knew the countryside so well and we could get out fast. That happened at Soi Cut, where they destroyed three villages while they were trying to catch us.

The Vietnamese Communists and the Americans had very different ideas about the war. When the Americans came to Vietnam, they didn't bring with them a hatred for the Vietnamese people. But we had it for them! Stalin said, "In order to defeat the enemy, one must build up hatred." We had been thoroughly exposed to anti-Saigon and anti-American propaganda in the North. We had seen pictures of the South Vietnamese people being beaten, arrested, and tortured. We had seen documentary movies of Ngo Dinh Diem's cruel suppression of the Buddhists, of people being shocked with electricity and women being raped. These pictures had built up our rage and our determination to liberate the South.

5.10 Nguyen Van Be (member of an NLF demolition platoon), personal papers, 1966

One of the new generation of homegrown NLF fighters, Be belonged to the NLF's 514th Battalion operating in My Tho province. Be's platoon had the dangerous task of spearheading attacks on enemy bases. He appears to have had ties to two villages in the province, Hau My, with a population of around

10,000, and Vinh Kim, with about half that population. Thanks to the NLF postal system, he corresponded with family and friends, using the nickname Be Danh. His exact relationship to his correspondents is not clear; the terms "brother" and "sister" used liberally here applied to anyone close and not necessarily siblings. The letters together with a poem found in his papers offer a poignant reminder of the lines of affection that sustained Vietnamese no less than American soldiers through their deadly ordeals. Be's poem is not unusual. Vietnamese commonly expressed themselves through poems—some soulful, others heroic.[3] Be's papers were captured by U.S. forces in mid-May 1967. His fate is not known.

[Older sister Chin Thuan to Be Danh, 30 May:] Hau My, our native village, is no longer as happy as before—it's become very desolate. The Americans pour their bombs and shells on the village every day without stopping. But the people in Hau My still maintain their revolutionary tradition and still cling to their rice fields and orchards. They devote themselves to the production task in order to contribute large quantities of resources to the Revolution. But in the last sweep operation, many people in Hau My were shot dead by the enemy. The other older sisters and I and our families fortunately escaped unhurt. . . .

Dear Danh, don't be pessimistic when you read this letter. Instead you should intensify your hatred. The front line and the rear areas should join hands to increase our strength to fight harder and avenge the people of South Vietnam in general and the people of Hau My in particular. . . .

P.S. . . . I think that you should go ahead with your marriage announcement. What do you think?

[Younger sister Minh Anh to Be Danh, Van Tri Phung, and "the rest of the older Brothers," no date:] I was overjoyed when I learned that you were getting married, and I was happy at the thought that soon I would have a deserving sister-in-law who would contribute to the Revolution to liberate the people. But my joy was shortlived, because I have just heard that she has been killed by the enemy's shelling and bombing. I'm writing you to share your sorrow, my dear older brother.

Dear Danh, I think you should put your sorrow aside in order to con-

---

3. Telling testimony on this point can be found in *Poems from Captured Documents*, trans. and comp. Thanh T. Nguyen and Bruce Weigl (Amherst: University of Massachusetts Press, 1994).

centrate on fighting the enemy and avenge the death of the girl who is now lying peacefully in her grave. Don't give way completely to sadness, because this will have a bad effect on your health and because it won't do you any good. The deeper your sorrow is, the deeper your hatred against the enemy should be, don't you think so, dear Danh?

[Be Danh to older sister, 13 July, describing an operation that night:] It was raining and the path was very slippery. I had to carry a heavy load, and so had to proceed very slowly and carefully on the muddy path in the middle of an isolated and deserted forest. Our column of troops, back from a victorious battle, were the only people moving in the forest. The sky was without stars and hung like a black blanket overhead. The night was pitch black and quiet. I heard the chirping of crickets and insects, a sad song echoing in the quiet night.

At that moment I thought of you in the rear area, and wondered if you and all the other older and younger sisters knew the hardships that your brother had to go through. I wondered whether you were sleeping peacefully or sitting at the openings of shelters, ready to take cover if you were shelled? . . . I wondered whether you talked about your brothers on the front line, or whether you had forgotten completely about them. . . .

Good-bye to my very dear sister. Loving you for ever.

[Thanh Van to Be Danh, Manh, Phouc, Met, and Kim, 2 August:] Let me give you some news about Vinh Kim village. The enemy are still holed up in their strategic hamlet. The other hamlets that used to be under firm enemy control are now being destroyed by the people and by our active supporters even during the day. We have destroyed a number of enemy officials and inflicted many defeats on the enemy. . . . The enemy shells the village every night, but we don't have time to count and see how many lizards have been killed in these shellings.

[Older sister Tu Tuyet to Be Danh, day 23 of the lunar month (probably latter part of 1966):] Many years have gone by since the time you and I shared our bowls of rice and rice gruel — I will never forget this. Dear Danh, you and I are separated from each other because of the American imperialists, and this is why both of us will have to stand up to take revenge and to fulfill our duty. When there are no American imperialists left, then parents will be reunited with their sons and you and I will see each other again, and only then will we be the deserving and grateful children of the nation. When this day comes, how glorious and bright and beautiful will it be.

[Undated poem in Nguyen Van Be's notebook:]

> Autumn passes away, winter comes, and then spring returns.
> I am as always enraptured by my mission.
> Before me, flowers bloom in brilliant colors in front of someone's house,
> A bamboo branch sways gracefully, reminding me of the native village I love.
> Our unit stops to rest in an isolated area.
> My shoes are still covered with dust gathered during the march.
> I hurriedly compose this letter to you
> And send you all my love.

5.11 Le Thi Dau (NLF nurse), recollections of service in the resistance, late 1950s–late 1960s

This account adds to Nguyen Thi Dinh's (document 1.8) on the revolutionary appeal to young women eager for adventure and escape from the confines of family and village. Le Thi Dau served in an NLF village, where she met and married an experienced, older cadre, Trinh Duc (see document 5.20). The difficult situation in the countryside after the Tet Offensive forced her to move to Saigon to work and raise the couple's three children.

I joined the revolution when I was fifteen. My mother hated the idea. She told me to think about marriage, think about having a family. I told her I had other things to do. I did, too. Of course I ended up in prison. They arrested me . . . when I was sixteen. I was in prison for six years. . . .

When I got out I went to school to become a nurse. After that I worked in Saigon for a while. Then I left for the jungle, to be trained at COSVN. This was at the end of 1965 or the beginning of 1966. My first assignment after COSVN was as a nurse in Bao Binh village. I was told that our first mission was to win the people's sympathy. If we helped them as much as we could we would win them over. After we won them over, they would help us.

When I got to Bao Binh I opened up a little infirmary, myself and two assistants from the village. One of the problems at first was that the people were illiterate. They weren't used to Western medicine at all. They relied mostly on prayers and superstitions, so we had to educate them. I took care of minor health problems, taught basic hygiene, baby care, things like that.

I was friendly with almost all the women I treated. . . . The ones who had husbands in the main force were under terrible stress. They never knew if their husbands were dead or alive. The Party didn't inform them, and they had to live with the constant uncertainty.

Many of these women suffered from chronic depression. Mostly they kept it to themselves. But my good friends would talk to me about it. I couldn't really do anything to comfort or console them—just let them talk, give them sympathy and someone whom they could talk to freely about what they were going through.

When I had my first child, my husband sent me back to Saigon [in 1969] to live with his brother. He thought it would be better not to try to raise the child in the village, that it was too dangerous. But I was unhappy about leaving. I felt a terrible guilt about going back to safety myself and leaving my friends. But of course my husband sent me, so I had to go.

The war was horrible. But it excited me too. I liked the adrenaline. I had originally joined the revolution when I was young because it was exciting, interesting. It gave me something to do that was out of the ordinary.

THE WAR GOES SOUR, 1968–1971

Through the latter phase of the war, Americans soldiers struggled to keep the faith. They were aware of mounting antiwar protests at home and declining popular support for the Vietnam commitment. They more and more doubted the effectiveness of the military operations they conducted. They began defying and even threatening their immediate leaders. The Tet Offensive, followed by Nixon's commitment to a complete U.S. withdrawal, deepened an already heavy pall of anger and frustration, which was often directed at Vietnamese.

5.12 Soldiers of Lieutenant William Calley's platoon, testimony on the My Lai massacre of 16 March 1968

The My Lai massacre, carried out in two hamlets of Son My village in Quang Ngai province along the central coastal plain, revealed the rising strain

U.S. soldiers were under. Elements of the Americal Division — from Charlie
Company, First Battalion, Eleventh Infantry Brigade — committed not just
the wanton killing of some 500 villagers but also rape. They also shot all live-
stock, destroyed all houses, and poisoned the wells. A steady loss of comrades
to mines and snipers in the name of a cause they could not grasp had helped
set the stage for the massacre. The difficulty they had distinguishing friend
from foe in the countryside was another key cause, as was poor leadership
that extended from platoon leader Calley up the chain of command. My Lai
was one of a kind, but the many little acts of brutality, deepening disillusion-
ment, and spasms of rage recorded by American soldiers testify to an army
that had suffered a deep psychological wound.

a. Dennis I. Conti (rifleman in March 1968), sworn testimony, 2 January 1970

[During a briefing before the My Lai operation, company commander Captain Ernest Medina said] that we should be careful because he expected strong resistance, and that the area was booby trapped. . . .

[Platoon leader Second Lieutenant William Calley] said that when we go in, . . . any men found there will have a weapon, any women will have a pack, any cattle is VC food, and to destroy it. . . .

. . . I figured myself that there was going to be strong resistance. I figured there would be men in the village, but I figured the men would be armed, and I figured that they would be supported by the women. . . .

. . . I think we were "psyched up", ready for battle more or less. . . . [W]e were ready to meet a foe of equal military strength, if not greater. And we prepared to give our best.

. . . [Calley] said something to the effect that [the children] would be future VC. . . .

. . . I assume he meant the children were the same as the mothers and fathers, they were VC. . . .

[Asked whether Calley meant men, women, and children would be shot:] . . . [T]hat's the way I interpreted it.

b. Herbert L. Carter (rifleman in March 1968), sworn testimony, 6 November 1969

We landed outside the village in a dry rice paddy. There was no resistance from the village. There was no armed enemy in the village. We formed a line outside the village.

The first killing was an old man in a field outside the village who said some kind of greeting in Vietnamese and waved his arms at us. Someone — either Medina or Calley — said to kill him and a big heavy-set white fellow killed the man. . . .

Just after the man killed the Vietnamese, a woman came out of the village and someone knocked her down and Medina shot her with his M16 rifle. I was 50 or 60 feet from him and saw this. There was no reason to shoot this girl. . . .

Then our squad started into the village. We were making sure no one escaped from the village. Seventy-five or a hundred yards inside the village we came to where the soldiers had collected 15 or more Vietnamese men, women, and children in a group. Medina said, "Kill everybody, leave no one standing.["] . . .

Just after this shooting, Medina stopped a 17 or 18 year old man with a water buffalo. Medina said for the boy to make a run for it — he tried to get him to run — but the boy wouldn't run, so Medina shot him with his M16 rifle and killed him. . . . Medina killed the buffalo, too. . . .

We went on through the village. [Rifleman Paul] Meadlo shot a Vietnamese and asked me to help him throw the man in the well. I refused and Meadlo had [rifleman Billy] Carney help him throw the man in the well. I saw this murder with my own eyes and know that there was no reason to shoot the man. . . .

Also in the village the soldiers had rounded up a group of people. . . . Calley came up and said that he wanted them all killed. . . . Calley had two Vietnamese with him at this time and he killed them, too, by shooting them with his M16 rifle on automatic fire. I didn't want to get involved and I walked away. There was no reason for this killing. These were mainly women and children and a few old men. They weren't trying to escape or attack or anything. It was murder.

A woman came out of a hut with a baby in her arms and she was crying. She was crying because her little boy had been in front of her hut . . . and someone had killed the child by shooting it. . . . [Radio operator Frederick] Widmer shot her with an M16 and she fell. When she fell, she dropped the baby and then Widmer opened up on the baby with his M16 and killed the baby, too.

I also saw another woman come out of a hut and Calley grabbed her by the hair and shot her with a caliber .45 pistol. He held her by the hair for a minute and then let go and she fell to the ground. Some enlisted man standing there said, "Well, she'll be in the big rice paddy in the sky." . . .

I also saw a Vietnamese boy about 8 years old who had been wounded,

I think in the leg. One of the photographers attached to the company patted the kid on the head and then [Platoon Sergeant David] Mitchell shot the kid right in front of the photographer and me. . . .

About that time I sat down by a stack of dying people and Widmer asked me if he could borrow my caliber .45 pistol and finish off the people. . . . He used three magazines of caliber .45 ammunition on these people. These were men, children, women, and babies. . . .

We went on through the village and there was killing and more killing.

5.13 David W. Mulldune (private in the First Marine Division), letters home, May–October 1968

This young California native was a high school dropout who enlisted in the marines to get some structure and direction into his life. He arrived in Vietnam in mid-May 1968. His experience fighting in the Da Nang area proved a shock. The letters that follow were written around his nineteenth birthday. He survived to return home — and to grapple with the images of war burned into his brain.

[To best friend Dennis Bacon (himself later wounded in Vietnam), 18 June:] Things here are the same old bullshit. You don't know if your next step is going to be your last, and that wears on your fucking nerves. I still believe we are fighting for the freedom of the South Vietnamese but I don't know that they care and if they don't then why should I? I can tell I'm salty because when one of our guys gets killed or maimed all I can think about is that I'm glad it was him and not me and I no longer feel guilty about it. I am already pissed off how this war is dragging on. If just the Marines were allowed to kick ass we could march all the way to Hanoi and hand Ho Chi Minh's head on a platter and this war would be over A-fucking-SAP and our guys wouldn't be dying like they are! I'm frustrated and worn down.

[To Dennis, 13 July:] Yes, I've heard that we are being called shell-shocked baby killers. It's convenient that a lot of those guys became protestors after they became eligible for the draft. They act holier-than-thou by calling us names in order to ease their consciences because they know deep down that they are chickenshit, coward mother-fuckers! They can't even face themselves so there is no way in hell that they have the guts to step in our boots for even two minutes. Fuck them! We had a memorial service this week for the guys who have been killed but I didn't go. I don't want to be reminded about them and I don't want to think about the fact that the next memorial service could be for me. . . .

P.S. Don't tell Mama about what I write you.

[To Mama, 27 September:] I'm really sorry for having not written but I have been very busy. We have been going on operation after operation and it is really rough and physically tiring. I get so mad at times because they never let up; it's always go, go, go. . . . A lot of my friends from boot camp days are either dead or have been maimed for life. I just can't describe how much I despise this war.

[To Mama, 23 October:] It seems like I'm always saying I'm sorry for not writing but I'm saying it again. Most of the time I am out in the bush and I can't but there are time when I can but I just don't. You get so used to putting your mind in neutral and becoming numb that it is hard to sit and write a letter like you are a human again. It's hard to put this into words when I haven't been able to figure it out myself. Not a week goes by without someone being killed or wounded or maimed and your nerves are raw. I try not to let it affect me because that is when you make mistakes.

————

5.14 Clarence Fitch (African American enlisted marine), interview on discontent in the military in 1968

This native of Jersey City, New Jersey, joined the marines in 1966 right out of high school. He arrived in Vietnam in time for the Tet Offensive. He was then nineteen. By the time he left in January 1969, he had seen intensifying racial tensions on bases as well as growing caution on the part of combat units. He brought home a couple of wounds, a heroin habit that would take fifteen years to kick, and a taste for political activism that he would channel into the American Postal Workers Union and the Vietnam Veterans against the War.

We weren't living in no vacuum in Vietnam. There was a certain growing black consciousness that was happening in the States, and also over there in Vietnam. People was aware of what was going on. . . .

The militancy really grew after Martin Luther King got killed in '68. It made black people really angry. . . . People were saying it doesn't pay to be nonviolent and benevolent. There were a lot of staff NCOs [noncommissioned officers], the type of so-called Negro that would be telling you to be patient, just do your job, pull yourself up by the bootstraps. So we called them Uncle Toms and that was that. People were saying, "I'm black and I'm proud. I'm not going to be no Uncle Tom."

There was a whole Black Power thing. There was Black Power salutes and handshakes and Afros and beads. It was a whole atmosphere. All that was a way of showing our camaraderie, like brothers really hanging together. When a new brother came into the unit, we used to really reach out for the guy, show him the ropes and tell him what's happening. It was like a togetherness that I ain't never seen since.

I think people really listened to Martin Luther King. . . . [S]omehow or another we got a copy of the speech [document 6.4], and we was really impressed. He talked about how blacks were dying in Vietnam at a greater rate. . . .

. . . It was like more white guys was in the rear with the easy jobs. They were driving trucks and working in the PX and shit like this, and we're out there in the bush, and that's why we was dying. A lot of the line companies over there were mostly black. There were white grunts, too, assigned to infantry units, but there was a *lot* of black grunts.

And then, as jobs became available in the rear, they would pull people back for jobs like company driver, stuff like that. . . . Black guys were staying their whole tour in the field. You just looked around you and said, "Well, they're just using us as cannon fodder." . . .

The form the militancy took most often was brothers just saying, "We're not going back in the bush." And we'd come up with all sorts of ways to avoid going back in the bush. It would be, like, instead of going out two klicks [kilometers] on a patrol, you'd say, "Hey, I'm going to stay back. It's dark. We're squatting right here, and we don't want no contact."

There were people that would go so far as to hurt themselves enough to get out of going into the bush. I seen people shoot themselves in the arm or the foot or the legs to get one of those Stateside wounds. I seen people fake injuries. . . .

There were fragging incidents for the same reason. It didn't happen every day, but after a while it got to be an unwritten rule. A lot of times you get these boot-camp second lieutenants, just out of Quantico, the officer training school, no field experience, and they just give them a platoon. The smart ones would come over and take suggestions, use their NCOs and squad leaders—guys that have been in the bush six, seven, eight months and really know what's going on—to show them until they get the ropes. But you get these guys that want to come over with school-book tactics, and they might want to do something that's detrimental to the company. Then you're talking about people's lives. Well, hey, the first firefight you get in, somebody takes him out. "Killed in action." ...

I saw a lot of craziness there.

_____

5.15 Rose Sandecki (army nurse), reflections on caring for casualties, October 1968–October 1969

Sandecki was an experienced nurse when, in her late twenties, she decided she wanted to work in Vietnam. She was one of about 10,000 American women who served in the military during the war, most as nurses. Hospital work was relatively safe but carried with it the psychological burdens of watching the dying and maimed cycle through the wards during duty hours and coping with men desperate for the company of women during off-duty hours. Interviewed in February 1983, Sandecki described her experience as head nurse in an intensive care unit in Cu Chi (a fiercely contested area northwest of Saigon) and later in a Da Nang medical facility.

I couldn't believe the numbers of people coming in, the numbers of beds and the kinds of injuries that I saw in front of me—I really wasn't prepared for that. . . . As long as an individual didn't lose a leg, arm, or an eye, as long as they were walking, they would go back to the boonies. . . .

. . . I learned a lot very quickly, seeing the types of casualties and the numbers of them. They were all so young. Seeing this on a daily basis twelve to fourteen hours a day, six or seven days a week, I think that I became somewhat callous and bitter. You also learned that you became almost like a commodity because you were a woman. After working twelve-hour shifts with all the blood and gore, you would change into a civilian dress to go to one of the local officers' clubs. . . . You couldn't sit still, just have a drink and relax. There would be one guy after another coming up and more or less doing his number on you: "I haven't seen a round-eye in six months. Would you dance with me?" You'd say, "No, I'm tired. I just want to sit and put my feet up." They wouldn't take no for an answer and would play this guilt thing like, "God, you don't know how bad I'm feeling. Just one dance, that's all." So you would dance and drink until two or three in the morning, then at six go back to the blood and guts of the war again. The initial two or three months was getting used to the pace of the twelve to thirteen hours of work and then the three or four hours of play. And it was a pressure kind of play because if you didn't go to the officers' club there was something wrong with you. If you stayed back in your hooch by yourself or stayed and talked to a couple of the other nurses, you were accused of being a lesbian, or you would be accused of having an affair with one of the doctors. . . .

The way of dealing with the sheer amount of patients, the long hours in the hospital, was by putting up a wall, the emotional numbing that we talk about. I think it built up over a period of time. Each day I went in and the more I saw, the thicker this wall became; it was sort of a skin protecting me from what was going on. . . .

. . . [T]he general comes in and gives [the 20,000th admission to an army hospital in Vietnam] a watch. They have this little ceremony, give him a Purple Heart and the watch. I'm standing off in the corner watching all this, and as the general handed him the watch — "From the 25th Infantry Division as a token of our appreciation"—the kid more or less flings the watch back at him and says something like, "I can't accept this, sir; it's not going to help me walk." I couldn't really see the expression on the general's face, but they all left after this little incident. I went over and just put my arms around him and hugged him . . . and if I remember correctly, I started crying . . . and I think he was crying. I really admired him for that. That was one time that I let the feelings down and let somebody see what I felt. It took a lot for him to do that, and it sort of said what this war was all about to me. . . .

. . . I felt that twelve months over there was probably one of the most rewarding nursing experiences in my life, that I'll never equal that again.

It was incredible coming back a real changed person, one who was sarcastic and bitter about what was happening in America. . . .

. . . I had a real "attitude problem" working in a civilian hospital. There was this need for the recreation of the push. . . . "adrenaline junkies" . . . that we are; the nurses who were in Vietnam. I really mean that. That certain rush of adrenaline, the excitement; there were all these casualties coming in that you have got to work . . . and the adrenaline starts going. So you try to perpetuate that. Nothing meant anything when I came back from Vietnam. The phrase "Don't mean nothin'" was very descriptive of the way I felt. I found it was getting in my way of jobs when I came back. Twelve to fourteen jobs in fourteen or fifteen years. . . .

. . . [T]hat war really did a number on all of us, the women as well as the men.

5.16 William Kahane (junior army officer), recalling conditions in support bases, late 1970–early 1971

William Kahane was commissioned an officer right out of college in 1967. He spent his last months of military service in Vietnam, arriving in late 1970 and working as a supply officer at Long Binh, the largest army base in Vietnam, located just northeast of Saigon. From his relatively comfortable post, he observed an increasingly troubled, dysfunctional expeditionary force.

[On drug and alcohol abuse:] [M]ost of my guys were using heroin. They were using it by smoking it and the Vietnamese were openly selling it. There was also a lot of marijuana use, which I indulged in myself, but the heroin, I stayed away from that. . . . [T]he military cracked down hard on marijuana use, because it was detectable. They could smell it, and so, there were lots of raids and, in a way, it kind of pushed these guys into smoking heroin, which didn't have an odor. . . .

Most of the officers did not use drugs, not even smoked marijuana. . . . Most of them drank heavily. Alcohol was their drug of choice and it was legal, of course. . . . [A]mong the enlisted men, mostly, it was marijuana and heroin. There was a lot of drug use. . . . I'm sure it cut down on the effectiveness [of U.S. units]. . . .

[On relations with Vietnamese:] [M]ost of the guys that I was around . . . hated the Vietnamese. They called them "gooks," "slopes." There were a lot of derogatory words for the Vietnamese and this was [appalling]. . . . I've had anti-Semitic slurs called to me, and I knew that it was wrong to think of a people in that way and talk of a people in that way. . . . [W]hen I was in Saigon once . . . with some other officers, . . . we went into a hotel, . . . a very famous hotel that was from the French period. . . . [W]e were sitting there, having drinks, gin and tonic, whatever, and I thought to myself, "I am like occupation here," you know. "I'm in the American occupation," and I found it very uncomfortable, not only that moment, but the whole time I was there.

[On living conditions:] They provided for us, they provided very well for us, in Long Binh. We had the best of food. We had an outdoor movie theater, with, like, bleachers and a screen, and . . . they would show a movie every night. . . . They had a swimming pool, . . . and I could go there at lunch hour and . . . go for a swim. . . . We had an officers' mess hall. For a while, we had a Hungarian cook who made tremendous food. . . . We had Vietnamese ladies, . . . older women who would shine our boots every day, press our uniforms. We'd get a new, pressed uniform every day, shined boots, every day. We lived, really, like royalty there, you know. . . . I feel bad, in a way, saying this, because I know how hard it was for some of the guys out . . . in the jungle and it was a really bad time for them, but, for me, it was a very, very easy experience and . . . not a hardship.

[Divisions within units:] I think that the military didn't really trust the troops very much, because there was a big divide. . . . The draftees, privates, corporals, lower grade sergeants, non-career people, they were, you know, using drugs and they were anti-war . . . for the most part, and the sergeants and the officers were pro-war. . . .

. . . [W]e had a few junior officers who were involved in the anti-war movement. . . . We looked at the anti-war movement as our friends. . . . "Anything that shortens this war is good for us."

STAGGERING THROUGH AN ENDLESS WAR, 1968–1971

For Vietnamese the post-Tet period was difficult. Hanoi's fighters suffered heavy losses in three offensives launched in 1968, and the interminable war promised more carnage to come. Some defected, but most displayed a determined stoicism that stood in marked contrast to the Americans' desperation, division, and bitterness. At the same time, in Saigon and other urban strongholds of the Thieu regime, a sense of malaise took hold as the war dragged on inconclusively and then deepened as the Americans packed up and shifted the burden of dying to the ARVN.

5.17 Trinh Cong Son (South Vietnamese songwriter), popular antiwar song "A Lullaby of the Cannons for the Night"

A telling barometer of sentiment in the urban South can be found in the popular songs of Trinh Cong Son. He had begun reacting to the war in the mid-1960s (then in his late twenties) — cities filled with U.S. soldiers and millions of refugees, the constant rumble of nearby fighting, and then the direct encounter with death and destruction during Tet in 1968. His antiwar songs, including "Lullaby" from 1967, had a special appeal among young urbanites, artists, intellectuals, ARVN soldiers and officers, and even troops on the other side furtively listening to the radio. Reflecting the cosmopolitan character of the urban South, the songs mixed Buddhist and existential philosophy with

a strong preoccupation with love and the land. Banned by the Saigon gov-
ernment in 1968, they still circulated widely thanks to cassette recordings.
Son himself evaded military service and, after the war, wrung a degree of tol-
eration for his work from Communist cultural bureaucrats suspicious of his
apolitical humanism.

Every night cannons resound in the town
A street cleaner stops sweeping and listens
The cannons wake up a mother
The cannons disturb a young child
At midnight a flare shines in the mountains

Every night cannons resound in the town
A street cleaner stops sweeping and listens
Each flight of the planes frightens the child
Destroying the shelter, tearing golden skin
Each night the native land's eyes stay open wide

Thousands of bombs rain down on the village
Thousands of bombs rain down on the field
And Vietnamese homes burn bright in the hamlet
Thousands of trucks with Claymores and grenades
Thousands of trucks enter the cities
Carrying the remains of mothers, sisters, brothers

Every night cannons resound in the town
A street cleaner stops sweeping and listens
Every night cannons create a future without life
Cannons like a chant without a prayer
Children forget to live and anxiously wait

Every night cannons resound in the town
A street cleaner stops sweeping and listens
Every night cannons sing a lullaby for golden skin
The cannons sound like a prelude to a familiar sad song
And children are gone before they see their native land

To fend off the war weariness reflected in Son's songs, Hanoi relied on a well-developed system of morale building. The determined effort to get soldiers to see the political cause behind the military struggle began with basic training that took up themes already sounded in public propaganda. Sustaining morale was the job of the political officers assigned down to the company level. Lower down, at the basic unit level, the task fell to the three-man cell. Headed by a party member, it created cohesion and confidence and quickly integrated replacements. In addition, units held regular criticism sessions to get complaints and difficulties into the open, and before and after operations the men had a chance to ask questions and raise concerns. Finally, soldiers could be confident of the priority given the recovery of the dead and wounded and of the help given to soldiers' families far away in the DRV.

A private first class designated by his Rand interview team "K-11" offers a perspective on the state of morale amid hardship and heavy losses in 1968. He came from a large family in Phu Tho province (in the Red River Delta, about fifty miles from Hanoi). In March 1967, then age seventeen and still a student, he was called to duty. His infantry unit, which arrived in the South the following October, fought in the Saigon area during the Tet Offensive and in the attack on the capital of Tay Ninh province the following May. Wounded in battle and taken prisoner in October 1968, K-11 was interviewed in January 1969.

[On the political officer and political commitment:] The political officer's main job was to motivate the men's morale. He educated the men on the Party's policies. Sometimes he even commanded the unit during the fighting. His deputy was in charge of removing the wounded and dead soldiers. During the fighting, the deputy political officer motivated the men to move their wounded comrades out from the battlefields for medical care, and to move the dead ones out from the battlefields for burying them properly. . . .

After each battle, the political officer gathered the men in the unit together to motivate their morale. The political officer informed the men about the good results that the men had gained from their action, this made the men feel enthusiastic. . . .

We all liked the political officer. He was a nice person, he was very gentle and very modest. He treated all of us like brothers. . . .

I had fought very enthusiastically in the army rank for a year because I fully understood the revolutionary line of the Party and of Uncle Ho, I was told about the political situation and about the American aggression in Vietnam, I am strongly determined to take the way the Party had planned in order to liberate the country from the American imperialist. I always believe that the Liberation Front and our army have been fighting for the just cause, and sooner or later the people who fight for the just cause will win the war. . . .

. . . [E]ven if I know that I would be killed in fighting, I wouldn't hesitate to keep on fighting because I fight for the just cause, and dying for the just cause, for the nation and for the people is glorious.

[On the three-man cell:] The three-man cell was the smallest unit in the army. It helped the men in the unit stay close and be friendly to each other. . . .

. . . [I]n combat the three men in the cell always kept close to each other. They moved forward together and withdrew together in case they had to. . . .

. . . [W]hen I had [a] problem, the other men in the cell helped me to solve [it]. When I quarreled with someone, the other two men helped me to calm down and they explained to me about the problem. When I got sick, the other two men called the nurse and got medicine for me.

[On support for the families of soldiers:] Before I left for the South, I was told that the government was going to help my family. When I was still in the North, I had known many families who had sons and husbands fighting in the South, they were not only helped by the government, but were also helped by the people living in their areas. Sincerely speaking, I don't worry about my people, they should now be in good shape.

5.19 Dang Thuy Tram (doctor caring for NLF personnel), diary entries, May–July 1969

Tram was a dedicated surgeon in her mid-twenties. Just out of medical school, she volunteered for service in the South. She arrived in spring 1967 and served for three years in Quang Ngai province near Duc Pho, caring for sick and wounded NLF soldiers and training local medical personnel. Enemy patrols, air attacks, and shelling posed constant dangers and repeatedly forced Tram to move her clinic to safer ground. A year after making these entries, she was killed by a U.S. patrol. An American intelligence officer rescued a portion of her diary. Published in Hanoi in 2005, it became a best seller. The diary may in the end have served as Tram intended: in the words of a Vietnamese literary scholar, as "the soul that she hopes to leave behind if her body dies."[4]

[18 May:] The other day I met some very young scouts, their skin still fair, the hair on their cheeks still soft and downy— probably high school students who recently dropped their pens to take up guns, embarking on the journey to fight the Americans and save the country.

That's it, the whole nation is on the road, the whole nation is throwing itself into battle. We certainly must defeat the American invaders, must bring ourselves to the days of independence and freedom.

[20 May:] Close to death once more. This morning several HU-1As and a small scout plane circled very close to Deep Hole [a clinic so named because it was partially underground]. The intensity of their search worried me very much. After a search close to the treetops, they found a patients' ward. The sounds of exploding grenades burst in our ears, fire broke out, and smoke covered the whole house. Everybody rushed down to the shelter—the shelter is very shallow, but there was no other alternative—I think perhaps it will be hard to escape this time.

When the gunship had circled out farther, I ran back to the room for the wounded soldiers, everyone had gone down to the shelter, including immobile patients. The gunship approached again, circling closer. Its occupants showered grenades down around the house. The sounds of rockets exploding on the slope shook the sky.

I turned to brother Minh, a wounded soldier from the clinic and asked, "What do we do now?"

"Sit here, what else?" . . .

After thirty minutes of shooting, the devils went away. I ran back and moved the injured in a hurry.

[11 June:] All day and night, the sounds of bombs, jet planes, gunships, and HU-1As circling above are deafening. The forest is gouged and scarred by bombs, the remaining trees stained yellow by toxic chemicals [for defoliation]. We're affected by the poison, too. All cadres are severely fatigued, their arms and legs weary, their appetites gone. They can nei-

4. Doan Cam Thi, "Dang Thuy Tram, a Variable and an Unknown: Opening *The Diary of Dang Thuy Tram* Forty Years Later," *Journal of Vietnamese Studies* 3 (Summer 2008): 209.

ther move nor eat. We want to encourage one another, but there are moments when our worries become clear and undeniable, and the shadow of pessimism creeps upon us.

[16 June:] Received letters from home. . . . I feel sad reading your letters.

[25 June:] The enemies begin their sweep very early this morning. I just wake up and crawl underground, no time to eat. . . . The heat in the earth is exhausting, stifling. The situation is very precarious. Enemy forces have spread all over the three hamlets of the village, American soldiers, traitors, and field combat police. My shelter is not far from the enemy.

[16 July:] This afternoon, like other afternoons, an OV-10 [light U.S.] plane circles several times above the hamlets, then launches a rocket down to Hamlet 13 in Pho An [a village on the coast of Quang Ngai province]. Immediately, two jets take turn[s] diving down. Where each bomb strikes, fire and smoke flare up; the napalm bomb flashes, then explodes in a red ball of fire, leaving dark, thick smoke that climbs into the sky. Still, the airplanes scream overhead, a series of bombs raining down with each pass, the explosions deafening.

From a position nearby, I sit with silent fury in my heart. Who is burned in that fire and smoke? In those heaven-shaking explosions, whose bodies are annihilated in the bomb craters? The old lady sitting by me stares at the hamlet and says, "That's where Hung's mother-in-law lives."

5.20 Trinh Duc (NLF cadre), recollections of his rural work, 1968–1971

Trinh Duc represents the political cadres whose efforts were critical to sustaining the resistance in the countryside through the difficult post-Tet period. He was born into a peasant family on the southern Chinese island of Hainan. Politically active as a youth during World War II, he fled the dangers of China's civil war to the safety of Saigon's Chinese quarter (known as Cholon), where his brother had long been settled. There Trinh Duc became involved in the anti-French resistance, joined Vietnam's Communist Party, and after the 1954 Geneva division of Vietnam was designated a "stay behind." He soon landed in one of Ngo Dinh Diem's prisons. Released in 1964, he became an NLF rural organizer, and by 1967 he was in charge of three villages in Long Khanh province, approximately fifty miles northeast of Saigon. Looking back a decade and a half later, he recalled the difficult circumstances he faced during and after the Tet Offensive.

First of all, casualties everywhere were very, very high, and the spirit of the soldiers dropped to a low point. Secondly, [the enemy] . . . began to reoccupy posts they had abandoned before — they mostly let the ARVN do that. Then they began to send out guerrilla forces to ambush us in the jungle. . . . After a while there was nowhere to turn. I would send units out on supply missions and they would disappear. People would be killed while they were cooking or going for water. Sometimes I could find out what happened to them, sometimes I couldn't.

During the period 1968–70, I was ambushed eleven times and wounded twice. It seemed the enemy had learned a lot about how to fight in the jungle. . . .

So many were killed in 1969 and 1970. There was no way we could stand up to the Americans. Every time they came in force we ran from them. Then when they turned back, we'd follow them. We practically lived on top of them, so they couldn't hit us with artillery and air strikes. During those years I had to reorganize my unit three times. Twice, the entire unit was killed. Each time I reorganized, the numbers were smaller. It was almost impossible to get new recruits. . . .

There's no doubt that 1969 was the worst year we faced, at least the worst year I faced. There was no food, no future — nothing bright. But 1969 was also the time I was happiest. I destroyed several American tanks from the "Flying Horses" tank battalion that was stationed in Suoi Ram. I did it with pressure mines that our bombmakers made from unexploded American bombs. . . .

The year 1969 was also the period when the true heroism of the peasants showed itself. Although we were isolated from the villagers, many of them risked their lives to get food to us. They devised all sorts of ingenious ways to get rice through the government checkpoints. Their feeling for us was one of the things that gave me courage to go on.

Another thing was the conviction the Americans couldn't last. In 1969 they began to pull out some of their troops. We believed that eventually they would have to withdraw altogether. We knew that even though we faced tremendous difficulties, so did they. They had terrible problems, especially at home. We didn't think their government could stand it in the long run. . . .

Toward the end of 1970 things began to get better. We started gaining more control. I could feel the optimism starting to return. One of the ways you could tell this was that the peasants felt more comfortable about contacting us and giving us support. They didn't have to be heroes to do that anymore, especially after 1971. ARVN was taking over from the Americans at that time. . . .

The supply situation also got a lot better. . . . I was able to supply the North Vietnamese main forces in my area as well as my own people.

The War
Comes Home,
1965–1971

All wars have profound effects on the societies fighting them, and the longer the wars last and the closer they come to home, the deeper their impact. The social ramifications of Vietnam's long struggle are evident in the previous chapters. By the time the Americans arrived, Vietnamese had known warfare for several decades. But against the Americans the fighting would become all consuming, a total war. The North mobilized; the South was subject to massive bombing; dislocation, privation, and death were commonplace all over the country. The pervasive effects of war are abundantly clear in the words encountered earlier of Vietnamese North and South, young and old, elite and popular, men and women, combatants and bystanders. None escaped the convulsion.

The war on the U.S. home front had an entirely different character. It arrived late. It deeply touched some and completely spared others. It merged with other areas of ferment in American life. It provoked deepening bitterness. And it remains hugely controversial. Social, cultural, and political fissures that opened or widened in the course of the Vietnam conflict continued to reverberate for decades and are evident even today.

Hints of serious trouble coincided with Johnson's decision to escalate the war during the first half of 1965. His actions set off teach-ins on college campuses and the first of what would prove to be many demonstrations in Washington. U.S. foreign policy observers and Vietnam specialists expressed doubts. Even the public seemed hesitant. Two in five Americans polled just after Johnson's July decision on a major troop increase said they thought the Vietnam commitment a mistake or had no opinion.

Over the following two years, a distant conflict would unsettle the country just as it unsettled the Johnson administration and the soldiers on the front line. A relatively small number of young people — most from major Northeast, upper Midwest, and West Coast universities — got the earliest public protests going. Soon demonstrations were attracting larger and more diverse crowds. Polls revealed that the broader public was turning against Johnson's war, at first embracing a hawkish alternative (greater military effort than Johnson was ready to make) and then increasingly shifting to the dovish option (a negotiated settlement and an early U.S. troop withdrawal). By the latter part of 1967, over half of poll respondents for the first time called the Vietnam commitment a mistake.

The downward trend in popular support both responded to and accentuated the misgivings of policy makers and troops in complicated interplay. Influential political figures doubtful of Johnson's course at the outset were emboldened by the polls to speak out publicly, and their public criticism in turn deepened popular doubts about the war. The news from Vietnam, often conveyed in the voices and images of the troops, was not encouraging, and as opponents of the war grew louder, soldiers found it easier to question their mission or feel betrayed.

The post-Tet period brought domestic tensions to a new high. The failure of the Democratic Party to accept a peace candidate or even a peace platform discredited conventional political activity in the eyes of many activists. Some turned their backs on the war, while others shifted toward significantly more radical and violent antiwar activity. The prominence of veterans in the last phase of public protest added fuel to the fire. They began to appear in a new round of demonstrations at the end of 1969 set off by Nixon's failure to deliver on his promise of peace. Pro-war patriots recoiled at the sight of protesting veterans and denounced them as phonies and "crybabies." Nixon's appeal to the "real" Americans in the heartland, his denigration of protesters, and his calls to support the troops were understandable attempts to hold back the rising antiwar tide. But they also underlined the deep divisions that had developed over the meaning of the intervention in Vietnam and the acceptability of democratic dissent.

These developments on the U.S. home front raise a set of critical questions:

- What arguments did U.S. critics make about the Vietnam commitment? How did the doubts expressed in public compare with the criticisms offered in private by policy makers in chapter 3 and by soldiers in chapter 5?
- If it is fair to say that dissent opened up a great debate within the American body politic over national identity and the U.S. role in the world, what were the terms of that debate?

- How should we evaluate the critics of the war? For example, in terms of their perceptiveness on the nature of the war, their success in influencing policy and the public, or their effectiveness in rebutting the claims of interventionist presidents?

OPENING SHOTS, 1965

The march toward war provoked public dissent that was searching in its critique of U.S. society and strikingly skeptical of military action. Those who showed up for the early protests and read appreciatively the first critiques of Johnson's policy were products of a particular moment. The civil rights movement and rising levels of activism on campuses had begun to politicize a small but influential group of students. The fear of nuclear war and the talk of better relations with the Soviet Union were at the same time acting as solvents of the old Cold War certitudes that had shaped the Vietnam commitment.

6.1 Paul Potter (president of Students for a Democratic Society), speech against the war, Washington, D.C., 17 April 1965

This thoughtful twenty-five-year-old had grown up in the Midwest (in an Illinois farm town) and attended college there (Oberlin). He had done graduate work at the University of Michigan, participated in the southern civil rights struggle, taken an early activist role in the Students for a Democratic Society (SDS), and thrown himself into community organizing in Cleveland. The SDS took the lead in organizing this first major antiwar demonstration, and Potter as its head offered the concluding remarks. In an argument that was warmly received by an audience of about 20,000 drawn to the event, he made what would become the trademark SDS linkage between opposition to the Vietnam War and far-reaching political and social change in the United States.

[I]n recent years, the withdrawal from the hysteria of the Cold War era and the development of a more aggressive, activist foreign policy have done much to force many of us to rethink attitudes that were deep and basic sentiments about our country. The incredible war in Vietnam has provided the razor, the terrifying sharp cutting edge that has finally severed the last vestige of illusion that morality and democracy are the guiding principles of American foreign policy. . . .

The President says that we are defending freedom in Vietnam. Whose freedom? Not the freedom of the Vietnamese. The first act of the first dictator, Diem, the United States installed in Vietnam, was to systematically begin the persecution of all political opposition, non-Communist as well as Communist. . . .

What in fact has the war done for freedom in America? It has led to even more vigorous governmental efforts to control information, manipulate the press and pressure and persuade the public through distorted or downright dishonest documents. . . . It has led to the confiscation of films and other anti-war material and the vigorous harassment by the FBI of some of the people who have been most outspokenly active in their criticism of the war. . . .

. . . What is exciting about the participants in this march is that so many of us view ourselves consciously as participants as well in a movement to build a more decent society. There are students here who have been involved in protests over the quality and kind of education they are receiving in growingly bureaucratized, depersonalized institutions called universities; there are Negroes from Mississippi and Alabama who are struggling against the tyranny and repression of those states; there are poor people here — Negro and white — from Northern urban areas who are attempting to build movements that abolish poverty and secure democracy; there are faculty who are beginning to question the relevance of their institutions to the critical problems facing the society. Where will these people and the movements they are a part of be if the President is allowed to expand the war in Asia? What happens to the hopeful beginnings of expressed discontent that are trying to shift American attention to long-neglected internal priorities of shared abundance, democracy and decency at home when those priorities have to compete with the all-consuming priorities and psychology of a war against an enemy thousands of miles away? . . .

. . . [T]he freedom to conduct that war . . . depends on the construction of a system of premises and thinking that insulates the President and his advisors thoroughly and completely from the human consequences of the decisions they make. I do not believe that the President or Mr. Rusk or Mr. McNamara or even McGeorge Bundy are particularly evil men. If asked to throw napalm on the back of a ten-year-old child they would shrink in horror—but their decisions have led to mutilation and death of thousands and thousands of people.

What kind of system is it that allows good men to make those kinds of decisions? What kind of system is it that justifies the United States or any country seizing the destinies of the Vietnamese people and using them callously for its own purpose? What kind of system is it that disenfranchises people in the South, leaves millions upon millions of people throughout the country impoverished and excluded from the mainstream and promise of American society, that creates faceless and terrible bureaucracies and makes those the place where people spend their lives and do their work, that consistently puts material values before human values—and still persists in calling itself free and still persists in finding itself fit to police the world? What place is there for ordinary men in that system and how are they to control it, make it bend itself to their wills rather than bending them to its?

We must name that system. We must name it, describe it, analyze it, understand it and change it. For it is only when that system is changed and brought under control that there can be any hope for stopping the forces that create a war in Vietnam today or a murder in the South tomorrow or all the incalculable, innumerable more subtle atrocities that are worked on people all over—all the time....

... If the people of this country are to end the war in Vietnam, and to change the institutions which create it, then the people of this country must create a massive social movement—and if that can be built around the issue of Vietnam then that is what we must do.

... What we must do is begin to build a democratic and humane society in which Vietnams are unthinkable, in which human life and initiative are precious. The reason there are twenty thousand people here today and not a hundred or none at all is because five years ago in the South students began to build a social [civil rights] movement to change the system. The reason there are poor people, Negro and white, housewives, faculty members, and many others here in Washington is because that movement has grown and spread and changed and reached out as an expression of the broad concerns of people throughout the society. The reason the war and the system it represents will be stopped, if it is stopped before it destroys all of us, will be because the movement has become strong enough to exact change in the society.

6.2 Hans J. Morgenthau (University of Chicago professor), articles on the perils of intervention in South Vietnam, April and July 1965

This political scientist was noted for his advocacy of realism in international affairs. Already during the 1950s he had warned that U.S. policy makers' Cold War obsessions might obscure the nationalist and anticolonialist thrust behind revolution in Vietnam. That oversight, he feared, might in turn lead to a commitment that would be beyond U.S. means to sustain and harmful to U.S. interests in the world. Lyndon Johnson's public defense of his policy in early April (document 3.7) prompted Morgenthau to renew his stand against what he saw as a misguided crusade.

a. "We Are Deluding Ourselves in Vietnam," 18 April 1965

[W]e are under a psychological compulsion to continue our military presence in South Vietnam as part of the peripheral military containment of China. We have been emboldened in this course of action by the identification of the enemy as "Communist," seeing in every Communist party and regime an extension of hostile Russian or Chinese power. . . .

Thus [U.S. policy makers] maneuver themselves into a position which is antirevolutionary per se and which requires military opposition to revolution wherever it is found in Asia, regardless of how it affects the interests — and how susceptible it is to the power — of the United States. . . .

. . . In South Vietnam there is nothing to oppose the faith of the Vietcong and, in consequence, the Saigon Government and we are losing the civil war. . . .

The United States has recognized that it is failing in South Vietnam. But it has drawn from this recognition of failure a most astounding conclusion.

The United States has decided to change the character of the war by unilateral declaration from a South Vietnamese civil war to a war of "foreign aggression." . . .

Our very presence in Vietnam is in a sense dictated by considerations of public relations; we are afraid lest our prestige would suffer were we to retreat from an untenable position.

One may ask whether we have gained prestige by being involved in a civil war on the mainland of Asia and by being unable to win it. Would we gain more by being unable to extricate ourselves from it, and by expanding it unilaterally into an international war? . . . Does not a great power gain prestige by mustering the wisdom and courage necessary to liquidate a losing enterprise? In other words, is it not the mark of greatness, in circumstances such as these, to be able to afford to be indifferent to one's prestige?

b. "Globalism: Johnson's Moral Crusade," 3 July 1965

The domestic "consensus" supports [U.S. anticommunist foreign policy with its fear of all revolutionary movements], and it makes but minimum demands on moral discrimination, intellectual subtlety, and political skill. Its implementation is in essence a problem of military logistics: how to get the requisite number of armed men quickly to the theater of revolution. That task is easy, and we have shown ourselves adept at it. Yet the achievement of that task does not solve the problem of revolution. It smothers, as it were, the fire of revolution under a military blanket, but it does not extinguish it. And when that fire breaks out again with increased fury, the assumptions of our policy have left us with no remedy but the commitment of more armed men trying to smother it again.

This policy is bound to be ineffective in the long run against the local revolution to which it is applied. It is also ineffective in its own terms of the anti-Communist crusade. For the very logic which makes us appear as the anti-revolutionary power *per se* surrenders to Communism the sponsorship of revolution everywhere. Thus the anti-Communist crusade achieves what it aims to prevent: the exploitation of the revolutions of the age by the Soviet Union and China.

Finally, our reliance upon a simple anti-Communist stance and its corollary, military intervention, is bound to corrupt our judgment about the nature and the limits of our power. We flatter ourselves to defend right against wrong, to discharge the self-imposed duty to establish a new order throughout the world, and to do so effectively within the limits of military logistics. Thus we may well come to think that all the problems of the political world will yield to moral conviction and military efficiency, and that whatever we want to do we shall be able to do so because we possess those two assets in abundance.

CRITICISM GOES MAINSTREAM, 1966–1968

By early 1966 doubts about the war were both deepening and spreading. This shift was reflected not just in the public opinion polls but also in the willingness of prominent national leaders to speak out.

6.3 Senator J. William Fulbright (chair of the Senate Foreign Relations Committee), decrying "the arrogance of power," 1966

This Arkansas Democrat played a pivotal role in legitimizing public opposition. In early 1966 Fulbright held Senate hearings in which prominent critics appeared alongside leading Johnson administration officials. Soon after, he forcefully articulated his own deepening doubts in a set of lectures, which became the basis for a best-selling book. Vietnam and other interventions overseas figured in his view as a fundamental betrayal of basic U.S. values.

The attitude above all others which I feel sure is no longer valid is the arrogance of power, the tendency of great nations to equate power with virtue and major responsibilities with a universal mission. The dilemmas involved are pre-eminently American dilemmas, not because America has weaknesses that others do not have but because America is powerful as no nation has ever been before, and the discrepancy between her power and the power of others appears to be increasing. . . .

I have not the slightest doubt of the sincerity of the President. . . . What I do question is the ability of the United States or any other Western nation to go into a small, alien, undeveloped Asian nation and create stability where there is chaos, the will to fight where there is defeatism, democracy where there is no tradition of it, and honest government where corruption is almost a way of life. . . .

If America has a service to perform in the world — and I believe she has — it is in large part the service of her own example. In our excessive involvement in the affairs of other countries, we are not only living off our assets and denying our own people the proper enjoyment of their resources, we are also denying the world the example of a free society enjoying its freedom to the fullest. This is regrettable indeed for a nation that aspires to teach democracy to other nations. . . .

There are many respects in which America, if she can bring herself to act with the magnanimity and the empathy appropriate to her size and power, can be an intelligent example to the world. We have the opportunity to set an example of generous understanding in our relations with China, of practical cooperation for peace in our relations with Russia, of reliable and respectful partnership in our relations with Western Europe, of material helpfulness without moral presumption in our relations with developing nations, of abstention from the temptations of hegemony in our relations with Latin America, and of the all-around advantages of minding one's own business in our relations with everybody. Most of all, we have the opportunity to serve as an example of democracy to the world by the way in which we run our own society. America, in the words of John Quincy Adams [early-nineteenth-century U.S. secretary of state and president], should be "the well-wisher to the freedom and independence of all" but "the champion and vindicator only of her own."

If we can bring ourselves so to act, we will have overcome the dangers of the arrogance of power. It will involve, no doubt, the loss of certain glories, but that seems a price worth paying for the probable rewards, which are the happiness of America and the peace of the world.

6.4 Martin Luther King Jr., address at the Riverside Church, New York City, 4 April 1967, making the Vietnam War a matter of conscience

Just as the public was approaching an even split on the wisdom of the Vietnam intervention, Martin Luther King Jr. threw his moral authority against the war. He spoke out reluctantly, fearing his views would hurt his campaign to secure civil rights for African Americans. He appeared in New York to take his stand at the invitation of one of the leading antiwar organizations, Clergy and Laity Concerned about Vietnam.

There is at the outset a very obvious and almost facile connection between the war in Vietnam and the struggle I and others have been waging in America. . . . I knew that America would never invest the necessary funds or energies in rehabilitation of its poor so long as adventures like Vietnam continued to draw men and skills and money like some demonic, destructive suction tube. . . .

. . . [I]t became clear to me that the war was doing far more than devastating the hopes of the poor at home. It was sending their sons and their brothers and their husbands to fight and to die in extraordinarily high proportions relative to the rest of the population. We were taking the black young men who had been crippled by our society and sending them eight thousand miles away to guarantee liberties in Southeast Asia which they had not found in southwest Georgia and East Harlem. . . .

. . . As I have walked among the desperate, rejected, and angry young men, I have told them that Molotov cocktails and rifles would not solve their problems. . . . They asked if our own nation wasn't using massive doses of violence to solve its problems, to bring about the changes it wanted. . . .

[The Vietnamese people] must see Americans as strange liberators. . . .

. . . Now they languish under our bombs and consider us, not their fellow Vietnamese, the real enemy. They move sadly and apathetically as we herd them off the land of their fathers into concentration camps where minimal social needs are rarely met. They know they must move on or be destroyed by our bombs. . . .

. . . I am as deeply concerned about our own troops there as anything else. For it occurs to me that what we are submitting them to in Vietnam is not simply the brutalizing process that goes on in any war where armies face each other and seek to destroy. We are adding cynicism to the process of death, for they must know after a short period there that none of the things we claim to be fighting for are really involved. . . .

Somehow this madness must cease. We must stop now. I speak as a child of God and brother to the suffering poor of Vietnam. I speak for those whose land is being laid waste, whose homes are being destroyed, whose culture is being subverted. I speak for the poor of America who are paying the double price of smashed hopes at home and death and corruption in Vietnam. I speak as a citizen of the world, for the world as it stands aghast at the path we have taken. I speak as one who loves America, to the leaders of our own nation: The great initiative in this war is ours; the initiative to stop it must be ours.

6.5 Senator John C. Stennis, speech to the American Legion National Convention, Boston, 30 August 1967, calling for a more forceful war strategy

Stennis, a Democrat from Mississippi, was an influential voice on the Senate Armed Services Committee. Here he expresses the view of hawks who were critical of Johnson's handling of the war. They favored unleashing U.S. military power and especially lifting the restrictions the president had personally imposed on the bombing of North Vietnam. The Stennis strategy — one shaped by military rather than civilian leaders and directed toward achieving victory in a relatively short period — had wide public appeal during the first years of the war. Like other hawks, Stennis had no patience with antiwar sentiment. National unity and determination were essential to victory.

Casualties in our forces committed to mortal battle continue to mount. At this moment we find ourselves pinned down by a small third-rate nation in a contest that may determine whether all the people of Asia will live under communism. Certainly the outcome of this conflict will decide whether the United States maintains its position as the strongest nation in the world willing and able to meet its commitments.

. . . We do not want to develop a permanent policy of fighting long, restricted, limited, diplomatic wars. While we are lovers of peace and never aggressors, let it be known to friend and foe alike that if we enter a war, our purpose will be to prevail to win, and that we will follow whatever course is necessary to attain that end. . . .

I do not suggest that we should indiscriminately bomb North Vietnam, but I do maintain that we must hit every significant military target that our *military commanders* consider to be necessary to the enemy's war-making capability. . . .

Far too long we let the enemy freely use railroad bridges, storage areas, power plants, cement factories, main highways and ocean ports. These military targets in North Vietnam were for many months untouched while the enemy used them to produce and transport hundreds of thousands of tons of weapons, ammunition and other war materiel for battle against American men. Some of these targets have not yet bee[n] bombed. . . .

However, in addition to heavily bombing more military targets in North Vietnam, we must also develop an overall plan to win the war, or an honorable settlement. This war-ending plan which should be prepared by military men should include the use of all conventional ground, naval and air power necessary to win as quickly as possible and bring our men home.

I see no prospect of early success under a policy of applying military pressure in a limited, gradual and piecemeal fashion. This only lengthens the war and makes it far more costly to us in men, money and equipment. . . .

This is the hour for a national decision and for personal dedication. The time has passed when it was useful to argue whether, and to what extent, we should have become involved in Vietnam. We are there — to turn back is unthinkable. . . .

. . . Americans everywhere should now close ranks and give our fighting men the support and backing they need and deserve. Continued criticism will only cause our enemy to mistake our national purpose, and lead to more casualties. It will decrease, not improve, the chances for peace.

6.6 Walter Cronkite (CBS television news anchor), editorial comment on the Tet Offensive, 27 February 1968

The Tet Offensive shook the U.S. political landscape. The veteran journalist Walter Cronkite toured South Vietnam to see for himself what had happened and then shared with his many evening viewers his pessimistic appraisal. President Johnson, who put great stock in television news and monitored it closely, was dismayed to hear so respected a figure call for a negotiated peace just as he was about to begin his own policy review (document 4.5a).

Who won and who lost in the great Tet offensive against the cities? I'm not sure. The Vietcong did not win by a knockout, but neither did we. . . . On the political front, past performance gives no confidence that the Vietnamese government can cope with its problems, now compounded by the attack on the cities. It may not fall, it may hold on, but it probably won't show the dynamic qualities demanded of this young nation. Another standoff.

We have been too often disappointed by the optimism of the American leaders, both in Vietnam and Washington, to have faith any longer in the silver linings they find in the darkest clouds. . . .

To say that we are closer to victory today is to believe, in the face of the evidence, the optimists who have been wrong in the past. To suggest we are on the edge of defeat is to yield to unreasonable pessimism. To say that we are mired in stalemate seems the only realistic, yet unsatisfactory, conclusion. . . . [I]t is increasingly clear to this reporter that the only rational way out then will be to negotiate, not as victors, but as an honorable people who lived up to their pledge to defend democracy, and did the best they could.

6.7 Marvin Dolgov (Democratic Party activist on Long Island), recollections of the "dump Johnson" movement

This account suggests how the antiwar movement gradually broadened and reached into the Democratic Party base. University educated, with a record of military service during the Korean War, Dolgov had gradually turned against Johnson's war and by 1968 was actively opposing Johnson's reelection. This "dump Johnson" movement culminated in March when the antiwar senator Eugene McCarthy from Minnesota nearly defeated the incumbent president in the New Hampshire primary. Seeing an opening, New York senator Rob-

ert Kennedy quickly declared his candidacy. Johnson's announcement that he was withdrawing from the race came at the end of the month (document 4.5b).

After the 1964 election [against Barry Goldwater], Lyndon Johnson was a hero to partisan Democrats like myself. On his coattails our very [R]epublican county elected many Democratic officials for the first time in history.

Sometime after that election I remember rumblings of disapproval from our Democratic youth group. We (other party leaders and myself) took the position with them that — *although we could not see the reasoning behind Johnson's policies, he is our leader and must know things that we don't.* I would guess that around 1966 we were convinced that we knew what Johnson didn't and that the kids were right. My doubts started then.

We were greatly influenced by a charismatic figure, Allard Lowenstein. He lived locally but had a national reputation as a civil rights and social justice leader and soon to be a leader of the "dump Johnson" movement. I remember clearly attending one of his inspiring speeches in which he exhorted all anti-war groups to put aside differences and work together to end the war. Lowenstein was the darling of college students throughout the country. . . .

Our community had an ad hoc anti war group. We (the Democratic Party leaders) had a meeting with them in my home. We subsequently "gave birth" to a letter sent to every household in the community urging an anti war attitude. We referred to this effort as giving birth because we had so many differences to work out. Our approach was always to present our views as an official position of the local Democratic Party and our goal was to show opposition by a main-stream group, and that the movement was not limited to radicals, counter culture groups and college students. As you see, my efforts were not so much in the form of demonstrations, but a lot more was going on that received much less notice in the media.

. . . About two or three weeks before Johnson announced that he would not run in 1968, I wrote him a letter in my official capacity as Democratic Party Club President and Zone Leader. In it I drew some comparisons between President of the United States and President of a Democratic Club. (Yes I did, I was young then.) Perhaps it's best that I didn't save a copy. What I did, which was not stupid, was to explain why the war was bad for both the Party and the Country. I am convinced that he read my letter and it persuaded him not to run. That's my story and I'm sticking to it. No one can prove it isn't so.

. . . [T]hat announcement by Johnson was one of those defining moments where you remember where you were and what you were doing. [My wife] Terry and I turned to each other at that moment to confirm that we both heard the same thing. We thought that all our efforts were coming to fruition. Little did we know what would follow. It's my personal belief that the radicals, and their insistence on having it all their way, cost us the 1968 election. Politics is the art of compromise. . . .

Why did Terry and I and thousands of others feel so passionate about ending this war? Politically active people like ourselves feel partially responsible for what ever our government does. The deaths and atrocities without acceptable reason was something we felt a personal obligation to stop.

A philosophical point—The old adage is correct "Truth is the first casualty of war, any war." View government with skepticism because citizens must make judgments based on critical instincts. You never get courtroom proof. If it looks like a duck, walks like a duck and quacks like a duck, don't let the government tell you it's a chicken.

RISING CONTENTION AND POLARIZATION, 1969–1970

Relentlessly destructive, the Vietnam commitment had already divided Americans by 1968. As the war continued and as demonstrations flared in late 1969 against Nixon's lack of progress toward peace, the division among Americans grew deeper and more bitter. Fewer and fewer approved of the war, but many could not stomach the prospect of defeat any more than Nixon could.

6.8 Weathermen manifesto issued at the SDS convention, Chicago, 18 June 1969

Frustration over the war that would not end helped fracture the SDS and propelled one faction, known as the Weathermen (formally the Revolutionary Youth Movement), in a sharply radical direction. The group took its name from the lines of a Bob Dylan song, "You don't need a weather man / To know which way the wind blows." The new organization announced itself in mid-1969 with a revolutionary statement prepared by a collective, with John

Jacobs playing the leading role. Applying an explicitly Marxist framework, this statement focused on U.S. imperialism locked in conflict with the forces of national revolution in Vietnam and elsewhere in the third world and opposed at home by a radical movement of African Americans and young people.

We are within the heartland of a world-wide monster, a country so rich from its world-wide plunder that even the crumbs doled out to the en-slaved masses within its borders provide for material existence very much above the conditions of the masses of people of the world. The US empire, as a world-wide system, channels wealth, based upon the labor and resources of the rest of the world, into the United States. . . .

The goal [of the Weathermen] is the destruction of US imperialism and the achievement of a classless world: world communism. Winning state power in the US will occur as a result of the military forces of the US overextending themselves around the world and being defeated piece-meal; struggle within the US will be a vital part of this process. . . .

The struggle of black people — as a colony — is for self-determination, freedom, and liberation from US imperialism. Because blacks have been oppressed and held in an inferior social position as a people, they have a right to decide, organize and act on their common destiny as a people apart from white interference. . . .

In general, young people have less stake in a society (no family, fewer debts, etc.), are more open to new ideas (they have not been brainwashed for so long or so well), and are therefore more able and willing to move in a revolutionary direction. Specifically in America, young people have grown up experiencing the crises in imperialism. They have grown up along with a developing black liberation movement, with the liberation of Cuba [in 1959], the fights for independence in Africa and the war in Vietnam. . . . This crisis in imperialism affects all parts of the society. America has had to militarize to protect and expand its empire; hence the high draft calls and the creation of a standing army of three and a half million, an army which still has been unable to win in Vietnam. Further, the huge defense expenditures — required for the defense of the empire and at the same time a way of making increasing profits for the defense industries — have gone hand in hand with the urban crisis around wel-fare, the hospitals, the schools, housing, air and water pollution. The state cannot provide the services it has been forced to assume responsi-bility for, and needs to increase taxes and to pay its growing debts while it cuts services and uses the pigs [police] to repress protest. . . .

. . . [T]he war against Vietnam is not "the heroic war against the Nazis"; it's the big lie, with napalm burning through everything we had heard this country stood for. Kids begin to ask questions: Where is the Free World? And who do the pigs protect at home? . . .

. . . A revolution is a war; when the Movement in this country can defend itself militarily against total repression it will be part of the revolutionary war.

This will require a cadre organization, effective secrecy, self-reliance among the cadres, and an integrated relationship with the active mass-based movement. To win a war with an enemy as highly organized and centralized as the imperialists will require a (clandestine) organization of revolutionaries, having also a unified "general staff"; that is, combined at some point with discipline under one centralized leadership. Because war is political, political tasks — the international communist revolution — must guide it.

6.9 The Nixon administration appeals for public support, November 1969

By fall 1969 Nixon had failed to deliver on his election promise to end the war. Popular impatience led to a revival of protest. Millions joined in demonstrations nationwide, first on 15 October and then on 15 November, in what would prove the high tide of the antiwar movement. The president was so worried by the first round of demonstrations that he felt obliged to push back. Nixon personally appealed to a patriotic majority to back him up as he maneuvered for an honorable settlement. Vice President Spiro Agnew followed close behind with an attack on media distortions and biases. His charges would echo in later controversies over the Vietnam War.

a. President Nixon, address from the White House, 3 November 1969

I would be untrue to my oath of office if I allowed the policy of this Nation to be dictated by the minority who hold [an antiwar position] and who try to impose it on the Nation by mounting demonstrations in the street.

. . . If a vocal minority, however fervent its cause, prevails over reason and the will of the majority, this Nation has no future as a free society. . . .

I know it may not be fashionable to speak of patriotism or national destiny these days. But I feel it is appropriate to do so on this occasion.

Two hundred years ago this Nation was weak and poor. But even then,

America was the hope of millions in the world. Today we have become the strongest and richest nation in the world. And the wheel of destiny has turned so that any hope the world has for the survival of peace and freedom will be determined by whether the American people have the moral stamina and the courage to meet the challenge of free world leadership.

Let historians not record that when America was the most powerful nation in the world we passed on the other side of the road and allowed the last hopes for peace and freedom of millions of people to be suffocated by the forces of totalitarianism.

And so tonight — to you, the great silent majority of my fellow Americans — I ask for your support. . . .

Let us be united for peace. Let us also be united against defeat. Because let us understand: North Vietnam cannot defeat or humiliate the United States. Only Americans can do that.

b. Vice President Spiro Agnew, speech in Des Moines, Iowa, 13 November 1969

When the President completed his address — an address that he spent weeks in preparing — his words and policies were subjected to instant analysis and querulous criticism. The audience of seventy million Americans — gathered to hear the President of the United States — was inherited by a small band of network commentators and self-appointed analysts, the *majority* of whom expressed in one way or another their hostility to what he had to say. . . .

. . . [T]his little group of men . . . not only enjoy[s] a right of instant rebuttal to every presidential address, but more importantly, wield[s] a free hand in selecting, presenting, and interpreting the great issues of our nation. . . .

I am not asking for government censorship or any other kind of censorship. I am asking whether a form of censorship already exists when the news that forty million Americans receive each night is determined by a handful of men responsible only to their corporate employers and filtered through a handful of commentators who admit to their own set of biases. . . .

. . . The American who relies upon television for his news might conclude that the majority of American students are embittered radicals, that the majority of black Americans feel no regard for their country; that violence and lawlessness are the rule, rather than the exception, on the American campus. . . .

. . . How many marches and demonstrations would we have if the marchers did not know that the ever-faithful TV cameras would be there to record their antics for the next news show? . . .

In this search for excitement and controversy, has more than equal time gone to the minority of Americans who specialize in attacking the United States, its institutions, and its citizens?

6.10 Kent State and the polarization of public opinion, May 1970

Nixon's April 1970 decision to invade Cambodia (document 4.10) provoked campus protests. An angry president threw fuel on the fire when he made an off-the-cuff but widely publicized reference to protesters as "bums." At Kent State University in Ohio, the situation turned ugly. On-campus demonstrations had begun on 1 May and had led to the destruction of the campus building used to train future officers. On 4 May Ohio National Guard troops deployed on campus fired shots into a crowd, hitting both protesters and bystanders. Four students died and nine were wounded. News of Kent State ignited already volatile campuses all across the country; well over a million students on well over a thousand campuses went on strike. In an extended interview conducted by New York Times reporters in the immediate aftermath of the shooting, Kent State students expressed a mix of anger, alienation, and pessimism. But in a nation more deeply divided than ever over the war, some citizens blamed the protesters, not the guardsmen, not the president, and not his policy. The revulsion toward unruly students is evident in letters sent to the Record-Courier, *the newspaper for Kent as well as Ravenna, Ohio.*

a. Kent State students, interview in the wake of the campus killings

ELLEN GLASS [a twenty-three-year-old senior majoring in art]: I'm not saying he [Nixon] gave the direct order. But I'm saying he was sympathetic to those people who wanted something to happen. It's his general attitude toward students and his general attitude toward dissent.

TOM DIFLOURE [a twenty-one-year-old political science major who grew up in an air force family and who described his views as having shifted from far right to far left]: . . . But it's not just Nixon. It's the whole system.

BUZZ [TERHUNE, a twenty-two-year-old Vietnam veteran pursuing a degree in biology and describing himself as a political "moderate"]: You want to jump up and scream, "Do something. Somebody do something." But the somebody we scream to is Mr. and Mrs. Front Porch America, who haven't done anything for the last how many years. When I came home from Vietnam, I was very much for mother, dad, country, apple pie and that sort of stuff. . . .

And now I feel like I've stood by too long and haven't done anything. I'm not a militant. . . . But I can't see where anybody can sit still and let Nixon and his boys cook another Vietnam in Cambodia. . . . . I don't want this, and I'm going to do everything I can to change it. . . .

RON [ARBAUGH, a twenty-two-year-old sophomore and former first lieutenant in the Army Special Forces who characterized himself as a "conservative"]: Last week, I suppose I didn't have any views pro or con to a great degree. . . . Then came Nixon's speech on Cambodia and I thought, well, for crying out loud, I voted for the guy because I wanted to get it over and then he turns around and makes it bigger. . . .

[After the shooting] I felt I really ought to do something. . . . Later on I called a guardsman a "pig" and then I felt better.

Q. A graduate of Fort Benning calls a guardsman a pig?

RON: Well, I did and I felt very mean about it. I almost had tears in my eyes. I felt that disappointed and mad. . . .

LUCIA [PERRY, an eighteen-year-old art major with limited engagement in politics]: . . . [F]rankly I feel about as alienated from my Government as you can get. . . .

ELLEN: I think that a basic problem with this country is that it's a world power and sees itself as a policeman of the world. And I think this country has to be reduced to something other than a world power. . . .

JEFF [ZINK, a twenty-one-year-old senior who was a member of the student senate and had plans to go to law school]: The question I have is this: There are four people dead, the universities are closed down, and we're still fighting the war, aren't we? So even violence didn't do any good, did it? . . .

JEFF TETREAULT [a twenty-year-old sophomore biology major]: . . . I'm planning to go to Canada, British Columbia, and go to school there. . . .

I don't like the way this country's going. There's too much hate in this country, too much control on my life. I don't like all the hate between the blacks and the whites and all the economic oppression. . . .

TOM: . . . I made up my mind a long time ago that I'm leaving. . . .

LUCIA: . . . I don't feel that I am a citizen of the United States. . . .

ELLEN: A lot of women, young women, are making personal commitments not to have children. . . . [T]his is not the kind of world I would want to bring a child into.

b. Ohio citizens, letters to the editor on the National Guard killings at Kent State

[Ravenna housewife:] Authority, law and order are the backbone of our society, for its protection. Would you want authorities to stand by if your home were threatened? Well, Kent State is my home by virtue of taxes spent funding it. What's more, it's their home by virtue of tuition paid. Playful children destroying a disenchanting toy.

How dare they! I stand behind the action of the National Guard! I want my property defended. And if dissenters refuse to obey the final warning before the punishment, hurling taunts, rocks (stones, they say), sticks, brandishing clubs with razor blades imbedded, then the first slap is a mighty sting.

Live ammunition! Well, really, what did they expect, spitballs? . . .
. . . America, support it or leave it.

[Concerned citizen:] When radical students are allowed to go through a town smashing windows, terrifying the citizens, and are allowed to burn buildings belonging to the taxpayers to the ground, I think it is high time that the Guard be brought in to stop them—and stop them in any way they can.

The sooner the students of this country learn that they are not running this country, that they are going to college to learn, *not teach*, the better.

[Mother of a guardsman:] Congratulations to the Guardsmen for their performance of duty on the Kent University Campus. I hope their actions serve as an example for the entire nation. The governors of our states cannot waste the taxpayers' money playing games. . . .

I extend appreciation and whole-hearted support of the Guard of every state for their fine efforts in protecting citizens like me and our property.

[Ravenna citizen:] Kent has tolerated these so-called misunderstood students long enough. The city of Kent should be off-limits to students. Keep them on the university grounds, and when they have completely destroyed it, they can go home and we will be rid of them.

If the National Guard is forced to face these situations without loaded guns, the silent majority has lost everything. The National Guard made only one mistake — they should have fired sooner and longer.

[Attorney-at-law:] It is too bad that a small minority of students feel that these damnable demonstrations must take place. If the slouchily dressed female students and the freakishly dressed, long-haired male students would properly dress and otherwise properly demean themselves as not to make show-offs of themselves, such trouble could be and would be avoided. It is difficult to understand why female students must get out and make such fools of themselves as they do, but it is understandable that male students do so largely to get their screwball mugs on television and in the press.

THE VIETNAM VETERANS MOVEMENT, 1971

The Vietnam Veterans against the War, organized in 1967, developed a nationwide network with thousands of members. It launched an exposé of war crimes in early 1971 in what the organizers called the Winter Soldier Investigation. Angry, depressed, repentant former servicemen gathered in Detroit to testify to the atrocities they had witnessed. Their suggestion that My Lai, which had become public in late 1969, was part of a broader pattern offended many Americans. The Vietnam Veterans against the War followed up in April with demonstrations in Washington, including a heavily publicized gathering of angry veterans who threw away their medals on the steps of the Capitol.

6.11 John Kerry, statement before the Senate Foreign Relations Committee, 23 April 1971

One of the most memorable statements during the April protest came from John Kerry. This decorated navy veteran and protest organizer appeared before the Senate Foreign Relations Committee. He spoke out of an intimate sense of what fellow antiwar veterans were burning to say and with the knowledge that other Americans were still fighting in a war gone wrong.

[S]everal months ago in Detroit, we had an investigation at which over

150 honorably discharged and many very highly decorated veterans testified to war crimes committed in Southeast Asia, not isolated incidents but crimes committed on a day-to-day basis with the full awareness of officers at all levels of command. It is impossible to describe to you exactly what did happen in Detroit, the emotions in the room, the feelings of the men who were reliving their experiences in Vietnam, but they did. They relived the absolute horror of what this country, in a sense, made them do.

They told stories that at times they had personally raped, cut off ears, cut off heads, taped wires from portable telephones to human genitals and turned up the power, cut off limbs, blown up bodies, randomly shot at civilians, razed villages in [a] fashion reminiscent of Genghis Khan, shot cattle and dogs for fun, poisoned food stocks, and generally ravaged the countryside of South Vietnam in addition to the normal ravage of war, and the normal and very particular ravaging which is done by the applied bombing power of this country. . . .

In our opinion, and from our experience, there is nothing in South Vietnam, nothing which could happen that realistically threatens the United States of America. And to attempt to justify the loss of one American life in Vietnam, Cambodia, or Laos by linking such loss to the preservation of freedom . . . is to us the height of criminal hypocrisy, and it is that kind of hypocrisy which we feel has torn this country apart. . . .

We rationalized destroying villages in order to save them. We saw America lose her sense of morality as she accepted very coolly a My Lai and refused to give up the image of American soldiers who hand out chocolate bars and chewing gum.

We learned the meaning of free fire zones, shooting anything that moves, and we watched while America placed a cheapness on the lives of orientals.

. . . [W]e watched while men charged up hills because a general said that hill has to be taken, and after losing one platoon or two platoons they marched away to leave the [hill] for the reoccupation by the North Vietnamese. . . .

Each day to facilitate the process by which the United States washes her hands of Vietnam someone has to give up his life so that the United States doesn't have to admit something that the entire world already knows, so that we can't say that we have made a mistake. Someone has to die so that President Nixon won't be, and these are his words, "the first President to lose a war."

... [H]ow do you ask a man to be the last man to die in Vietnam? How do you ask a man to be the last man to die for a mistake? ...

We wish that a merciful God could wipe away our own memories of that service as easily as this administration has wiped their memories of us. But all that they have done and all that they can do by this denial is to make more clear than ever our own determination to undertake one last mission, to search out and destroy the last vestige of this barbaric war, to pacify our own hearts, to conquer the hate and the fear that have driven this country these last 10 years and more, and so when 30 years from now, our brothers go down the street without a leg, without an arm, or a face, and small boys ask why, we will be able to say "Vietnam" and not mean a desert, not a filthy obscene memory but mean instead the place where America finally turned and where soldiers like us helped it in the turning.

6.12 President Nixon, address from the White House, 7 April 1971

As the critical veterans' voices grew louder, Nixon sought to blunt atrocity charges by praising the troops. Just days earlier, the president had responded to the popular outcry against the conviction of Lieutenant William Calley for murder at My Lai by ordering his transfer from prison to house arrest. (Calley's life sentence was soon reduced, and in 1974 he received parole.)

I understand the deep concerns which have been raised in this country, fanned by reports of brutalities in Vietnam. . . .

. . . I feel it is my duty to speak up for the two and a half million fine young Americans who have served in Vietnam. The atrocity charges in individual cases should not and cannot be allowed to reflect on their courage and their self-sacrifice. War is a terrible and cruel experience for a nation, and it is particularly terrible and cruel for those who bear the burden of fighting.

But never in history have men fought for less selfish motives — not for conquest, not for glory, but only for the right of a people far away to choose the kind of government they want.

While we hear and read much of isolated acts of cruelty, we do not hear enough of the tens of thousands of individual American soldiers — I have seen them there — building schools, roads, hospitals, clinics, who, through countless acts of generosity and kindness, have tried to help the people of South Vietnam. We can and we should be very proud of these men. They deserve not our scorn, but they deserve our admiration and our deepest appreciation.

Outcomes and Verdicts

The war ended in early 1973 for American soldiers — but not for Vietnamese. The program of reconciliation outlined in the Paris peace accords collapsed into renewed fighting between the forces of Hanoi and Saigon. In early 1975 the PAVN launched a carefully prepared offensive in the Central Highlands. Caught off guard, then confused, and finally badly outmaneuvered, ARVN units panicked and fled south. In April PAVN tanks rolled into Saigon. As the long war came to an end, most Americans looked away, while Vietnamese who had fought for national unity exulted and many on the losing side fled the country.

The guns had fallen silent, leaving Vietnamese and Americans to grapple with difficult questions. In both countries, anxious nationalists went to work either to preserve the memory of a glorious victory or to redeem the shame of defeat. Just as determined and increasingly vocal were the veterans on both sides whose lives were shadowed by the private memories of war. They became in time implacable public witnesses to what they and their comrades had experienced and to the special ways those experiences had marked them.

For Vietnam the postwar turmoil was manifold and profound. The wounds of war on the land and people were deep and widespread. Le Duan and his colleagues faced the tasks of political reunification and reconciliation as well as economic reconstruction. Heavy-handed assertion of Hanoi's rule in the South created political disaffection, while clumsy efforts to integrate the country's two long-separated economies resulted in disruption, shortages, and hardship. In what amounted to a referendum on the new order, many Vietnamese voted with their feet. Saigon loyalists, anticipating the worst, had been the first to flee. They were followed by ethnic Chinese dispossessed of their businesses as part of Hanoi's imposition of a state-directed economy on the South. Ethnic Chinese were also suspected of disloyalty as tensions rose between

Hanoi and Beijing. Postwar refugees of all kinds totaled well over 1 million, perhaps close to 2 million.

International rivalry added to domestic difficulties as former revolutionary allies turned on each other. The new Cambodian regime installed by the Khmer Rouge and headed by Pol Pot proved a serious thorn in Hanoi's side, with its oppression of Vietnamese residents and its armed incursions into Vietnamese territory. With patience at last exhausted, Le Duan dispatched forces to end Pol Pot's bloody rule and set up in early 1979 a government of Khmer Rouge defectors that was friendly to Hanoi. The price was substantial: the costly burden of the occupation itself, international condemnation and isolation, and China's retaliatory invasion of northern Vietnam.

Against this troubled backdrop, three kinds of postwar Vietnamese perspectives emerged. Soul searching was the order of the day among those closely tied to the Saigon government. They had lost all—position, honor, country—and many faced uncertain futures either as exiles or as inmates in Vietnam's "reeducation centers." The Communist Party leadership clung to its well-honed and deeply ingrained patriotic picture of the war as a just cause in yet another heroic Vietnamese struggle against outsiders. This picture was reflected in popular celebrations, public memorials, and literary mythmaking. Finally, soldiers who had fought the good fight began expressing their own, less positive views of what war meant. Veterans organized to demand better care, and they insisted on communicating their wartime experiences. Their dark narratives were at odds with the upbeat government orthodoxy and thus encountered official disapproval and censorship.

For Americans, Saigon's fall represented a challenge to national narratives of righteousness and great achievements. In what amounted to a national psychic ordeal, the ghosts of the lost war kept coming back—on Veterans Day, on the campaign trail, in debates over the use of U.S. forces abroad, in the design of memorials, and in literary and historical polemics. Retrospective views divided along three main interpretive lines, each rooted in positions developed during the wartime controversies.

Some, echoing Stennis, Nixon, and Agnew, saw in the war primarily a betrayal of a good cause. The U.S. mission in Vietnam had been to stop human oppression and promote freedom. The blame for failure rested on decision makers who had been reluctant to bring American power fully to bear and on elites who had sowed public doubt and disunity. Those determined to avoid another betrayal called for giving a free hand to the president as commander in chief and to the military as the agent of the president's will, for mobilizing public support, for controlling dissent and the media, and for offering troops in the field unwavering support.

The more critical perspective, harking back to Potter, Morgenthau, Fulbright, and King, roundly denounced the war as a criminal act of aggression, as a betrayal of U.S. values, as immoral and racist, as fundamentally misconceived, and as ultimately foredoomed. What all these charges have in common is the conviction that avoiding other Vietnams would involve effecting profound changes in American society and attitudes.

The middle ground sought to transcend wartime acrimony by embracing the notion of a no-fault tragedy. Americans and Vietnamese came to blows because of who they were and how as a result they misunderstood each other. Their experiences and their convictions, however well or ill intentioned, set them at odds, with terrible results. The impulse to draw lessons was here turned into a search for patterns of miscalculations and misperceptions that might make future policy makers wiser and more prudent.

In the postwar period, two groups of Americans loomed especially large. One was veterans who spoke out in an extraordinarily creative stream of memoirs, oral histories, novels, and poetry. Like the accounts of their Vietnamese counterparts, what they had to say coexisted uneasily with political retrospectives and at once inspired and transcended the entertainment industry's vision of the war. The other, more practically consequential group consisted of policy and political types bent on drawing lessons. Their pronouncements perpetuated a long-standing tendency to imagine the war as a largely if not exclusively American affair. Hawks still proclaimed their faith in the decisive role of force while seldom looking carefully at the will and capacity of the foe whom American power was meant to compel or persuade. Doves continued to profess sensitivity to the costs of intervention while failing to question whether the Vietnamese case could in fact be generalized.

Readers now have a chance to reflect on the close of the war and the diverse assessments offered in its aftermath.

- How did Le Duan conceive victory and Gerald Ford defeat in the closing phase of the Vietnam War?
- In the estimate of those aligned with the Saigon government, what

was the decisive element in their defeat? How much blame did they put on the United States?

- What memories did Vietnamese and American veterans carry from the war? How different were their memories from each other?
- Of the divergent lessons drawn by American and Vietnamese leaders, which are the most compelling in light of the evidence presented in earlier chapters?

ENDGAME, 1974–1975

With U.S. combat forces gone by early 1973, Hanoi went through a period of posturing over political reconciliation stipulated by the Paris peace agreement and, in 1974, worked out plans for a final campaign in the South to extend over 1975 and 1976. PAVN had some 400,000 troops there with a good logistical network behind them. The Saigon government had been weakened by diminished U.S. support and afflicted by war weariness and economic crisis. Nixon had been immobilized by the Watergate scandal and had resigned. The hands of his successor, Gerald Ford, were tied by a popular and congressional aversion to Vietnam. The DRV's Pham Van Dong whimsically predicted in December 1974 that "the Americans would not come back even if you offered them candy."[1]

7.1 Le Duan, letter to Pham Hung (head of COSVN), 10 October 1974, laying out the thinking behind "the last general offensive and uprising"

In early October the Politburo gathered to consider plans formulated under Giap's supervision for a new offensive. Le Duan's letter, based on his speech on that occasion, provides insight not only on military calculations but also on Hanoi's view of the Paris accords and its concerns over U.S.-China collusion.

[T]he US still entertains the hope that its henchmen in the South can hold out thanks to one million puppet troops, 20,000 US advisers and a huge amount of US aid, and will be able to control the cities and a large part of the countryside. Thus, *the Americans entered South Vietnam be-*

---

1. Dong quoted in *William J. Duiker, Sacred War: Nationalism and Revolution in a Divided Vietnam* (New York: McGraw-Hill, 1995), 244.

cause they thought they were strong and we were weak, that they would win and we would be defeated. Now the Americans have to pull out because we are strong and they are weak, we have won and have made a big stride forward; they have been defeated and have to back down. . . .

What was our strategic intention when we signed the Paris Agreement?

While saying that the Americans had to pull out because they were defeated, we knew that the US still had great potentials and many wicked schemes. We never indulged in wishful thinking and never said that they were "out of steam". Though we had won repeated victories and had gained in strength, we still met with many difficulties. At that time, the aid from our camp [China and the Soviet Union] was not sufficient and timely as we had expected. The compromise and collusion between the US and China has rendered our war of resistance more complicated. In that conjuncture, we had to create for ourselves a posture for steady advance and for certain victory. It was for that reason that we signed the Paris Agreement.

For us, the importance of the Paris Agreement does not lie in the admission that there are two administrations, two armies and two areas of control, the future formation of a three-faction government, but essentially in the fact that US troops have to pull out while our forces can stay on, that the North-South corridor remains open, the great rear is firmly linked to the great front, that our offensive battle array is imposing. . . .

. . . Our main task now is to topple the puppet regime, and in concrete terms, to overthrow the Nguyen Van Thieu clique, who represent the interests of the feudal class, the compradores, bureaucrats and militarists.

We are resolved to *enlist the greatest efforts of the whole Party, the whole army, the whole nation in both zones in order to launch the last general offensive and uprising, bring the revolutionary war to its climax, wipe out and disband the whole puppet army, occupy Saigon — the central den of the enemy — and all other cities, topple the puppet administrations at all levels, seize all the power for the people, completely liberate South Vietnam, complete the people's national democratic revolution in the whole country and proceed to reunify our homeland.* From now on preparations should be made with a sense of urgency, thus creating the best material basis for a powerful and rapid offensive to win brisk and complete victory in the years 1975 and 1976.

7.2 Nguyen Van Thieu, speech, 21 April 1975, resigning as president in the face of crumbling ARVN defenses

The major offensive anticipated by Le Duan and named in honor of Ho Chi Minh began in March 1975. Much more quickly than the Communist leaders hoped and the American leaders feared, the Thieu regime collapsed. With defeat looming, Thieu abandoned his office and fled the country — but not before taking a final swipe at the Americans who had let him down. His long, extemporaneous parting remarks were delivered before the National Assembly in Saigon and broadcast over national television.

The Americans have asked us to do an impossible thing. . . . You have asked us to do something you failed to do with half a million powerful troops and skilled commanders and with nearly $300 billion in expenditures over six long years. If I do not say that you were defeated by the Communists in Vietnam I must modestly say that you did not win either. But you found an honorable way out. And at present, when our army lacks weapons, ammunition, helicopters, aircraft, and B-52s, you ask us to do an impossible thing like filling the ocean up with stones. . . .

Likewise, you have let our combatants die under the hail of shells. This is an inhumane act by an inhumane ally. . . .

The United States is proud of being an invincible defender of the just cause and the ideal of freedom in this world. . . . I asked [a visiting U.S. congressional delegation]: Are U.S. statements worthy? Are U.S. commitments still valid? Some $300 million is not a big sum to you. Compared to the amount of money you spent here in ten years, this sum is sufficient for only ten days of fighting. And with this sum, you ask me to score a victory or to check the Communist aggression — a task which you failed to fulfill in six years with all U.S. forces and with such an amount of money. This is absurd.

7.3 President Gerald Ford, address at Tulane University, New Orleans, 23 April 1975, on the eve of the fall of Saigon

With U.S. Vietnam policy reaching its dead end and with a longtime client facing imminent demise, Ford publicly suggested that the best response was to look away.

Today, America can regain the sense of pride that existed before Vietnam. But it cannot be achieved by refighting a war that is finished [enthusiastic response by a heavily student audience] as far as America is concerned. As I see it, the time has come to look forward to an agenda for the future, to unify, to bind up the Nation's wounds, and to restore its health and its optimistic self-confidence. . . .

I ask that we stop refighting the battles and the recriminations of the past. I ask that we look now at what is right with America, at our possibilities and our potentialities for change and growth and achievement and sharing. I ask that we accept the responsibilities of leadership as a good neighbor to all peoples and the enemy of none. I ask that we strive to become, in the finest American tradition, something more tomorrow than we are today. . . .

We, of course, are saddened indeed by the events in Indochina. But these events, tragic as they are, portend neither the end of the world nor of America's leadership in the world.

7.4 Le Duan, speech in Hanoi celebrating victory, 15 May 1975

Unlike American leaders, Le Duan had a glorious victory to celebrate. His stress here on national reconstruction provides a reminder that the war was not just about political unification; it was also about an international system in which capitalism was faltering and about Vietnam's development along socialist lines. At the same time, this speech looks back, invoking the spirit of the early resistance treated at the outset of this volume.

Viet Nam became the testing ground for the power and prestige of US imperialism. Viet Nam became the area of the fiercest historic confrontation between the most warlike, the most stubborn aggressive imperialism with the most powerful economic and military potential on one side, and the forces of national independence, democracy and socialism of which the Vietnamese people are the shock force in this region on the other. The victory of Viet Nam, therefore, is not only a victory of national independence and socialism in Viet Nam, but has also a great international significance, and an epoch making character. It has upset the global strategy of US imperialism. . . .

Our people have made countless sacrifices and overcome untold hardships and difficulties to recover our country. . . . Let us prove ourselves worthy of being the real masters of the country. Let our compatriots in the North step up socialist construction. Let our compatriots in the South unite and strive to build there a fine national democratic regime, a prosperous national and democratic economy, a progressive and healthy national and democratic culture. In the spirit of national reconciliation and concord, our people have shown leniency to all those who have strayed from the right path and who are now returning to the people, no matter what their past was. Provided they sincerely mend [lend?] their abilities to the service of the homeland, their place among the people will be guaranteed and all the shame put on them by criminal US imperialist[s] will be washed away. . . .

In the four thousand years of our nation's history, the last hundred years were the hardest and fiercest period of struggle against foreign aggression, but they were at the same time the period of our most glorious victories. Our people have overthrown the domination of the Japanese fascists, defeated the old colonialism of France and have now completely defeated the neo-colonialism of the United States. By those splendid exploits, our nation has joined the ranks of the vanguard nations of the world and has won the affection and esteem of the whole of progressive mankind. A nation which has recorded such splendid exploits deserves to enjoy peace, freedom and happiness. Such a nation surely has enough determination and energy, strength and talent to overcome all difficulties and reach the great heights of our times, to turn a poor and backward country heavily devastated by war, in which US imperialism has perpetrated so many crimes, into a civilized, prosperous and powerful country, an impregnable bastion of national independence, democracy and socialism in Indochina and Southeast Asia. . . .

Long live the Viet Nam Workers' Party!

President Ho Chi Minh will live forever in our cause!

SOUTH VIETNAMESE LOOKING BACK ON A LOST CAUSE

The losers in a war generally get written out of the historical record. The following interviews provide often neglected insights on Vietnamese tied to the Saigon government — why they lost and what they felt in defeat.

7.5 Nguyen Cao Ky (former Saigon government leader), interview conducted in 1977

Ky was born in the North in 1930 into a scholar-official family, which moved south in 1954 when the Communists gained full control north of the seven-

*teenth parallel. Trained as a pilot by the French, Ky participated in the coup
against Ngo Dinh Diem and was made head of South Vietnam's air force. An
outspoken and flamboyant figure, Ky served as premier between 1965 and
1967 and then as vice president under the shadow of the increasingly powerful Nguyen Van Thieu. Ky withdrew from politics in 1971 and, after the fall
of Saigon, settled in Los Angeles. In this passage he reflects on Saigon politics
and the U.S. role.*

I always thought that my responsibility was to build a strong Vietnam, to
stop Communist aggression, and second to bring to the people happiness and justice, social justice. . . .

. . . Myself and my family, we are not Catholic, but I really encouraged all my family to go and vote for [Ngo Dinh Diem]. Before he came
to power, he was very popular, he had a very good reputation as a nationalist, and I think we really respected him. . . . But then . . . in 1963, after
five years in power, absolute control, I think Mr Diem thought that he
was God. At least he believed that he had some message from God to stay
there and govern the way he thinks was God's policy. . . .

. . . [I]t was a big turn of history, whether the overthrow of Mr Diem was
wrong or right. But right after that you see a big big enthusiastic atmosphere among the population. . . . [W]hat was wrong was that you eliminate Diem and replace him by a bunch of generals who were more dumb
than Mr Diem himself. I still believe that at least Mr Diem had some ideal
to serve, but the group of general officers who replaced him had no ideals
at all. . . .

. . . I think most of them, the Vietnamese generals, had the feeling that
they owed something to America. And . . . there is no way that they could
go against the rule of the Americans because they will be eliminated right
away. Even Thieu, Thieu after he became President. . . . Every time he
discussed a problem with me, . . . he only asked me what the Americans
think about it. Thieu always worried about America. He believed that the
Americans could do everything. That's why most of the time he tried to
please America. . . .

. . . After I become Premier I have many meetings with American officials — including President Johnson on many occasions — and on each
occasion I told him what I think was the right way to deal with the war and
to deal with the Communists and to deal with South Vietnamese people.
Most of the time the Americans just smile, and very politely, but the problem is they never listened to me. They never did the things that I asked. . . .

. . . I remember I mentioned to Ambassador Cabot Lodge when he asked me: "What is your government program [or] policy?" and I told him just two words. I said: "Social revolution". After the session he said to me, he said: "Well you know, I don't think it is good to mention the word 'social' and the word 'revolution' to the Americans. They are reluctant about 'revolution'; and about 'social' because it sounds like Communism." . . . So you see that is, in my opinion, the basic difference between Americans and we, the Vietnamese. I see the need of a complete change in South Vietnam in everything, but the Americans didn't see it or they saw it a different way. . . .

. . . [The war gave rise to] a lot of profiteers, particularly among the officers in the government. So what happened to the Vietnamese society at that time was a minority on the top profit everything from war while the vast majority, particularly the military, had nothing. So when you see a captain going to the front and leaving behind a big family and knowing that his wife, his children didn't have enough to eat you can't expect him having a high spirit for fighting; so my idea at that time was to give the best to those who deserve it. I mean the military, the fighting soldiers. . . .

. . . [I]t was true when the Communists' propaganda condemn[ed] us as not nationalists but "a puppet and lackey of America". The way that the Vietnamization was implemented was the wrong way. When they handed the fighting responsibility to the Vietnamese, they handed [it] to the people that they felt comfortable with. One general officer, Vietnamese, he was well known among the Vietnamese as the most corrupted and incapable officer. Every American who came to me said: "Oh, he is a real tiger". That is the reason why at the end [in spring 1975] within 30 days the whole army of a million men collapsed, not because the poor soldiers are less courageous than the North Vietnamese but because all the commanding officers at that time were cowardly and corrupted.

7.6 Ly Tong Ba (ARVN brigadier general), interview from the late 1980s

General Ba spoke from long experience with the Vietnamese army created by the French and sustained by the Americans. Born in 1931, this southerner attended the French-run military academy in Dalat. Commissioned as an army officer in 1952, he began his service in the Red River Delta fighting the Viet

Minh and rose to command an ARVN division in the heavily contested terri-tory northwest of Saigon.

The soldiers of the ARVN by [1975] . . . had a kind of sickness, a mental sickness. . . . The soldiers of the ARVN in the end believed that they had been lied to. Look, they were in a bad situation. To fight a good war, they could not be led by a man like Nguyen Van Thieu. The Americans were not helping them any more and their own government was not helping them, either. They were fighting and dying, and for what?

Some of my soldiers finally started to run. The sickness got them. And when I saw that, I could not do anything else. The Army was finally gone. I decided to walk back on foot from Cu Chi to Saigon. . . .

. . . The commanders' mentality was not a fighting mentality. When the fight became tough, they didn't want to fight any more. They wanted to depend on America, and when they could not depend on America they ran away. That was the sickness that they had caught. . . .

I fought for my country. I did my duty. I did the best I could. And I lost. Yet I am proud, still. When I could not perform my job any more I still tried to fight. I lost my army, but I was never defeated. I just did my job for Vietnam. And when the [PAVN] General that I fought against said to me, "What do you think now?" I said, "I am Vietnamese. I want to see Vietnam rich and the people happy and free." . . .

. . . Vietnam lost many good citizens in the war and now look at the country. I must say that we got nothing from the war. . . . I still say to the leaders of the country, "I did my part. You won and I lost. And now you do what you wanted to do. If you do good, if the people become free and prosperous, then I have nothing against you. . . ."

. . . [T]he new regime has [this sickness] in the way that the old regime had. Corruption—a sickness that eats away at the people. If you don't like someone, or if you don't like what he says, then today they put him in prison.

―――――

7.7 Vu Thi Kim Vinh, interview from the late 1980s

Here the daughter of an apolitical ARVN officer offers the perspective of a less prominent Catholic family. She recounts the confusion surrounding the occupation of Saigon and the transition to northern rule as she experienced it as a teenager.

I am very proud of my dad. He had retired before 1975. After he fought in 1968 he received many certificates and awards from Nixon and Westmoreland, because he was the one who took back Binh Duong province [just north of Saigon] and opened the road for other troops so the Communists were defeated. He was a very brave man. After that he retired. It was too political, he thought. . . .

When we heard rumors about the Communist victories in 1974 and 1975 my father wasn't concerned, so we didn't worry either. Even when they came close to Saigon, we didn't worry, because my father believed that the Communists would never win.

. . . This was at the beginning of April [1975]. Even after the twenty-first we didn't think there was a way we could lose; we had a strong army and a strong military. Even though we did not like the Thieu government, we did not like the Communists, either. . . . But we were tired of the war. We were afraid that if the Communists took over, our family and our lives would be in danger. The problem was, after mid-April, all the important people in the government started to become refugees, and it made everything chaotic at that time. Everybody got scared. After the first wave of refugees left the country, many people panicked. . . .

After April 30 you could still leave Vietnam easily. . . . My parents tried to pay a boat to take our family. But on the way they met some Communist soldiers who were hitchhiking and my parents talked to them, and they said that everything would be all right and there would be no bloodbath. My parents asked them about being sent to concentration camps if you were in the Army, and they said, "No, no! Everything will be all right." They told us about how beautiful the North Vietnamese girls were and how much nicer they dressed than the South Vietnamese girls. They said that there would be no revenge: "Don't make us out to be monsters, because we aren't."

But the first day of May was a very sad day. The day was very heavy and sobering. The electricity was out and the Communists could not fix it. We heard on the radio the voice of a Northerner, very high-pitched and loud, and he condemned America and the people who cooperated with them. He humiliated us by saying that we had been the servants and the dogs of the American government because we had worked with them and against the Communists. We were very hurt to hear that. . . .

At that time if your family had someone who worked for the government in the North, even just a regular soldier, you could feel safe at last, and say, "Oh, we have somebody who fought against South Vietnamese!"

... Everybody was suddenly wearing the Vietcong flag. The flag was security or a credit card that could save your life. Everybody had one. . . .

After a week they divided us into sections and we had a political guy on our block. He told us about Marxism and Leninism and we had to discuss it in a meeting. What was humiliating about this was that they made us criticize ourselves. Even my father at these meetings had to criticize his own behavior. He had to say that he killed innocent people. But I knew he didn't kill innocent people, because if he hadn't killed them they would have killed him. But he said that he was a guilty man and asked for forgiveness for killing what he called "innocent people." And I watched him cry in front of them. It was the first time I had ever seen my father cry. I had to do the same thing. . . . So I said that I hated people like my parents who did what they did. I said that to survive.

LIVING WITH THE GHOSTS OF A LONG WAR

In this war as perhaps all others, veterans carried their own perspective, carved by the sharp blade of combat. At its most psychologically severe, that perspective was manifested in post-traumatic stress disorder (PTSD), a diagnosis formally recognized by psychiatrists in 1980. We know a good deal about the postwar perspective of U.S. soldiers from oral histories and memoirs. But perhaps more important for them and more important still for Vietnamese veterans has been fiction. It has allowed former soldiers on both sides to speak eloquently about how they have grappled with memories and about how they have felt not so much rejected or dishonored as disconnected from and neglected by the society for which they fought.

7.8 Micheal Clodfelter, essay from the 1980s reflecting on his Vietnam experience

The seventeen-year-old Clodfelter enlisted in the army in 1964, and by July the next year he was in Vietnam. After spending his first year with an artillery unit, he volunteered to stay on and serve as an infantryman in the 101st Airborne Division. A punji stick wound in December 1966 finally ended his Vietnam career. Mounting disillusionment with U.S. policy pushed him into the antiwar movement. Here he reflects, as many veterans did, on the powerful and painful memories he carried home.

Fifteen years later I still have trouble dealing with that old man [whom Clodfelter had seen killed by fellow soldiers angry over their own losses]. He confronts me sometimes in my dreams, his face always ill-defined.... But I haven't forgotten his final expression, the one frozen on his face and in my soul, the one that he carried with him out of this world of the living when that M-79 buckshot round shattered his back.

But the old man's image comes and goes, just as the guilt comes and goes. Sometimes I have to remind myself of it; sometimes I have to hide from myself because I can't get away from it. That's because part of me, the part that made me question the war, that made me turn against the war, that made me work against the war, that part of me finds me guilty, an accessory to the crime of murder, guilty through inaction, through acquiescence, through acceptance. But another part of me, the part that loved the thought of war, that even kept a little bit of that love for the experience of war, that part excuses my act of non-action, buries the guilt, tells me it's all understandable and forgivable, given the circumstances of war, given the savagery of war, given the strange but special loyalties of war.

Back then, when it happened, something bright and burning inside me flickered and went out, leaving not even a warm cinder, leaving only a pile of cold cold ashes.

I went home four months later. It was not a happy homecoming. I suppose I would have come out of any war disillusioned. Even when fought for the most glorious cause, even when resulting in the most magnificent victory, war can never be the creature of dash and daring, of adventure and admiration, that young minds might imagine. And to the misfortune of our egos and aspirations—though probably ultimately to the good fortune of our souls—the only war offered our generation was Vietnam, surely the most disillusioning war ever fought by Americans. Had it been World War II or Korea maybe we could have salvaged some scrap of our former favorable opinion of war; maybe we could have looked back as middle aged vets sitting in VFW [Veterans of Foreign Wars] clubs and recalled some higher purpose to our sacrifices and proposed a toast to the good fight, to "our war." But ours was not WWII or Korea; ours was Vietnam, and it would have required a far greater leap from reality—and a dishonest one at that—than that of our adolescent fantasies, now that our opinion was no longer based on ignorance, for us to bless a war that could bear no blessing.

Though separated geographically, the war stayed with me down through all the following years. In all that time, in all those years while I was either fighting in the Vietnam War or against it,. . . . I could not fathom how Vietnam could be anything to all Americans but the central concern of their lives; how it could be anything less than the dark sun around which we were all in unbreakable orbit as its doomed and somehow hopeless satellites. But I had to face the fact, the appalling fact, that to the vast majority of Americans, even those of my age, families and homes and careers, and even cars, cocaine, connections and the next piece of ass, were greater concerns than all that muck and madness in Southeast Asia. . . . For most of my family, friends and acquaintances, the war had an impact upon them similar to that made by a pebble dropped into the depths of the ocean.

But for me and for most of the men who fought there, the war was everything. It had been the worst experience of my life and it had been the best. I never wanted out of any place so bad as I wanted out of Vietnam. But after I left I felt an immediate and overwhelming sense of loss for Vietnam and its war. After all these years, this nostalgia, this strange yearning to return to it all, still persists, still haunts me. Looking at it in terms of good or bad is all wrong. It was simply the most awesome experience of my life and will probably remain so to the end of my years. It is a mountain range rising up abruptly and sharply from the more or less level plains that make up the topography of the rest of my life. These are heights desolate and depressing, more like the mountains of the moon than some snow-capped range, magic and majestic. They are there, undeniable and unscalable, and though time and fading memory may erode them to foothills, they will never entirely disappear from my life's landscape until the gray glacier of death wears everything down to dust.

7.9 Bao Ninh (PAVN veteran), novel on the sorrow of war, 1991

The novel The Sorrow of War *conveys one PAVN veteran's melancholy perspective. Hanoi-born Bao Ninh uses his hero, Kien, to carry readers into a world of hardship and death. His account is at odds with the official version that celebrates the heroic war of resistance and that has no room for battlefield reverses, personal trauma, and generational sacrifice. His novel became a best seller in Vietnam following its publication in 1991, but censors struck back and banned the book. However much it evokes the specifically Vietnamese experience of war, this novel eerily parallels accomplished U.S. veterans' fiction such as Tim O'Brien's* The Things We Carried *(published just a year after* Sorrow*). Both men are haunted by memories of lost comrades, see writing as a way to appease their ghosts, and highlight the fractured, quicksilver quality of memory.*

[Ghosts of lost comrades:] It was here [in the Central Highlands], at the end of the dry season of 1969, that [Kien's] Battalion 27 was surrounded and almost totally wiped out. Ten men survived from the Unlucky Battalion, after fierce, horrible, barbarous fighting.

That was the dry season when the sun burned harshly, the wind blew fiercely, and the enemy sent napalm spraying through the jungle and a sea of fire enveloped them, spreading like the fires of hell. Troops in the fragmented companies tried to regroup, only to be blown out of their shelters again as they went mad, became disoriented and threw themselves into nets of bullets, dying in the flaming inferno. Above them the helicopters flew at tree-top height and shot them almost one by one, the blood spreading out, spraying from their backs, flowing like red mud.

The diamond-shaped grass clearing was piled high with bodies killed by helicopter gunships. Broken bodies, bodies blown apart, bodies vaporised. . . .

In the days that followed, crows and eagles darkened the sky. After the Americans withdrew, the rainy season came, flooding the jungle floor, turning the battlefield into a marsh whose surface water turned rust-coloured from the blood. Bloated human corpses, floating alongside the bodies of incinerated jungle animals, mixed with branches and trunks cut down by artillery, all drifting in a stinking marsh. When the flood receded everything dried in the heat of the sun into thick mud and stinking rotting meat. . . . After that battle no one mentioned Battalion 27 any more, though numerous souls of ghosts and devils were born in that deadly defeat. They were still loose, wandering in every corner and bush in the jungle, drifting along the stream, refusing to depart for the Other World.

[Writing to exorcise postwar nightmares:] [Kien] became bored with his university studies. One morning he simply decided he wouldn't attend. From that point on he ended his easy student life, quietly, and for no apparent reason. He stopped reading newspapers, then books, then let everything go. He lost contact with his friends, then with the outside world in general. Except drink. And cigarettes. He couldn't care less that he was penniless, that he drank and smoked almost non-stop. He wandered around outside, pacing the lonely streets. When he did sleep, it was a heavy, drunken slumber.

. . . Horrible, poisonous nightmares brought back images that had haunted him constantly throughout the war. During the twilights of those cold nights the familiar, lonely spirits reappeared from the Screaming Souls Jungle, sighing and moaning to him, whispering as they floated around, like pale vapours, shredded with bullet holes. They moved into his sleep as though they were mirrors surrounding him. . . .

It was that spring [1979] . . . when something moved within Kien's heart, taking him from turmoil to peace. Something inside him, powerful and urgent, pumped life back into his collapsed spirit and snapped life back into him. It felt like love. Perhaps it was recognition of some wonderful truth deep inside him.

That same chilly dark spring night Kien started to write his first novel. . . .

. . . In [his] derelict room he wrote frantically, non-stop with a sort of divine inspiration, knowing this might be the only time he would feel this urge.

He wrote, cruelly reviving the images of his comrades, of the mortal combat in the jungle that became the Screaming Souls, where his battalion had met its tragic end. . . .

One by one they fell in that battle in that room, until the greatest hero of them all, a soldier who had stayed behind enemy lines to harass the enemy's withdrawal, was blown into a small tattered pile of humanity on the edge of a trench.

The next morning rays from the first day of spring shone through to the darkest corner of his room.

[Victory for whom, for what:] After 1975, . . . [t]he wind of war had stopped. The branches of conflict had stopped rustling. As we had won, Kien thought, then that meant justice had won; that had been some consolation. Or had it? Think carefully; look at your own existence. Look carefully now at the peace we have, painful, bitter and sad. And look at who won the war.

To win, martyrs had sacrificed their lives in order that others might survive. Not a new phenomenon, true. But for those still living to know that the kindest, most worthy people have all fallen away, or even been tortured, humiliated before being killed, or buried and wiped away by the machinery of war, then this beautiful landscape of calm and peace is an appalling paradox. Justice may have won, but cruelty, death and inhuman violence had also won.

Just look and think: it is the truth.

Losses can be made good, damage can be repaired and wounds will heal in time. But the psychological scars of the war will remain forever.

POLITICAL VERDICTS

A conflict as long and costly as the Vietnamese-American war has cried out for lessons and conclusions — and observers, pundits, and political leaders of all stripes have eagerly, insistently obliged.

7.10 President Ronald Reagan, Veterans Day remarks at the Vietnam Veterans Memorial, 11 November 1988

Reagan's comments encapsulated a view of the Vietnam War with broad appeal. Like Hollywood filmmakers, this former actor was bent on redeeming the war by holding up the soldiers as models of sacrifice and patriotism. Like many others in the Republican Party, he thought the war a just cause fought in the name of freedom. The lesson he drew, popular among the military and armchair strategists, was beguilingly simple: any war, once begun, had to be fought all out and to a successful conclusion. He spoke against a backdrop — Maya Lin's recently completed severe black marble slabs naming the dead in row after row — that carried a more ambiguous message.

[We] embrace the gentle heroes of Vietnam and of all our wars. We remember those who were called upon to give all a person can give, and we remember those who were prepared to make that sacrifice if it were demanded of them in the line of duty, though it never was. Most of all, we remember the devotion and gallantry with which all of them ennobled their nation as they became champions of a noble cause.

. . . Unlike the other wars of this century, . . . there were deep divisions about the wisdom and rightness of the Vietnam war. Both sides spoke with honesty and fervor. And what more can we ask in our democracy? And yet after more than a decade of desperate boat people, after the killing fields of Cambodia, after all that has happened in that unhappy part of the world, who can doubt that the cause for which our men fought was just? It was, after all, however imperfectly pursued, the cause of freedom; and they showed uncommon courage in its service. Perhaps at this late date we can all agree that we've learned one lesson: that young Americans must never again be sent to fight and die unless we are prepared to let them win.

But beyond that, we remember today that all our gentle heroes of Vietnam have given us a lesson in something more: a lesson in living love. Yes, for all of them, those who came back and those who did not, their love for their families lives. Their love for their buddies on the battlefields and friends back home lives. Their love of their country lives. . . .

. . . [T]his place . . . reminds us of a great and profound truth about our nation: that from all our divisions we have always eventually emerged strengthened. Perhaps we are finding that new strength today, and if so, much of it comes from the forgiveness and healing love that our Vietnam veterans have shown.

. . . [A]s I approach the end of my service and I see Vietnam veterans take their rightful place among America's heroes, it appears to me that we have healed. And what can I say to our Vietnam veterans but: Welcome home.

7.11 Vo Nguyen Giap and Nguyen Co Thach clash with Robert McNamara over how to evaluate the war, 1995 and 1997

Ever since leaving the Pentagon, Robert McNamara had been intensely preoccupied with identifying missed opportunities that might have averted what he called a tragic war. To explore this isue, he arranged meetings with high-level Vietnamese leaders in the mid-1990s. What he discovered was not missed opportunities but an understanding of the war that was fundamentally at odds with his own. His first meeting was with the eighty-four-year-old Vo Nguyen Giap at the Ministry of Defense in Hanoi in November 1995. In a follow-up conference in June 1997, McNamara sat down with Nguyen Co Thach. Part of the anti-French resistance in his early teens, Thach had become Giap's close aide right after World War II. As a foreign affairs specialist, he had kept an eye on U.S. policy between 1962 and 1968 and participated in the Paris peace talks between 1968 and 1973.

[Exchange of views in November 1995:]

ROBERT MCNAMARA: General, I want us to examine our mindsets, and to look at specific instances where we — Hanoi and Washington — may each have been mistaken, have misunderstood each other. . . .

GEN. VO NGUYEN GIAP: I don't believe we misunderstood you. You were the enemy; you wished to defeat us—to destroy us. So we were forced to fight you—to fight a "people's war" to reclaim our country from your neoimperialist ally in Saigon—we used the word "puppet," of course, back then—and to reunify our country.

ROBERT MCNAMARA: . . . Were we—was I, was Kennedy, was Johnson—a "neoimperialist" in the sense you are using the word? I would say *absolutely not!* Now, if we can agree on an agenda focused on episodes like Tonkin Gulf, where we may have misunderstood each other, then—

GEN. VO NGUYEN GIAP: Excuse me, but we *correctly* understood you. . . .

ROBERT MCNAMARA: . . . [W]e need to reexamine each other's misunderstandings—for two reasons. First, we need to identify missed opportunities; and second, we need to draw lessons which will allow us to avoid such tragedies in the future.

GEN. VO NGUYEN GIAP: Lessons are important. I agree. However, you are wrong to call the war a "tragedy"—to say that it came from missed opportunities. Maybe it was a tragedy for you, because yours was a war of aggression, in the neocolonialist "style," or fashion, of the day for the Americans. You wanted to replace the French; you failed; men died; so, yes, it was tragic, because they died for a bad cause.

But for us, the war against you was a noble sacrifice. We did not want to fight the U.S. We did not. But you gave us no choice. Our people sacrificed tremendously for our cause of freedom and independence. There were no missed opportunities for us. We did what we had to do to drive you and your "puppets"—I apologize, Mr. McNamara, for again using the term "puppet"—to drive you and your puppets out. So I agree that *you* missed opportunities and that *you* need to draw lessons. But us? I think we would do nothing different, under the circumstances. . . .

ROBERT MCNAMARA: . . . [I]t seemed obvious to us [in the Kennedy and Johnson administrations] that the communist movement in Vietnam was closely related to the guerrilla insurgencies being carried on in the 1950s in Burma, Malaya, and the Philippines. We viewed those conflicts not as nationalistic movements—as I think they were, with hindsight—we viewed them as signs of a unified communist drive for hegemony in Asia.

[NGUYEN CO THACH's comments in June 1997:]

I want to thank Mr. McNamara . . . for giving us such a clear picture of the U.S. mindset toward Vietnam—toward the government in Hanoi I mean, after the country was split into two parts at Geneva in 1954. . . .

In my way of thinking, the principal problem in the evolution of these mindsets was that—especially in the 1950s and 1960s—the U.S. seemed to want to become the world's policeman. Mr. McNamara correctly quotes President Kennedy's inaugural address [calling for Americans to "pay any price, bear any burden"] as evidence of a certain anticommunist mindset—a fear that communism would overrun the U.S., or something of the sort. Actually, it seemed to us that in Kennedy's inaugural, he was asserting that the U.S. wished to become something like the "master of the world." In this way, the U.S. would replace the British and the French, who had previously based their policies on such a wish. In our part of the world, this "fear of falling dominoes" was joined to the "threat of the yellow skin" [yellow peril]—so those were two reasons, or excuses, really, why the U.S. felt justified in taking over as the new imperialists.

Now, where did the war come from—from what did the American War emerge? The answer is not difficult to find. In Geneva in 1954, other countries—large and powerful countries [alluding to the Soviet Union and China], not only the U.S.—decided that Vietnam should be divided into two countries. The U.S. installed Ngo Dinh Diem in Saigon and decided to keep him in power at all costs, because of the fear of the communists in the North, ignoring the fact that many, many people in the southern part of Vietnam did not want Diem, would not have voted for Diem, in fact feared Diem. When Diem, backed by the U.S., became increasingly brutal, the people in the South organized themselves, at last, to fight Diem, because they were given no alternative by the U.S.-backed dictator. And so, beginning with the struggle against Diem, the conflict grew, as the U.S. gradually took over Diem's functions, including the military ones, eventually, and the southern resistance—the NLF—turned to its northern allies for assistance in their struggle. That is more or less how the war came about, I think. There is no big mystery about it.

Therefore, I would say, with all due respect to Mr. McNamara, that the U.S. mindset, as he says, was incorrect, but also that the Vietnamese mindset—our assessment of the U.S.—was essentially correct.

CONCLUDING REFLECTIONS

The blunt, matter-of-fact Vietnamese indictment of the United States, articulated at the end of the last selection, may wound some readers, but the charge may seem less preposterous after exposure to the evidence in this documentary survey. Gaining a historical perspective — knowing an event in a deeper and more rounded way — can turn narrow, fixed, reassuring, reflexive judgments into more complex and contingent (and, yes, less comfortable) ways of thinking. In this sense a genuinely historical view of the war is a long way from the popular conceptions reflected in the Hollywood films and polling data discussed in the introduction. It now goes without saying that the war was long in the making and that it was as much a Vietnamese story (or stories) as an American one. U.S. soldiers are no longer simply victims but more complicated characters in a larger drama. However readers may now choose to construct their own particular version of the Vietnam War and whatever evaluation they may place on it, the result is very likely to be far more profound and revealing than the lamentable distortions and shallow awareness that appear in what usually passes for the history of this war.

Now is the time to return to the big, controversial questions that opened this volume. Seven major issues call out for special attention:

- The problem of dates: Usually wars have clearly defined beginnings and ends — but not this one. Is July 1965 the starting point, or do we have to look to an earlier moment (such as Hanoi's 1959 decision on the South or the Gulf of Tonkin episode) to make sense of this conflict? When did the war end: With the Paris peace agreement in 1973, by which time the U.S. public and Congress had turned their backs on the war effort? Or with the fall of Saigon in April 1975?

- The search for fitting labels: Which of the general appraisals offered by prominent Americans works best: The Vietnam War as an aggressive, counterrevolutionary effort driven by a "self-righteous moralism" (SDS leader Paul Potter)? As a morally justified struggle to defend freedom (President Ronald Reagan)? Or as a "tragic mistake" made by well-intentioned leaders (Robert McNamara in retrospect)?

  Looking at the war from the Vietnamese perspective, should we describe the conflict that raged between 1945 and 1975 as fundamentally a civil war, a revolutionary war, a war of Communist aggression, or a war for national independence or unification?

Is there one label that captures the nature of the conflict across its whole sweep and encompasses the experience of both sides?

- The inevitability issue: Were the aspirations of Vietnamese Communists and U.S. policy makers so at odds that war became virtually unavoidable? Were there no major turning points, only a large number of minor, incremental decisions leading to an ever greater likelihood of a violent collision? Did decisions on one side or the other do more to drive the two countries toward war?
- The responsibility question: Does a judgment on blame for the war clearly emerge from the evidence? If so, is that blame to fall on one side or the other, on a particular leader or group, or on some abstraction, such as the political culture of one country or the pressures generated by international rivalry? Alternatively, does a forgiving, no-fault approach make more sense in light of what we now know?
- An explanation for the military outcome: Should we focus on the motivation and techniques that enabled relatively weak NLF and PAVN forces to take on and outlast their stronger U.S. opponent? Should we look for some defect in the approach of the stronger party? Or was it the relative weakness of the ARVN that was crucial, at least in the origins and the last stage of the war?
- The function of misperceptions: How well did Vietnamese and Americans understand each other? How large does misperception loom in any explanation for the origin and conduct of the Vietnam War?

What did the Americans overlook or misconstrue that might help account for their going to war and for their subsequent difficulties? It may be worth considering in particular their general view of Vietnamese, the appeal of communism and nationalism, the conflict for control of the countryside, and the roles of China and the Soviet Union.

Were there serious misconceptions of a comparable nature on the Vietnamese side — for example, the perception of the United States as an exponent of self-determination in the 1940s or later as an exploitative, calculating, and doomed capitalist power?

- The lure of lessons: Does the Vietnam War carry any practical implications for dealing with other conflicts? Are the circumstances of this case so unique that parallels are likely to prove problematic, making any resulting lessons dangerously misleading?

In wrestling with this set of questions, more is at stake than a better understanding of one war, however important it may be. Historical engagement, a sensitivity to cultural differences, and a cultivated international perspective bear important implications for all peoples, not least for Americans: Under what circumstances should a country go to war? What values are important enough to justify organized, state-directed violence? What is known of the risks and the possible outcomes? And who should bear the chief sacrifice? History done with a pronounced international bent cannot supply easy answers to these questions. But without the perspective and sensitivity afforded by this sort of history, any answers are more likely to be superficial, to lead to dubious conclusions, and ultimately to do unanticipated and perhaps terrible harm. History does matter!

Sources of Documents

CHAPTER 1

1.1: *Patterns of Vietnamese Response to Foreign Intervention: 1858–1900*, ed. and trans. Truong Buu Lam (New Haven, Conn.: Yale University Southeast Asia Studies, 1967), 68–70.

1.2: *Colonialism Experienced: Vietnamese Writings on Colonialism, 1900–1931*, ed. and trans. Truong Buu Lam (Ann Arbor: University of Michigan Press, 2000), 107–8.

1.3: *Colonialism Experienced*, 126, 128–30, 139.

1.4: Ho Chi Minh, "The Path Which Led Me to Leninism," April 1960, in *Ho Chi Minh: Selected Writings (1920–1969)* (Hanoi: Foreign Languages Publishing House, 1973), 250–51.

1.5: *Ho Chi Minh: Selected Works*, vol. 3 (Hanoi: Foreign Languages Publishing House, 1961), 39–41.

1.6: *Ho Chi Minh: Selected Writings*, 45–46.

1.7: *Ho Chi Minh: Selected Writings*, 53–56.

1.8: Nguyen Thi Dinh, *No Other Road to Take: Memoir of Mrs. Nguyen Thi Dinh*, trans. Mai V. Elliott (Ithaca, N.Y.: Cornell University Southeast Asia Program and Department of Asian Studies, 1976), 25–29.

1.9: Truong Nhu Tang with David Chanoff and Doan Van Toai, *A Viet Cong Memoir* (New York: Harcourt Brace Jovanovich, 1985), 3–5, 11–13, 20.

1.10: Gérard Chaliand, *The Peasants of North Vietnam*, trans. Peter Wiles (Baltimore: Penguin, 1969), 72–75 (a. Doanh) and 93–95 (b. Ha).

1.11: a. U.S. Department of State, *Foreign Relations of the United States* (hereafter cited as *FRUS*), *The Conferences at Cairo and Tehran, 1943* (Washington, D.C.: U.S. Government Printing Office, 1961), 485 (minutes by Roosevelt's interpreter Charles E. Bohlen); b. *FRUS*, *1945*, vol. 6 (Washington, D.C.: U.S. Government Printing Office, 1969), 567–68; c. *FRUS*, *1950*, vol. 6 (Washington, D.C.: U.S. Government Printing Office, 1976), 745–47.

1.12: Ho Chi Minh [under the pseudonym Din], "The Imperialist Aggressors Can Never Enslave the Heroic Vietnamese People," published in *For a Lasting Peace, for a People's Democracy*, 4 April 1952, and reproduced in *Ho Chi Minh: Selected Works*, 3:311–12.

1.13: a. *Department of State Bulletin* 30 (12 April 1954): 539; b. *FRUS*, *1952–1954*, vol. 13, pt. 1 (Washington, D.C.: U.S. Government Printing Office, 1982), 1239–40.

CHAPTER 2

2.1: *Ho Chi Minh: Selected Writings (1920–1969)* (Hanoi: Foreign Languages Publishing House, 1973), 177–79.

2.2: U.S. Department of State, *American Foreign Policy, 1950–1955: Basic Documents*, vol. 1 (Washington, D.C.: U.S. Government Printing Office, 1957), 785–87.

2.3: a. *Public Papers of the Presidents of the United States* (hereafter cited as *PPP*): *Dwight D. Eisenhower, 1954* (Washington, D.C.: U.S. Government Printing Office, 1960), 642, 647; b. and c. U.S. Department of State, *Foreign Relations of the United States* (hereafter cited as *FRUS*), *1952–1954*, vol. 13, pt. 2 (Washington, D.C.: U.S. Government Printing Office, 1982), 1869–70, 2157–58.

2.4: *The Emergence of Free Viet-Nam: Major Addresses delivered by President NGO-DINH-DIEM during his official visit to the United States of America, May 8–18 1957* (Saigon: Press Office of the Presidency of the Republic of Vietnam, 1957), 24–25, 28.

2.5: a. and b. Merle Pribbenow II's translation from *Van Kien Dang* [Collected party documents], vol. 20, *1959* (Hanoi: National Political Publishing House, 2002), 3–5, 27 (report), 82–84 (resolution). My thanks to Pribbenow for sharing his draft translation. c. *Vietnamese Studies* (Hanoi), no. 23 (1970): 247–50.

2.6: Jeffrey Race, *War Comes to Long An: Revolutionary Conflict in a Vietnamese Province* (Berkeley: University of California Press, 1972), 99, 110–11 (Communists on the defensive), 97–98, 129–30 (peasant reaction).

2.7: J. J. Zasloff, *Political Motivation of the Viet Cong: The Vietminh Regroupees* (Rand memorandum RM-4703/2-ISA/ARPA, May 1968), 57, 106–7 (a. interviewee 24), 152 (b. interviewee 51), 90–91, 136–37 (c. interviewee 29).

2.8: a. U.S. Department of Defense, *United States–Vietnam Relations, 1945–1967* (Washington, D.C.: U.S. Government Printing Office, 1971), 11:359–60; b. minutes of a National Security Council meeting in *FRUS, 1961–1963*, vol. 1 (Washington, D.C.: U.S. Government Printing Office, 1988), 607–10.

2.9: *FRUS, 1961–1963*, vol. 4 (Washington, D.C.: U.S. Government Printing Office, 1991), 642–45.

2.10: *PPP: John F. Kennedy, 1963* (Washington, D.C.: U.S. Government Printing Office, 1964), 569.

2.11: Interview by Robert Udick (United Press International) in *Press Interviews with President Ngo Dinh Diem, Political Counselor Ngo Dinh Nhu* ([Saigon]: Republic of Vietnam, 1963), 4.

2.12: a. "Who Will Win in South Vietnam?" published in *Hoc Tap* and translated in *Vietnamese Studies*, no. 1 (1964): 14–15; b. Meiczyslaw Maneli, *War of the Vanquished*, trans. Maria de Görgey (New York: Harper and Row, 1971), 154–55.

2.13: a. *FRUS, 1961–1963*, vol. 3 (Washington, D.C.: U.S. Government Printing Office, 1991), 628; b., d., and h. John Prados, "JFK and the Diem Coup," 5 November 2003, National Security Archive, http://www.gwu.edu/~nsarchiv/NSAEBB/NSAEBB101/index.htm (accessed 30 November 2006); c., e., f., and g. *FRUS, 1961–1963*, 4:21–22, 252, 379, 393.

3.1: U.S. Department of State, *Foreign Relations of the United States* (hereafter cited as *FRUS*), *1961–1963*, vol. 4 (Washington, D.C.: U.S. Government Printing Office, 1991), 635–36 (a. meeting notes by McCone), 732–35 (b. McNamara report).

3.2: Translation in *Viet-Nam Documents and Research Notes* (July 1971), 9–10, 13, 16, 18–19, 24, 30, 39–41, copy in folder 2, box 3, Douglas Pike Collection, available through Virtual Vietnam Archive, Texas Tech University, at http:// www.vietnam.ttu.edu/star/images/212/2120302009a.pdf (accessed 29 June 2009).

3.3: Konrad Kellen, *A Profile of the PAVN Soldier in South Vietnam* (Rand study RM 5013-1, June 1966), 55–60.

3.4: *Letters from Vietnam*, ed. Bill Adler (New York: Ballantine Books, 2003), 196–99.

3.5: *United States Statutes at Large* 78 (1964): 384.

3.6: *FRUS, 1964–1968*, vol. 2 (Washington, D.C.: U.S. Government Printing Office, 1996), 181–85.

3.7: *Public Papers of the Presidents of the United States* (hereafter cited as *PPP*): *Lyndon B. Johnson, 1965* (Washington, D.C.: U.S. Government Printing Office, 1966), 1:394–99. Minor corrections made and audience applause added on the basis of a full video version of the speech available at the Lyndon Baines Johnson Library and Museum, Austin, Texas.

3.8: *77 Conversations between Chinese and Foreign Leaders on the Wars in Indochina, 1964–1977*, ed. Odd Arne Westad, Chen Jian, Stein Tønnesson, Nguyen Vu Tung, and James Hershberg (Washington, D.C.: Cold War International History Project working paper, 1998), 72–73 (a. October 1964), 83 (b. April 1965).

3.9: U.S. Department of State, *American Foreign Policy: Current Documents, 1965* (Washington, D.C.: U.S. Government Printing Office, 1968), 852.

3.10: Le Duan, *Letters to the South* (Hanoi: Foreign Languages Publishing House, 1986), 23–24, 27–31, 44.

3.11: Transcript reproduced in *Reaching for Glory: Lyndon Johnson's Secret White House Tapes, 1964–1965*, ed. Michael Beschloss (New York: Simon and Schuster, 2001), 365–66, and compared against the audiotape declassified in April 1995 by the Johnson Library and Museum.

3.12: a. *The Pentagon Papers: The Defense Department History of United States Decisionmaking on Vietnam*, Senator Gravel ed., 5 vols. (Boston: Beacon Press, 1971–72), 4:609–10. Thanks to Lauren Anstey for bringing this document to my attention. b. *FRUS, 1964–1968*, vol. 3 (Washington, D.C.: U.S. Government Printing Office, 1996), 106–8.

3.13: *FRUS, 1964–1968*, 3:172–75, 178.

3.14: Meeting notes by Jack Valenti in *FRUS, 1964–1968*, 3:192–96 (a. 21 July meeting), 213–16 (b. 22 July meeting), 238 (c. Clifford comments on 25 July).

3.15: *PPP: Lyndon B. Johnson, 1965*, 2:794–95, 797–98.

4.1: Le Duan, *Letters to the South* (Hanoi: Foreign Languages Publishing House, 1986), 58–59, 71, 73.

4.2: "Tactics and Techniques for Employment of US Forces in the Republic of Vietnam," drafted for William Westmoreland by Brig. Gen. William E. DePuy (MACV operations officer), reproduced in John M. Carland, "Winning the Vietnam War: Westmoreland's Approach in Two Documents," *Journal of Military History* 68 (April 2004): 558, 560–63, 568.

4.3: a. U.S. Department of State, *Foreign Relations of the United States* (hereafter cited as *FRUS*), *1964–1968*, vol. 3 (Washington, D.C.: U.S. Government Printing Office, 1996), 591–94; b. *FRUS, 1964–1968*, vol. 5 (Washington, D.C.: U.S. Government Printing Office, 2002), 424–27, 437.

4.4: a. Ho comments in Merle L. Pribbenow II, "General Vo Nguyen Giap and the Mysterious Evolution of the Plan for the 1968 Tet Offensive," *Journal of Vietnamese Studies* 3 (Summer 2008): 16; b. Le Duan, *Letters to the South*, 94–95, 98–100.

4.5: a. Meeting notes by Tom Johnson in *FRUS, 1964–1968*, vol. 6 (Washington, D.C.: U.S. Government Printing Office, 2002), 318–21 (4 March meeting), 329, 331 (5 March meeting); b. *Public Papers of the Presidents of the United States* (hereafter cited as *PPP*): *Lyndon B. Johnson, 1968* (Washington, D.C.: U.S. Government Printing Office, 1970), 469–70, 473, 476.

4.6: "The Sixth Resolution, Central Office of South Viet-Nam," *Viet-Nam Documents and Research Notes*, no. 38 (July 1968): 3–5.

4.7: Transcript in *77 Conversations between Chinese and Foreign Leaders*, ed. Odd Arne Westad, Chen Jian, Stein Tønnesson, Nguyen Vu Tung, and James Hershberg (Washington, D.C.: Cold War International History Project working paper, 1998), 139, 143–44, 146, 148, 150–52.

4.8: a. Meeting minutes by Alexander Haig in *FRUS, 1969–1976*, vol. 6 (Washington, D.C.: U.S. Government Printing Office, 2006), 169–71, 173; b. *PPP: Richard Nixon, 1969* (Washington, D.C.: U.S. Government Printing Office, 1971), 370–72, 374.

4.9: "Resolution Issued by the 9th Conference of COSVN (July 1969)," in *Viet-Nam Documents and Research Notes*, July 1969, 2, 6.

4.10: *PPP: Richard Nixon, 1970* (Washington, D.C.: U.S. Government Printing Office, 1971), 407–10.

4.11: Le Duan, *Letters to the South*, 118–20, 122–23, 133–34, 139, 150, 152.

4.12: Memo of conversation reproduced in Jeffrey Kimball, *The Vietnam War Files: Uncovering the Secret History of Nixon-Era Strategy* (Lawrence: University Press of Kansas, 2004), 135–38.

4.13: Transcript in Kimball, *Vietnam War Files*, 162–65.

4.14: Transcript in Kimball, *Vietnam War Files*, 216–17 (25 April), 220–21 (4 May).

4.15: Luu Van Loi and Nguyen Anh Vu, *Le Duc Tho–Kissinger Negotiations in Paris* (Hanoi: The Gioi Publishers, 1996), 233 (a. 6 May), 254–55 (b. 22 July), 278–82 (c. mid-August), 302–3 (d. 4 October). Document 4.15c may be either a direct quote or a paraphrase.

4.16: a. Draft transcript of tape no. 793-6 produced by the Presidential Recordings Program, Miller Center of Public Affairs, University of Virginia, available at http://www.whitehousetapes.net/clips/1972-10-06%20-%20 nixon%20on%20thieu.swf (accessed 29 June 2009); b., c., and d. Nguyen Tien Hung and Jerrold L. Schecter, *The Palace File* (New York: Harper and Row, 1986), 377–78, 380, 386.

4.17: *Message of the President of the Republic of Viet Nam Delivered at the Joint Session of the National Assembly, 12th December, 1972* ([Saigon?]: n.p., 1972), 5–6, 8.

4.18: *United States Treaties and Other International Agreements*, vol. 24, pt. 1, 1973 (Washington, D.C.: U.S. Government Printing Office, 1974), 5–8, 11–12, 20.

CHAPTER 5

5.1: *Dear America: Letters Home from Vietnam*, ed. Bernard Edelman (New York: Norton, 1985), 205.

5.2: *Letters from Vietnam*, ed. Bill Adler (New York: Ballantine Books, 2003), 27–28.

5.3: *Dear America*, 53–54.

5.4: Interview by Sandra Stewart Holyoak and Shaun Illingworth, 8 October 2004, Manalapan, N.J., for the Rutgers Oral History Archives, transcript by Domingo Duarte, Carl Burns, and Shaun Illingworth, reviewed by Shaun Illingworth 16 February 2005 and by Carl Burns 28 April 2005, http:// oralhistory.rutgers.edu/Interviews/burns_carl.html (accessed 8 February 2008).

5.5: *Letters of 2nd Lt. Richard S. Johnson, Jr., U.S. Marine Corps* (Columbia, S.C.: R. L. Bryan, 1969), 34–35, 37, 45–46.

5.6: a. Rand interview, 14–15 December 1965, folder 7, box 8, John Donnell Collection, available through Virtual Vietnam Archive, Texas Tech University, at http://www.vietnam.ttu.edu/star/images/072/0720807001.pdf (accessed 29 June 2009), 3–5 (NLF reeducation), 8 (village reaction to NLF), 14–16 (arrival of the Americans), 22–23 (arrest); b. Rand interview, 12–13 December 1965, folder 6, box 8, John Donnell Collection, available through Virtual Vietnam Archive at http://www.vietnam.ttu.edu/star/images/072/0720806004.pdf (accessed 29 June 2009), 14–15 (first desertion), 2–3 (NLF February takeover), 12 (village reaction to NLF), 16–18 (second desertion), 1 (service as NLF guerrilla), 18–20 (arrival of Americans).

5.7: Translation in *Viet-Nam Documents and Research Notes*, document no. 13 (January 1968), 4–6.

5.8: David Chanoff and Doan Van Toai, *"Vietnam": A Portrait of Its People at War* (London: Tauris, 1996), 45–46.

5.9: Chanoff and Toai, *"Vietnam,"* 154–55 (no source indicated).

5.10: David W. P. Elliott and Mai Elliott, *Documents of an Elite Viet Cong Delta Unit: The Demolition Platoon of the 514th Battalion*, pt. 5, *Personal Letters* (Rand memorandum RM-5852-ISA ARPA, May 1969), 7, 23–26, 29, 31, 34–35, 44.

5.11: Interview by David Chanoff and Doan Van Toai, in Chanoff and Toai, *"Vietnam,"* 112–13.

5.12: a. William R. Peers, *Report of the Department of the Army Review of the Preliminary Investigation into the My Lai Incident*, vol. 2, bk. 24, Conti testimony, pp. 27–28, available through Library of Congress at http://www.loc.gov/rr/frd/Military_Law/Vol_II-testimony.html (accessed 22 February 2009); b. statement taken by army investigator Reis R. Kash in James S. Olson and Randy Roberts, *My Lai: A Brief History with Documents* (Boston: Bedford Books, 1998), 79–81, original available through Virtual Vietnam Archive at http://www.vietnam.ttu.edu/star/images/154/1540148002.pdf (accessed 29 June 2009).

5.13: Transcribed from copies of the original letters supplied by David W. Mulldune. Mulldune recalls his experience in *The Mailman Went UA: A Vietnam Memoir* (Bennington, Vt.: Merriam Press, 2009).

5.14: *From Camelot to Kent State: The Sixties Experience in the Words of Those Who Lived It*, ed. Joan Morrison and Robert K. Morrison, 2nd ed. (New York: Oxford University Press, 2001), 76–79.

5.15: Interview by Keith Walker in Keith Walker, *A Piece of My Heart: The Stories of 26 Women Who Served in Vietnam* (Novato, Calif.: Presidio Press, 1986), 9–12, 14–15, 17.

5.16: Interview by Sandra Stewart Holyoak, Shaun Illingworth, and Gino Namur, 5 March 2007, New Brunswick, N.J., for the Rutgers Oral History Archives, transcript by Domingo Duarte, Gino Namur, Jake Morano, Dan O'Boyle, Shaun Illingworth, William Kahane, and Sandra Stewart Holyoak, http://oralhistory.rutgers.edu/Interviews/pdfs/kahane_william.pdf (accessed 4 June 2009), 42, 48 (substance abuse), 46 (view of Vietnamese), 46–47 (living conditions), 43, 48 (internal divisions).

5.17: Translation by Cao Thi Nhu-Quynh and John C. Schafer in John C. Schafer, "The Trinh Cong Son Phenomenon," *Journal of Asian Studies* 66 (August 2007): 636–37 (with minor revisions suggested by Schafer in e-mail to editor, 8 March 2009).

5.18: Interview transcript in "Rand Interviews in Vietnam," series K, 8, 19, 31 (political officer and political commitment), 14 (three-man cell), 21 (family support). For more on this collection, see W. Phillips Davison, *User's Guide to the Rand Interviews in Vietnam* (R-1024-ARPA, March 1972, revised November 1972), available at http://www.rand.org/pubs/reports/2006/R1024.pdf (accessed 9 June 2009).

5.19: Dang Thuy Tram, *Last Night I Dreamed of Peace: The Diary of Dang Thuy Tram*, trans. Andrew X. Pham (New York: Harmony Books, 2007), 119–21, 125, 127–28, 135.

5.20: Interview by David Chanoff and Doan Van Toai, in Chanoff and Toai, "*Vietnam*," 107–10.

CHAPTER 6

6.1: Paul Potter, "Naming the System," Students for a Democratic Society (SDS) Document Library, http://www.antiauthoritarian.net/sds_wuo/sds_documents/paul_potter.html (accessed 12 June 2009), which follows the version of the Potter speech published by the SDS in May 1965 (pamphlet in box 9, folder 6, Students for a Democratic Society Records, 1958–1970, Wisconsin Historical Society, Madison). Those records also contain an audio record of the speech (tape 517A/15), which varies only slightly from the published version. Thanks to Sally J. Jacobs for help with these materials, especially the rescue of the tape.

6.2: a. *New York Times Magazine*, 18 April 1965, 85+; b. *New Republic*, 3 July 1965, 22.

6.3: J. William Fulbright, *The Arrogance of Power* (New York: Random House, 1967), 9, 15, 21, 257–58.

6.4: Martin Luther King Jr., "Beyond Vietnam," available at Martin Luther King Jr. Papers Project, http://mlk-kpp01.stanford.edu/kingweb/publications/speeches/Beyond_Vietnam.pdf (accessed 4 June 2009), 2–5, 7. This version follows the tape of the address as delivered.

6.5: File folder 8, box 14, speeches subseries, public series, John C. Stennis Papers, Congressional and Political Research Center, Mississippi State University Libraries. Copyright held by the Congressional and Political Research Center and Mississippi State University Libraries.

6.6: The full thirty-minute broadcast transcript is in *The War in Vietnam: A Multimedia Chronicle from CBS News and the New York Times* (New York: Macmillan Digital USA CD-ROM, 1995). The excerpts here come from pp. 7–8 of the transcript.

6.7: Marvin Dolgov, recollections in e-mail exchanges with editor, 7, 12, 17 November 2008.

6.8: "You Don't Need a Weatherman to Know Which Way the Wind Blows" in *Weathermen*, ed. Harold Jacobs ([Berkeley, Calif.]: Ramparts Press, 1970), 52–53, 55, 69–70, 87–88.

6.9: a. *Public Papers of the Presidents of the United States* (hereafter cited as *PPP*): *Richard Nixon, 1969* (Washington, D.C.: U.S. Government Printing Office, 1971), 908–9; b. John R. Coyne Jr., *The Impudent Snobs: Agnew vs. the Intellectual Establishment* (New Rochelle, N.Y.: Arlington House, 1972), 266–70.

6.10: a. Interview by Joseph Lelyveld, John Kifner, and Robert M. Smith, "The View from Kent State: 11 Speak Out," *New York Times*, 11 May 1970, 23; b. James A. Michener, *Kent State: What Happened and Why* (New York: Random House, 1971), 436–39, 441–42.

6.11: Senate Committee on Foreign Relations, *Legislative Proposals Relating to the War in Southeast Asia*, 92nd Cong., 1st sess., 1971 (Washington, D.C.: U.S. Government Printing Office, 1971), 180–83, 185.

6.12: *PPP: Richard Nixon, 1971* (Washington, D.C.: U.S. Government Printing Office, 1972), 525.

CHAPTER 7

7.1: Le Duan, *Letters to the South* (Hanoi: Foreign Languages Publishing House, 1986), 208–9, 220–21.

7.2: Nguyen Tien Hung and Jerrold L. Schecter, *The Palace File* (New York: Harper and Row, 1986), 331–32.

7.3: *Public Papers of the Presidents of the United States* (hereafter cited as *PPP*): *Gerald D. Ford, 1975*, vol. 1 (Washington, D.C.: U.S. Government Printing Office, 1977), 569–70.

7.4: *Le Duan: Selected Writings (1960–1975)* (Hanoi: The Gioi Publishers, 1994), 534, 537–40.

7.5: Interview by Michael Charlton, in Michael Charlton and Anthony Moncrieff, *Many Reasons Why: The American Involvement in Vietnam* (New York: Hill and Wang, 1978), 215–16, 219–22.

7.6: Larry Engelmann, *Tears before the Rain: An Oral History of the Fall of South Vietnam* (New York: Oxford University Press, 1990), 242, 244.

7.7: Engelmann, *Tears before the Rain*, 284, 287–89.

7.8: *Vietnam Voices: Perspectives on the War Years, 1941–1982*, comp. John Clark Pratt (New York: Penguin Books, 1984), 656–58. Micheal Clodfelter's later memoir is titled *Mad Minutes and Vietnam Months: A Soldier's Memoir* (Jefferson, N.C.: McFarland, 1988).

7.9: Bao Ninh, *The Sorrow of War*, trans. Phan Thanh Hao and ed. Frank Palmos (London: Minerva, 1994), 2–3 (ghosts), 64, 69, 79 (writing), 179–80 (meaning of victory).

7.10: *PPP: Ronald Reagan, 1988–89*, vol. 2 (Washington, D.C.: U.S. Government Printing Office, 1991), 1495–96.

7.11: Robert S. McNamara, James G. Blight, and Robert K. Brigham with Thomas J. Biersteker and Herbert Y. Schandler, *Argument without End: In Search of Answers to the Vietnam Tragedy* (New York: Public Affairs, 1999), 23–24 (transcript of Giap-McNamara meeting translated by Pham Sanh Chau), 41, 46–47 (Thach meeting with McNamara).

Index

and strategy of attrition, 85, 89–90, 100, 139; Tet Offensive and, 93, 94, 96, 143, 147; Twenty-fifth Infantry Division, 128–29. *See also* U.S. Military Assistance Advisory Group; Veterans of war